D1570330

PERFORMING AUTOBIOGRAPHY

Contemporary Canadian Drama

Performing Autobiography:

Contemporary Canadian Drama

JENN STEPHENSON

UNIVERSITY OF TORONTO PRESS
Toronto Buffalo London

© University of Toronto Press 2013
Toronto Buffalo London
www.utppublishing.com
Printed in Canada

ISBN 978-1-4426-4446-5

Printed on acid-free, 100% post-consumer recycled paper with
vegetable-based inks.

Library and Archives Canada Cataloguing in Publication

Stephenson, Jenn, 1971–
Performing autobiography : contemporary Canadian drama /
Jenn Stephenson.

Includes bibliographical references and index.
ISBN 978-1-4426-4446-5

1. Autobiographical drama, Canadian (English) – History and criticism.
2. Monodramas – Canada – History and criticism.   3. One-person shows
(Performing arts) – Canada.   I. Title.

PN1936.S74 2013   792.1   C2012-907734-8

University of Toronto Press acknowledges the financial assistance to its
publishing program of the Canada Council for the Arts and the Ontario
Arts Council.

This book has been published with the help of a grant from the Canadian
Federation for the Humanities and Social Sciences, through the Awards to
Scholarly Publications Program, using funds provided by the Social Sciences
and Humanities Research Council of Canada.

University of Toronto Press acknowledges the financial support of the
Government of Canada through the Canada Book Fund for its publishing
activities.

Contents

Acknowledgments   vii

Introduction   3

1 Narrative Failure and the Loss of an Autobiographical Self:
   Perfect Pie and *The Drawer Boy*   23

2 Performative Witnessing to Autobiographies of Trauma:
   Goodness   45

3 Setting Free Silenced Autobiographical Voices:
   Eternal Hydra and *Shadows*   68

4 The Autobiographical Body as a Site of Utopian Performativity:
   Billy Twinkle   103

5 Self-Authoring Characters in Recursive Autothanatography:
   In On It   131

Coda   154

Notes   171
Bibliography   199
Index   209

Acknowledgments

Just as no autobiography stands alone, aloof from the biographies of other people, a book like this, although it bears just a single name for the author, is in fact the work of many people. To them goes my most sincere appreciation.

I am fortunate to be surrounded by colleagues as knowledgeable and skilled as they are generous. They have given their time and expert feedback at every stage. Their friendship has been invaluable. My warm thanks go to Jill Scott, Julie Salverson, Lee Atkinson, Kim Solga, Marlis Schweitzer, Laura Levin, and Natalie Alvarez. Gloria Brumer (my mother) was the first reader of every word contained here. She brought an intelligent non-expert perspective to the work, compelling me to keep the prose clear and the arguments accessible. Ric Knowles and Sherrill Grace are my wise owls. It was Sherrill who redirected an amorphous research project on metatheatre, trauma, and identity towards autobiography, giving the work a strong spine. Ric has been a stalwart supporter and a reliable source of advice on myriad topics, from what the title should be to what goes in the index and things in between.

My students here in the Drama Department at Queen's are also owed a debt of gratitude for their curiosity and for sharing their fresh insights. Thank you to the Canadian Drama classes of 2008 and 2010 and to Julie Salverson's Cultures of Theatre class who invited me to talk about *Goodness* at a very early stage in my thinking about that play. Thanks also go to Ashley Williamson, Johanna Lawrie, Vanessa Brown, and Ashley Peoples, who together concocted a directed reading course on autobiography and theatricality and invited me to lead it. Some of these students continued with me on this path, working as research assistants over the years: Keith Bennie and Ashley Williamson were energetic chasers of materials and references, often bringing in rich new leads. Johanna Lawrie contributed practical help in readying the final manuscript for publication.

Over the years, many portions of this book have been aired as conference papers at the annual meetings of the Canadian Association for Theatre Research (formerly Association for Canadian Theatre Research). Without doubt, these ideas have been strengthened and augmented by this early exposure. Parts of chapter 1 first appeared in *Theatre Research in Canada* as 'Kneading You: Performative Meta-Auto/Biography in *Perfect Pie*.' Chapter 2, titled 'The Notebook and the Gun: Performative Witnessing in *Goodness*,' appeared previously in *English Studies in Canada*. Part of chapter 4 is forthcoming in French in *Régimes fictionnels et scéniques du solo contemporain: Nouvelles perspectives*, edited by Gilbert David and Hervé Guay. I would like to acknowledge the work undertaken by the editors of those journals and the peer reviewers who offered such productive feedback. Thank you for granting permission to extend those pieces further here.

Research for *Performing Autobiography* was supported by the Social Science and Humanities Research Council of Canada through the Senate Advisory Research Committee of Queen's University. Publication of this book was assisted by funding from the Awards to Scholarly Publications Program of the Canadian Federation for the Humanities and Social Sciences. Thank you to the anonymous readers for University of Toronto Press for their comments and their constructive suggestions for improvement. Thank you too to Siobhan McMenemy, my editor, who has been a diligent shepherd through the publishing process.

Finally, my love and gratitude to my family – my husband John and children, Jessica, Sarah, and Benjamin – who took me out to play. They are my autobiography.

PERFORMING AUTOBIOGRAPHY

Contemporary Canadian Drama

Introduction

On the bulletin board beside my desk, there is an untitled black ink on white paper sketch by cartoonist and illustrator Saul Steinberg that epitomizes the transformative promise of performed autobiography.[1] The spare sketch outlines the profile of a cartoonish figure with a balding head and prominent nose. The thin single line begins at the back of the head, curves over the forehead to the nose, continuing in a single line to draw one arm, running along the body and down the legs. Launching from the heel of the second foot, the line is set loose, leaving the rest of the body incomplete. It loops-the-loop around the page. The line comes to a stop finally at the tip of a brush or pen held in the hand of the figure it just drew. It is an amusing self-referential paradox; the drawn figure is both its own creator and creation.

Autobiography, then, is more than simply a recording or retracing of a fixed, pre-existing life experience. Indeed, if the principal aim of autobiography is to present a perfectly accurate portrait of its subject, then as Philippe Lejeune acknowledges, autobiography is impossible: 'Telling the truth about the self, constituting the self as a complete subject – it is a fantasy. In spite of the fact that autobiography is impossible, this in no way prevents it from existing.'[2] Like Steinberg's line figure, a self-story must always be incomplete. In the narrative of one's own life, events are selected, shaped, and sequenced. Other events are forgotten, elided, or intentionally omitted. Autobiography, thus, is always a fictional construction, featuring an inescapable gap between the real-world referent and its fictional twin.

In the moment of creating autobiography, in the moment of holding the pen or taking the stage, these two selves – the actual and the fictional – blend one into another. The past experience of the autobiographical author-subject is enacted again in the present. Events and impressions are brought forward and relived in my own words and with my own body. Tracing again the contours of my life, I am powerful – a small god in the heavens hovering above my own story. Just as Steinberg's drawn line breaks free to imagine new spiraling paths, so too autobiographical performance acts as a catalyst not only to revisit but also to revise and reinvent.

This book, *Performing Autobiography*, begins with the premise that autobiography is a uniquely powerful political act. Rather than impossibly documenting the backward-looking narrative of one's life, autobiography is understood here as an evolving process of self-creation and transformation. Through the invocation of performative power, it is possible to remake one's identity and write a new future or magically even a new past. Looking at nine recent plays – works by Canadian playwrights written and performed between 1999 and 2009 – I treat these dramatic texts as metacritical works, reading through the experience of fictional characters engaged with autobiography to comment on the expanding role of autobiography in contemporary culture. The performance-oriented dramaturgical analyses of *Performing Autobiography* have three primary objectives: (1) to describe the various self-performance strategies employed by these dramatic autobiographers, (2) to consider how these strategies engage major questions in the field of autobiography studies, and (3) to demonstrate the sometimes paradoxical ways that the fictionalizing act of self-storytelling can bring about profound actual-world effects.

Autobiography is everywhere. From tell-all talk shows to the reality television phenomenon of *Survivor* and its ilk, from mommy bloggers to YouTube, these early years of the new millennium are awash in autobiography.[3] Life narratives are being generated and consumed at an unprecedented rate. No longer the exclusive purview of social and political elites, the publishing and broadcasting of autobiography are becoming increasingly democratic.[4] And yet, as Sherrill Grace notes in her introduction to *Theatre and AutoBiography*, this process is far from complete: 'While it is not accurate to claim that anyone can write a memoir or keep a diary or create a blog or stage a performance piece on their life (economics, access, and education are not equally available), the autobiographical voice and eye/I are available to minorities and to groups, such as women, who have been excluded from the dominant discourse and whose stories have been dismissed as worthless.'[5] Correspondingly, our taste for consuming autobiography has become more popular, and in the media marketplace there is expanding demand for reading about or watching the mundane travails of the 'common man.'[6] (Although too frequently in the interests of creating novelty, either the travails are not so mundane, think *Survivor*, or the common man is not so common, think *Jon and Kate Plus 8*.) As Sidonie Smith and Julia Watson argue in *Getting a Life: Everyday Uses of Autobiography*, we are involved daily in sharing and shaping self-narratives. Candidates for political office use personal narratives to project character or values. The act of confession has spilled out of the private confines of the church or the therapist's office into daytime talk shows and community self-help groups. People don identity clothing to signify status, origin, occupation, political consciousness.[7] At every turn, we are asked to fill out personal profiles, medical histories, questionnaires, and polls.

The proliferation of autobiographical participation in the twenty-first century is attributable to several concurrent developments. First, new technologies implicitly encourage the composition of personal stories and profiles and then facilitate their dissemination, moving autobiography from print-based private journals and albums into the virtual public sphere. With the advent of Web 2.0, the online docuverse is no longer read-only.[8] The mission of this most recent wave of Internet applications is to transfer control away from a single authorial voice and instead redistribute that responsibility to the collective. The monolithic *Encyclopedia Britannica* has been replaced by Wikipedia, where the reliability of the information is dependent on the practice of 'crowd sourcing.' Data is no longer locked but is open to information-sharing and collaboration. Existing content can be reimagined through the creation of mash-ups, wikis, folksonomies, and tag clouds.[9] The overall thrust of this movement promotes broad-based participation as authority (theoretically) devolves to the populace. The effect is to make everyone (everyone with Internet access, that is) a contributor; everyone has a say. Offshoots of this new openness have blossomed as social networking sites (Facebook, Twitter, Pinterest) and self-publishing sites (blogs, YouTube, Flickr). Invited to shape the geography of the virtual environment, Internet citizens ('netizens') also have been flocking to post personal content, to document experiences online, to become visible and live in this digital space. Although they do not resemble traditional modes of autobiography, it is easy to see how these applications provide platforms for personal storytelling.[10] A blog is the online equivalent of a diary or journal; content can range from random musings sent into the ether to focused posts on a narrow topic aimed at an invested readership of cognoscenti. A Flickr album of images from a holiday is autobiography. The names of sites such as *Face*book and *You*Tube say it all about these applications as sites of autobiography. Personal profiles function as mini-autobiographies, featuring basic personal information (age, birthday, gender) but also status updates, images of the user and the user's friends, lists of likes and dislikes, details of recent social engagements, and announcements of future plans. Twitter is the ultimate in instant autobiography. Reducing autobiography to gnomic poems of 140 characters or less, it also shrinks the time between the experience and the recounting of it to almost simultaneity. (@queensjenn: At my desk writing intro re: #tweeting it's raining outside pitter patter on the 3rd floor gables gloomy in here listening to #RadioParadise.) Researchers in social media at Rutgers University have coined a new word to describe this kind of personal report, calling it 'meformation' as opposed to 'information.'[11]

Paradoxically, in the context of these burgeoning virtual worlds of autobiography, Amy Spaulding argues that as life becomes more and more technologized, storytelling is an antidote to impersonality.[12] Spaulding, a professional storyteller, is an advocate for the warm intimate encounter of an audience and raconteur in a physically shared time and space. Digital technologies per se may not be the principal foe, but even beyond the connection of embodied presence in the live encounter, narrative storytelling in general and autobiographical stories in particular still carry significant power to ameliorate the impersonal and alienating nature of contemporary culture. By recounting direct experience through the lens of a single participant, autobiography uses the personal to open a window of understanding on larger issues, helping to 'put a human face on the abstract, impersonal forces of globalization, terrorism, and the corporatism.'[13] As Robert Fulford argues in the 1999 Massey Lectures, published as *The Triumph of Narrative: Storytelling in the Age of Mass Culture*, 'Storytelling is an attempt to deal with and at least partly contain the terrifyingly haphazard quality of life.'[14] Novelist Ben Okri explains the power of autobiographical stories in times of crisis this way: 'When we have made an experience or a chaos into a story we have transformed it, made sense of it, transmuted experience, domesticated chaos.'[15] The world is an uncertain place.

Though our faith in traditional master narratives has been eroded in recent decades, the compulsion to narrative persists.[16] In place of the 'top-down' organization of those no longer satisfying grand motifs, we now rely increasingly on stories that shape our experience from the 'bottom-up.' With the contemporary expansion of genres like the memoir of crisis (memoirs about surviving rape, abuse, alcoholism, and so on), first-person documentary, and citizen journalism,[17] those narratives where the personal intersects with the larger flow of politics or social issues are finding an audience. For example, Carl Wilson's book *Let's Talk about Love* (2008) is a philosophical examination of what constitutes 'taste' in the arts, and particularly in popular music. The arc of the narrative is shaped by Wilson's own strong distaste for the music of Quebecois pop icon Celine Dion, which is transmuted by the end into an admiration without guilt. Common-man memoirs on the *Globe and Mail* 'Best Non-Fiction of 2008' list include autobiographical accounts that range from the comical to the poignant to the tragic, from a summer-student gravedigger to the widow of a 9/11 victim, from the literary self-reflections of Farley Mowat (looking back to 1937–48) and M.G. Vassanji (travels in India) to two Dutch sisters' account of Nazi occupation of their village and their subsequent immigration to Canada in the 1950s.[18] Whatever their actual content, these micronarratives re-establish the personal connection, forging empathetic bonds between the autobiographical storyteller and her audience. Correspondingly, when taken as a whole, the myriad of available grassroots micronarratives present a kaleidoscopic view of the world from which we assemble a collage of perspectives and see ourselves reflected and refracted through individual experience. Not only do we find security and stability in the stories of others, but the use of narrative to structure one's own story gives life a discernible pattern and assists us in finding meaning in an otherwise chaotic existence. By imposing cognitive narrative schemas like cause and effect or thematic reiterations on life, which in its arbitrariness and unpredictability does not innately possess these orderly schematic characteristics, we are able to create an impression of coherence. With a sense of a coherent past, we are able then to translate this map into future action. Charlotte Linde articulates this autobiographical tenet: 'Life stories express our sense of self: who we are and how we got that way. They are also one very important means by which we communicate this sense of self and negotiate it with others.'[19]

The field of dramatic performance in Canada has not been immune to this contemporary fascination with autobiography.[20] In her recent book *Autobiography and Performance*, Deirdre Heddon traces the development of autobiographical drama through the 1970s in the United States and the UK through feminist politics, which yoked the personal to the political. Through the confluence of experimental performance and the incorporation of explicitly autobiographical material into performance, 'the binary between art and life, just as between public and private, collapsed as feminists consciously incorporated their lives into their art making.'[21] In Canada, the history of autobiographical performance followed a similar path, but on a slightly later timeline.[22] Drama explicitly grounded in first-person autobiographical narratives began to flourish in Canada in the early 1990s, although there are some important precursors.

Moving from historical biography (*Walsh* [1973], *The Komagata Maru Incident* [1976], and *Blood Relations* [1980]) to auto/biography, Sharon Pollock was one of the first playwrights to explicitly reach into her own life for source material in the creation of her 1984 play, *Doc*. *Doc* is frequently described as 'semiautobiographical,' although perhaps a more cautiously correct categorization might be to call the play 'autofiction' rather than autobiography, recognizing the clearly fictional treatment of real-life situations and events in the playwright's life.[23] 'Neither autobiography nor fiction in the strict sense, autofiction rather functions as a go-between in the defined interstice – that place which is impossible and which can only exist in writing.'[24] With *Doc*, Pollock revisits the family of her youth, capturing the emotionally loaded dynamics between her largely absent father devoted to his demanding medical practice and her mother who had become depressed, turning to alcohol and ultimately suicide. Despite detailed similarities to Pollock's life, Pollock biographer Sherrill Grace warns against 'too literal a reliance on fiction to produce or reproduce facts.'[25] As Pollock herself wrote in the 'Playwright's Notes' for the premiere production at Theatre Calgary: 'It is not "my" story or the story of my family. There is a lot of my father in Ev, my mother in Bob, and me in Catherine, but Ev is not my father, Bob is not my mother, nor Catherine me. They are extensions of real people and through telling their story, my personal journey of discovery is hopefully made large enough to communicate itself to you.'[26] In this statement, Pollock participates in what Sidonie Smith calls '"I"-lying' – a strategic practice that 'gestures towards the fictiveness of the "I" that seems to speak in autobiography. Thus they disrupt, consciously or unconsciously, the surface of the unified, authoritative, essential "self," a fiction of a regime of truth that would specify identity, contain it, capture it, universalize it, essentialize it.'[27] In the sometimes dream-like world of the play, structured in multi-synchronous layered episodes as a memory play, Pollock herself appears as a character, represented simultaneously both as the adult Catherine and as a child, Katie. Thus, *Doc* functions, in my view, as a proto-autobiographical play. It employs a lightly fictionalized autobiographical story, equating the playwright with the protagonist. However,

Pollock does not complete the autobiographical circuit by setting aside the cultivated reservations of autofiction to produce a fully embodied autobiographical performance. Not only does she not share her name with her protagonist, she herself takes no part in the actual world of the play-as-event, leaving the roles of her alternate selves to other actors.[28]

Song of This Place (1987) is also an early autobiographical performance with some reservations. Like *Doc*, *Song of This Place* also rests on an autobiographical foundation, blending a biographical portrait of painter Emily Carr with an autofictive performance by playwright Joy Coghill. Working across levels of dramatic fiction and reality, the play sketches an associative vector from the subject-playwright to the actor to the protagonist character, but like *Doc* the play still leaves some connections unresolved. *Song of This Place* was first conceived as biography;[29] as playwright Joy Coghill wryly explains, 'When any Canadian actress reaches her 56th year, she develops a driving passion to play Emily Carr.'[30] To fulfil this ambition, Coghill began to write a role for herself as Carr. In the resulting play, however, the role of Carr (Millie) was played by Joan Orenstein; Coghill assumed the semiautobiographical role of Frieda – an older actress who seeks communion with Carr and who shares Coghill's desire to perform the brilliant but notoriously misanthropic artist.[31] The play explores several dialogic strategies as it progresses; Coghill as Frieda begins by rehearsing her own play about Millie Carr with puppets and a cast of young puppeteers. When Frieda reaches an impasse, unable to find the voice for the Millie puppet, Carr herself arrives ghostlike from the forest. Frieda and Millie first converse through the puppets with Frieda voicing Alice, Carr's sister, and Millie speaking through her own puppet likeness. Eventually, Frieda takes on the role of Carr, and the two artists blend, both speaking Millie's thoughts. The stage directions indicate: '*This is the "transfer" as MILLIE gives and FRIEDA takes over MILLIE'S "life" and memory*' (56). It is through this transfer that Millie in Frieda faces down the corrosive criticism of her father, Frieda finds her 'Small' – her artist self – and Millie acknowledges Frieda as a compatriot: 'You are a Singer. You are one of us' (60). Thus, it is through this strategy of double-voicing that Frieda uses Carr as an alter ego to gain insight both into Carr's life and her own.[32] Linda Griffiths in her 1999 solo performance *Alien Creature: A Visitation from Gwendolyn MacEwen* also makes use of the metacritical perspective of double-voicing to explore similar issues, linking the artistic aspirations of MacEwen to her own, while at the same time creating space in which to question her presumption to MacEwen's life story.

In the early 1990s, a number of established theatre artists took up the mantle of autobiography proper and embraced the one-to-one correspondence implicit in full-blooded autobiography, creating work that explicitly situated themselves as the central subject. Not necessarily limited exclusively to solo performance, these autobiographical works forge two ontologically distinct roles into one for the autobiographical artist-subject. The subject straddles both actual and fictional worlds, sharing a name and body as both performer and character are 'me' or 'I.' Notable plays in this style include Djanet Sears's *Afrika Solo* (1990), George Seremba's *Come Good Rain* (1990), Guillermo Verdecchia's *Fronteras Americanas* (1993), and Ken Garnhum's *Pants on Fire* (1994). Informed by the feminist credo that the personal is indeed political, autobiographical storytelling brings ordinary experience to the fore, claiming space in the public sphere for previously undervalued and neglected self-stories. In this mode, autobiographical performance was at that time and continues to be primarily the domain of voices from outside the mainstream, with the vast majority of work being produced by women, gay, lesbian, or transgendered individuals, and performers from visible minority cultures. Around the turn of the millennium, autobiographical playwright-performers Sears, Seremba, Verdecchia, and Garnhum have been joined by d'bi young anitafrika (the sankofa trilogy), Lorena Gale (*Je me souviens*), Diane Flacks (*Bear With Me*), Nina Arsenault (*The Silicone Diaries, I am Barbie*), Monique Mojica (*Chocolate Woman Dreams the Milky Way*), Carmen Aguirre (*The Trigger, Blue Box*), and Fringe fixture TJ Dawe (*Totem Figures*), among many others.

A primary aspect of the consciousness-raising project of feminism, of bringing the quotidian into view through autobiographical acts, is simply to create visibility and awareness, to say, 'I exist. This is my life.' However, the public telling of self-stories quickly moves beyond mere description or demonstration to take on a profoundly performative quality. Autobiographical performance provides, for each of the performers listed above, a vehicle for the creation of identity, a way to speak oneself into being. The act of performance itself becomes a strategy to grant self-possessive agency to the performing subject and thereby avert objectification and marginalization. The conditions that make this generative act possible are embedded in the creative frame of performance itself, fostered by the innate duality of performer and protagonist. Suzanne Henke explains: 'Because the author can instantiate the alienated or marginal self into the pliable body of a protean text, the newly revised subject, emerging as the semifictive protagonist of an enabling counter-narrative, is free to rebel against the values and practices of a dominant culture and to assume an empowered position of political agency in the world.'[33]

Performing Autobiography locates this statement of the transformative power of autobiography at its core. Each of the nine contemporary Canadian plays discussed here features autobiographical subjects who take up the project of self-performance not only as a way to engage with their personal pasts but also as a catalyst to a newly imagined future. In selecting autobiographical performance texts that enact performative transformations of this kind, *Performing Autobiography* purposely eschews autobiography of actual-world persons telling actual-life histories. So, instead of 'straight' or unmediated autobiography, the plays discussed here are all works of what I am calling 'meta-autobiography,' that is, the autobiographers in these plays stand at one remove from the usual realm of autobiography. In each case, the autobiographical author-subjects examined in this study are fictional characters inhabiting already fictional worlds. Detaching autobiographical work from a real-world referent and treating these dramatic autobiographies as metacritical texts magnifies core challenges to autobiography, pertaining to expectations around the verifiable truth of the narrative offered and also to the way the separate personae of the autobiographical 'I' are ontologically organized.

Seeking to definitively establish a boundary between the genre of literary autobiography from first-person novels, Philippe Lejeune attempts to assert the foundational qualities of autobiography. Ultimately, the two essential criteria he proposes reflect his initial concern to distinguish a fact-based genre from a fictional one. First, he declares that the author of autobiography must be identical to the narrative voice and also to the protagonist of the related narrative. These three personae – author-subject, narrator, and protagonist – subsumed under the common identifier 'I' share a name and a history. Second, the subject must be a real person.[34] Together these criteria work to stabilize the tripartite roles of autobiographical subject, narrator, and protagonist and, by yoking them together, attach them firmly to a 'truth.' However, the innate stacked or nested structure of storytelling works to loosen these bonds and open substantial gaps among the layers. In the process of creating autobiography, the original subject is necessarily split into several ontologically distinct versions: The real-world subject residing in world[a] – the actual world occupied by you and me – decides to become an author and in an act of divine performative creation gives birth to a performer-narrator resident in world[b] who in her turn engenders the character-protagonist citizen of the nested world[c].[35] In this chain of increasingly fictional characters, only the primary subject of autobiography is solidly rooted in world[a]. For every subsequent version, the likeness to the original subject is diluted, as each creator makes choices about what to include, what to omit, what to emphasize or ignore, and in what order events are to be related. Moreover, as George Gusdorf points out, in addition to the decreasing faithfulness of replication, there is conversely increasing self-awareness and editorial intervention: 'The original sin of autobiography is first one of logical coherence and rationalization. The narrative is conscious, and since the narrator's consciousness directs the narrative, it seems to him incontestable that it has also directed his life. In other words, the act of reflecting that is essential to conscious awareness is transferred, by a kind of unavoidable optical illusion, back to the stage of the event itself.'[36] For Patrice Pavis, the dual presence of the author-subject and the character-protagonist creates a paradox in autoperformance: 'As soon as he [the autobiographical subject] appears to be there, present and real, he is also taking on a role as a character which at the same time prevents him from bearing autobiographical witness.'[37]

However, given that the conditions of identity across ontological levels and attachment to real-world referents are by their nature already not as tight as Lejeune might have hoped, I have chosen in *Performing Autobiography* to shift the terms of reference from the actually actual world of world[a] to the provisionally actual world, world[b] – a shift that does not mark a significant difference of kind but only of degree. It is in this difference of degree that these foundational aspects of autobiography – the promise of truth and the dialogic interplay of autobiographical personae across ontological levels – are opened up for critical observation, but also for manipulation and deconstruction.

The fictive origins of these meta-autobiographers also serve to augment the performative potential which lies at the heart of the autobiographical process; it is this potential that enables autobiographers to imagine new selves and to bring those selves into being. The term 'performativity,' then, is used here in its narrow sense. Rather than indicating broadly a set of qualities attached to performance in general, the performative underpinning of autobiography traces its history to J.L. Austin's *How to Do Things with Words*. As Austin points out, some words do actual work in and of themselves. For example, in the phrase 'I promise,' the act of promising is embedded in the words themselves. Naming works this way. So do cursing, betting, and banishing. Working out the particular conditions of sociolinguistic interaction under which a given speech act is felicitous or infelicitous, Austin sets out a strong exclusion specific to theatre: 'a performative utterance will ... be in a peculiar way hollow or void if said by an actor on the stage, or if introduced in a poem, or spoken in a soliloquy. This applies in a similar manner to any and every utterance – a sea change in special circumstances. Language in such circumstances is in special ways – intelligibly – used not seriously, but in ways parasitic upon its normal use – ways which fall under the doctrine of the etiolations of language.'[38] By highlighting the situation of the questionable utterance 'on the stage' or 'in a poem' or 'in a soliloquy,' Austin seems to be pointing towards the phenomenological recognition that transposes a work of art into an aesthetic object.[39] With this emphasis on the artistic context, Austin's prohibition can be better understood to refer to performative statements spoken within a fictional frame, that is, not merely by anyone standing 'on the stage,' but the significant criterion is that the speech is uttered by a character in a fictional world. Statements pronounced in this context will have no effect (lacking what Austin calls illocutionary force) in the actual world. That seems fair enough – an actor who makes a promise in his role as Hamlet is not reasonably expected to be bound by that promise when he steps out of the fictional world, removes his costume, and exits the theatre. The wording used by Austin describing language within fictional worlds as parasitic or as an etiolation – a blanching or fading, a bleaching out of the original – supports an understanding that fictional worlds, although similar perhaps to the actual world, are shadow copies, lesser than and dependent upon higher-order worlds. Thus, this restriction speaks to the projected inability of performative language to cross the boundaries between worlds; a speech act produced in world[b] has no force to effect change in world[a]. Yet, this restriction need not render all theatrical performatives void. Within the firm boundaries of a single fictional world, speech acts do successfully operate. For Hamlet, Ophelia, Claudius, and the other citizens of Shakespeare's play, their fictional world is unimpeachably real – real to them. And so in this provisionally actual world, promises may be made or broken, but the act of promising is not essentially void or infelicitous from the outset. Thus, as long as performatives function inside an ontologically homogenous environment – a single fictional world or level – they are valid.

The main cause of the hollowness of performative language across world boundaries is tied to the duality of the actor-character. Although they share one body and one voice, there are two distinct personae present. It is nonsensical to hold the actor accountable for the performative acts of her character. However, this situation changes in the context of autobiographical performance (pace Austin: a sea change in special circumstances) where the usual separation of the actor-narrator from the character-protagonist is elided by their common identity. For an autobiographical performer who is retelling and who is also re-enacting personal history, autobiographical narrative transcends its status as simply a story and becomes again lived experience. Reiterated experience is transferred across ontological levels from the fictional protagonist who is 'me' to the actual-world subject who is also 'me,' causing the 'new' secondary experience to resonate against the original historical event. In this way, what seems like 'pretending' or 'just saying so' can actually cause profound real-world change. For fictional characters, this cross-world performative potential of autobiographical performance is heightened. Autobiographers who are already made in performance are innately amenable to being changed by performance. Drawing on the flexibility of this different material existence, these characters challenge authorial power. Mimicking the work done by their first authors, they turn their creative will on themselves to craft new stories and new identities. If this kind of self-altering ability is offered to actual-world autobiographers, then how much more pliable and more powerful is an already fictive autobiographer who, usurping the power of the playwright, repeats the same constitutive process of her own fictional creation?

Psychologically speaking, there is no self without narrative. That is to say, the self does not possess an autonomous a priori existence that is passively described by self-narration. Rather, the self is continually being created, shaped, and reshaped through narrative, as the raw material of experience is sifted, sorted, and reorganized into stories. It is now an accepted principle in constructivist psychology that one's sense of self depends on autobiography.[40] At an essential level, we are our memories. I am the stories that I compose about myself. As Stephen Crites explains: 'Storytelling is not an arbitrary imposition upon remembered experience, altogether alien to its own much simpler form ... [This is not only because] consciousness has a form of its own, without which no coherent experience at all would be possible ... [but because] the form of active consciousness, i.e., the form of its experiencing, is in at least some rudimentary sense narrative.'[41] Although narrative naturally arises out of lived experience as we recount the stories of our lives, conversely, the storehouse of experience – the self – is not only recorded in autobiographical self-stories, but is in fact created out of those narratives. 'As narratives are apprehended, they give rise to the selves that apprehend them ... As narratives reach out to tap a preexisting identity, they construct a fluid, evolving identity-in-the-making. Spinning out their tellings through choice of words, degree of elaboration, attribution of causality and sequentiality, and the foregrounding and backgrounding of emotions, circumstances, and behaviour, narrators build novel understandings of themselves-in-the-world. In this manner, selves evolve in the time frame of a single telling as well as in the course of the many tellings that eventually compose a life.'[42] Thus, even the highest order self, the self who is a citizen of the actual world, is also under these parameters a kind of a fiction. The coloration of the word 'fiction' here then does not stress its connotations of pretence or untruthfulness, but it is meant to place emphasis on the constructed or manipulated nature of the self, suggesting that all selves are products of autobiography. Eakin reframes this interdependence of self and story as a question, asking, 'In what sense can a narrative about identity be said to be equivalent to that same identity? Or is it rather that identity can be said to be a narrative of some kind?'[43] Given this symbiotic relationship of self to narrative, the impulse to create autobiography becomes almost a basic human need.

Casual communications are peppered with autobiographical statements, regularly recounting the accomplishments, frustrations, successes, and scandals of one's day. Beyond these mundane 'housekeeping' self-stories that are told many times every day, the impetus to sustained public autobiography invariably arises from an unresolved crisis.[44] As Jean Starobinski notes, 'One would hardly have sufficient motive to write an autobiography had not some radical change occurred in his life.'[45] Anthony Paul Kerby adds, 'much of our own narrating can usefully be seen as driven by some ... conflict, tension, or crisis in our own lives.'[46] With crisis as a primary motivator to autobiographical reflection, the relative position of the author-subject to that crisis affects the potential scope for performative self-creation or revision. Crisis acts as the fulcrum across which the central tension in autobiography is expressed, balancing the documentary writing of a life story and the lifelong process of that identity under construction. Susanna Egan traces a change in this tension away from autobiography as documentation, pulling instead in the other direction to emphasize performative construction. She associates this change in the temporal orientation of the autobiographical narrator from past to future with a turn towards the anti-heroic. Contemporary autobiography as a field has progressively moved away from the teleological determinism of mapping the life achievements of great men and women (mostly men) to their well-documented and lauded end. Instead, the genre has shifted to the middle, becoming not only increasingly catholic and embracing more plebeian subjects, but also taking up lives that are far from finished. Autobiographers are not waiting for their later years to look back on crisis and its ultimate resolution. These younger autobiographers take up the story as a means to confront crisis head-on. 'Prompted to write by situations that will not go away, they can rarely invoke closure ... the writings being records in process, affirmations of survival so far, not of finite or final achievement.'[47] Autobiography in this context is very much an action undertaken, a verb, rather than the product of that act, a noun. 'Significantly, because the crisis in each case is current and continuing, it [the autobiographical work] seems to emphasize memory rather less than future possibilities, narratives of identity rather less than the presence of a survivor.'[48] Thus, the orientation of these autobiographical narratives taken up in medias res is decidedly Janus-faced. Standing at the point of crisis (or just immediately after), the narrator-performer is fixed in the immediate present, looking backward but also moving into the future. Autobiographical subjects delve into crisis to relive it but also to live it from a new perspective, to reshape their connection to this crisis, and to position themselves for survival. It is this kind of 'anti-heroic' autobiography that maximizes the performative potential of autobiography to be radically transformative, allowing autobiographical subjects to imagine a new future, or to be a new person. Moreover, while print and other recorded media, as fixed documents already located in the past relative to the moment of consumption by a reader or listener, are reflective of the retrospective vector of autobiography, the immediacy of live performance shared with a present audience fosters the sense of a life in progress and remains open to performative revision. 'Autobiographical performances ... capitalise on theatre's unique temporality, its here and nowness, and on its ability to respond to and engage with the present, while always keeping an eye on the future.'[49]

Looking at postmodern novels by Samuel Beckett, Christine Brooke-Rose, and Angela Carter, Debra Malina identifies a parallel between violent events within the content of these works and the repetition of this violence perpetrated against the work itself. This violence is inherent in the processes of subject creation, operating paradoxically as 'destructive construction.'[50] 'Narrative constitutes the subject in part by breaking down the very structures that apparently define subjects and lend them their air of stability.'[51] Not only is there violence in the 'marking off' of a subject through the erection of a boundary[52] but also in the transgression of these boundaries figured as rape or as a carnivalesque dissolution of hierarchy.[53] In Malina's chosen works, the penetration and disruption of constitutive narrative boundaries is paralleled in acts of physical violence against the characters themselves.

This same pattern appears in the millennial meta-autobiographies analysed here. Crisis in these plays is multiplied across the ontological levels of the performance. The characters experience some violent events – rape, wartime injury, a train crash, and a car crash; they are witness to single murders and to genocide. One character attempts suicide, a decision brought on by a loss of vocation. Another kills his old self metaphorically in a sex-change operation. Cynicism aside, these personal nightmares are not atypical subject matter for contemporary autobiography. Beyond the harm to self (both physical and psychological) within the story, which figures as autobiography's catalytic crisis, the autobiographical crises staged in these meta-plays work as metaphorical concretizations of threats to the story itself. Violence enacted in autobiographical narratives within fictional worlds (world^b) is reiterated at a structural level (world^a) as the boundaries between worlds are breached by metalepsis.[54] It is the perceptual border placed around a fictional world that brings that world into existence, cognitively carving out fictional space from the surrounding actual world.[55] However, when that border is compromised by metaleptic intrusions and migrations, the security of the fictional world contained within is at risk. If the border becomes too permeable and does not hold, the fictional world within may dissolve. For example, a fictional world will collapse if its author decides to discontinue the story or if the story is seriously destabilized through narrative inconsistency. And yet, as these plays show, cross-world connections and moments of ontological ambiguity between worlds grant the characters a certain freedom. In those moments, links are forged across ontologically distinct worlds connecting past, present, and future selves, links that enable the fragmented autobiographical self to gain insight from alternative positions or roles. Metaleptic crises that threaten autobiographical processes are invariably violent, but are also the source of autobiographical regeneration as the transformative process is recruited to create and protect narrative ability.

With this model of performatively regenerative autobiography in hand, the plays discussed in the following chapters function as critical texts in their own right, airing out and working through key challenges for the practice of autobiography. First performed and published in the first decade of the twenty-first century, these millennial plays – *Perfect Pie*

(Judith Thompson), *The Drawer Boy* (Michael Healey), *Goodness* (Michael Redhill), *Eternal Hydra* (Anton Piatigorsky), *Shadows* (Timothy Findley), *Billy Twinkle* (Ronnie Burkett), *In On It* (Daniel MacIvor), *Scorched* (Wajdi Mouawad), and *Written on Water* (Michel Marc Bouchard) – present metacritical views of autobiography. Even though I treat the plays as critical texts with theoretical insights into problems around autobiography, my approach to these plays is through their theatricality, using a method of production analysis described by Judith Milhous and Robert D. Hume (*Producible Interpretation: Eight English Plays, 1675–1707*). Producible interpretation invites the adoption of a distinctly theatrical perspective to generate a 'critical reading that a director could communicate to an audience in performance.'[56] By reading and viewing the plays as a potential director, at least in imagination, the critic is primed to interpret the possibilities inherent in the text with a sensitivity attuned to moments of choice. Following this methodology, the text, then, is not to be read as a literary artefact; the aim of this method is to envision the text in production. Moreover, Milhous and Hume encourage the conjuring of text into potential performance not as a singular ideal version but rather as a multiplicity of interpretations. It is incumbent on the critic to evaluate all possible choices suggested by the text: 'A production analysis is a series of architect's sketches, not the blueprints that would be necessary to bring any one of them to actuality.'[57] Through this approach, plays are reanimated through 'thick description,' combining textual analysis of the printed text's dialogue and stage directions with historical evidence and eyewitness accounts of multiple productions. Production analysis operates as an alternative to performance analysis. Performance analysis attempts to engage the full circumstances of a singular performance event. Andrew Sofer notes the strengths and weaknesses of this approach: 'Performance analysis enjoys the distinct advantage of dealing with actuality, with a production complete in all its details, with the experience of the real thing. Of course, the advantage is also a disadvantage: the critic is stuck with what the performance gives him. The production analyst is far freer to pursue hypothesis and speculation to envision interpretive possibilities.'[58] Rather than offer a single definitive interpretation, the goal of production analysis is to suggest viable possibilities for the text, enlivened in the theatre, and then to consider the critical implications of these various understandings.

One distinctive feature of the autobiographical project is that self-stories are contained in a fragile archive. Self-stories are, of course, highly dependent on memory. In addition to the natural memory erosion of simple forgetting, potential self-stories may be threatened by amnesia due to senility, dementia, brain damage, or emotional trauma. In Judith Thompson's *Perfect Pie* and Michael Healey's *The Drawer Boy*, protagonists Patsy and Angus both suffer from narrative dysfunction associated with trauma-related amnesia that inhibits the realization of an extended self. Following the pathology of dysnarrativias, described by Kay Young and Jeffrey L. Saver ('The Neurology of Narrative'), one may diagnose Angus's symptoms as consistent with what they call 'Arrested Narration,' limiting his memory to only the last few minutes, whereas Patsy manifests 'Unbounded Narration.' As Angus painstakingly acquires the procedure for autobiographical performance, Patsy relates a series of thematically associated episodes as she attempts to zero in on the lost memories. The first chapter begins by exploring the relation of identity to memory and asking the question: 'Can there be autobiography without memory?' Answering this question with a qualified yes, this analysis articulates the strategies whereby both characters are able to work across fictional world boundaries and across the ontological divide between autobiographer and autobiographical subject to heal both. For Angus and Patsy, the retrieval of an objectively verifiable past is beyond their reach. Nevertheless, the reflexive process of undertaking performative autobiography becomes not simply self-discovery but a radical act of self-creation.

Complementary to the ability of the autobiographical subject to remember and articulate their self-story is the willingness of an audience to listen to that story. Autobiography is dependent on communication; the autobiographical subject needs to be given voice and an audience. Another threat, then, to autobiography arises out of breaks in the transmission of the story, particularly with regard to stories that are hard to hear. Chapter 2 demonstrates how the play *Goodness* posits the development of an engaged morally responsible witness to autobiographical trauma narratives, who uses performative language to effect change. A play about an unnamed genocide in an unspecified country, *Goodness* by Michael Redhill centres on the encounter between Althea, a survivor who recounts her autobiographical tale, and Michael (the playwright as himself), who listens to that story and becomes the required performative witness. Issues around autobiography and the instability of truth are reflected in the play's structure, which is marred by metalepsis as borders between worlds collapse, opening the historiography of each remembered world to performative contingency. The problems of the preservation of memory and the potential for performative change are embodied in two key props, two objects which claim to house the past

and which attempt to transcend fictional and temporal world boundaries – Michael's notebook containing his notes for the play *Goodness* and
a gun, the only piece of evidence to a murder, now in Althea's possession.

Whereas the physical and emotional traumas experienced by Patsy
and Angus inhibit their narrative capacity, verbal attacks in *Eternal Hydra*
by Anton Piatigorsky and *Shadows* by Timothy Findley cripple the corpus of the story directly. It is no longer the fault of memory loss, which
cuts off the story at the root; rather, these stories are actively prevented
from blossoming and bearing fruit through such narratively hostile acts
as lying, silencing, and plagiarism. Although the impetus to self-narration may be essential to the actualization of that self, sometimes autobiographers are rendered vulnerable with regard to storytelling because
of physical, emotional, or intellectual disabilities or marginalization by
socio-economic, political, or cultural factors. In these cases, vulnerable
autobiographies can be hijacked – altered, co-opted, or lost entirely. The
situation of vulnerable autobiographies raises ethical questions pertaining to the relation of the dependent subject-autobiographer to those
who control the means of production or publication. After tracing several tactics for narrative coercion and control, chapter 3 will show how
some of these vulnerable subjects use metatheatrically 'messy' strategies
to manipulate the usual boundaries that contain fictional worlds and
successfully set their stories free in higher-order worlds.

Another distinctive feature of autobiographical storytelling is the dis-
junction in the performative 'now' of the self over time. The 'me' that
speaks now is not the same 'me' that experienced those events. In print,
autobiographical experience is translated into words alone, but in performance autobiographically invested objects complement and complicate the performance text. These objects enter into the performance and
cross the temporal divide, existing simultaneously as historically 'authentic' objects and as theatrical props of indeterminate provenance which
are then imbued with significance in the presently unfolding fiction. For
example, a knife is used to slice a grapefruit by an autobiographical performer who asserts that this is the knife that her father always used.[59]
On the one hand, the presence of the actual knife carries weight as an
actual thing bearing historical meaning. The presence of a world[a] object
performing itself in a world[b] setting sets up interpretative expectations
that are not part of the usual theatrical transposition of a perceptually
'blank' actual prop into a fictionally loaded object. On the other hand,
this is precisely the challenge to autobiographical objects since the claim
of the grapefruit knife to historical authenticity may in some cases be

unverifiable. It may, despite the performer's assertion of authenticity, be an ordinary knife from the prop storage room. This ambiguity appended to how objects transport experience across time is a persistent interpretive problem for autobiographical performance. The performer's body is, of course, the most potent of these variously temporally coded objects.

For the autobiographical solo performer, the inescapable presence of the authentic subject-body is an object of intense fascination for the audience. Perceived to hold 'the truth,' the physical body marked by experience competes for priority with the performatively generated self that is recounting those same experiences. Ric Knowles, drawing on Jill Dolan's concept of utopian performativity, describes particular moments of autobiographical solo performance rooted in the reality of the body that evoke a 'phenomenological frisson.'[60] But how does this bodily relationship at the heart of autobiographical performance work if the protagonist role is occupied by a puppet? In *Billy Twinkle*, created and performed by internationally acclaimed puppeteer Ronnie Burkett, the eponymous autobiographical subject is a cruise ship puppeteer stuck in the middle of his life. When he is fired from his job, he contemplates suicide. Pulling him back from the edge, his dead mentor Sid Diamond returns as a ghostly hand puppet. Sid forces Billy to take up the mantle of autobiography and perform his life as a marionette show. Ultimately, by separating the autobiographical roles of author-subject, narrator, and protagonist across human and puppet performers, questions around the autobiographical body come into focus. Considering the audience's perceptual 'frisson' through the lens of the puppet-body, this 'upsurge of the real'[61] constitutes the pivot in the arc of autobiographical transformation. It marks a moment of intersection between the historical subject-body and the re-enactment of the present-tense protagonist, thus opening up an intersubjective view to the future as the subject re-encounters and assimilates the initializing autobiographical crisis.

Although autobiography is the writing (performing) of a life (*bios*), life and autobiography are not fully synchronous. Gaps between experience and autobiography arise inevitably at the beginning and end of life. Memory starts only between ages three and six, and so it is impossible to present a direct account of one's birth or earliest years. The autobiographical accounting of one's first memory is a cliché of the genre. Likewise there is a similar impossible gap at the end of life. When the autobiographical subject dies, autobiography may simply stop, halting mid-story without the opportunity for summation. Alternatively, autobiography that ends before the death of its subject leaves another silent space, much like the inaccessible time in one's infancy. Sorting out this distinction between things that end and things that stop is the central concern of Daniel MacIvor's play *In On It*. The play is a work of autothanatography as the protagonists This One (Brad) and That One (Brian) rent a theatre to stage a series of scenes – both remembered and imagined – to try to give meaning to Brad's death, resulting from a car crash with a blue Mercedes. Folding time to cross over the usually impenetrable divide between life and death, Brad and Brian disrupt the containing frame of performance. Their convoluted Escher-like show presents several beginnings and several endings, testing the analogy between life itself and the autobiographical performance of that life to see what can be salvaged from beyond the parenthetical limits of autobiography. Paul John Eakin in his book *How Our Lives Became Stories* notes that 'there is always a gap or rupture that divides us from the knowledge that we seek.'[62] He explains that the knowledge we seek is the experience of catching ourselves in the act of becoming selves. Meta-autobiographies that self-reflexively depict or at least worry at this process of self-creation offer a way to look into this gap. These millennial metatheatrical autobiographies abandon the modern question of 'Who am I?' instead turning to ask the postmodern question 'How am I?' or simply 'Am I?' Placing the emphasis on the process of self-performance, rather than on the production of a definitive self, these plays suggest that identity is to be found not in the answers we seek but in the questions that we ask.

Chapter One

Narrative Failure and the Loss of an Autobiographical Self: *Perfect Pie* and *The Drawer Boy*

Self cannot be separated from narrative. It seems a bold claim, but there it is – we cannot live without stories. In the last two decades, it has become an accepted principle in psychology that the sense of self depends on autobiography.[1] Naturally, narrative arises out of experience as we tell stories of our lives; but conversely, the storehouse of experience – the self – is not only shaped by but actually created out of narrative. A major proponent of this constructivist theory of the narratively generated self, Jerome Bruner argues that worldmaking is the principal function of the mind. Just as physics or art or history are modes of making a world,[2] narrative is also a way of worldmaking and autobiography a way of 'life-making.'[3] Bruner goes on to argue that 'we seem to have no other way of describing "lived time" save in the form of a narrative. Which is not to say that there are not other temporal forms that can be imposed on the experience of time, but none of them succeeds in capturing the sense of *lived* time.'[4] Not only does narrative best describe life, but life itself is made out of narrative: '"Life" … is the same kind of construction of the human imagination as "a narrative" is. It is constructed by human beings through active ratiocination … In the end, it is a narrative achievement. There is no such thing psychologically as "life itself."'[5] And so, just as life is entwined with narrative for us, flesh-and-blood citizens of the actual world, it is even more so for citizens of fictional worlds since the lived experience of these characters is always already formed in words. Divorced from a specific, actual embodied self, a fictional self is a purely performative creation. Having already been created once through the performative act of a playwright, fictional characters experience auto/biography-within or what I am calling meta-auto/biography as a practically applicable reiteration of their own basic constitutive process. But, if one's self is dependent on performative auto/biography, then that same narratively constituted fictive self is especially vulnerable to erosion and erasure through memory loss and narrative disability.

Setting aside the idea of a unitary self, psychologist Ulric Neisser proposes a model comprising five aspects of self, reflected in the ways in which individuals know themselves: the ecological self, the interpersonal self, the extended self, the private self, the conceptual self. Among these disparate selves, it is the extended self that deals particularly with memory and anticipation, projecting the self forward or backward in time. Two kinds of memories contribute to the extended self: episodic memory, which is the recollection of specific experience (things I can remember having done), and procedural memory, which encompasses repeated and familiar routines (things I think of myself doing regularly).[6] Amnesia is the primary pathology of the extended self.

In two contemporaneous plays, *The Drawer Boy* (1999)[7] by Michael Healey and *Perfect Pie* (1999)[8] by Judith Thompson, characters Angus and Patsy suffer from trauma-related amnesia that inhibits the realization of a full extended self. Painted in broad strokes, the plays' precis share similar outlines. Both are set in rural farmhouses: one near Clinton, Ontario, and the other in eastern Ontario near Marmora. In both plays, the quotidian routines of these central characters are disrupted by the visit of a city dweller. And not coincidentally – I think – these urban catalysts, Miles and Francesca, are both professional actors. It is out of these transformational encounters that ultimately Angus and Patsy themselves become artists. Using storytelling and performance to access and rebuild self losses, they take up a therapeutic program of creating narrative. These meta-autobiographers actively challenge perceptions of autobiography as simply a one-way street where narrative captures and reflects the true circumstances of an actual life. Autobiographical performance-within opens opportunity to reverse the flow of causation. As performative autobiographers, Angus and Patsy tell stories not to document an extant self, but rather they create and recreate a fluid developmental self through ongoing reiterative narratives that privilege process over product. Memory loss in both Angus and Patsy jeopardizes the usual cognitive bridge between self and narrative, a bridge that joins the past experience of the subject and the present-tense recounting and re-performing of that experience. Because this traditional path is closed to them, both characters explore basic structures of autobiography in an attempt to access lost narratives and, more importantly, to participate in the narrative process. The break in memory manifests not simply as a temporal disruption of past and present but also represents a disconnect in the referential relationship between the actual-world author-subject of autobiography and his or her fictional representations. Angus and Patsy manipulate the ontological relations of these distinct roles, working across layered fictional worlds to reconcile the gaps in memory and heal the extended self.

Philippe Lejeune, in a seminal text for autobiographical studies, proposes a kind of social contract that directs the veridical expectations of a reader engaged with autobiography. In an attempt to distinguish autobiography proper from first-person novels, Lejeune sets out a number of criteria, but ultimately only two are definitive: First, the author, narrator, and protagonist must be identical; and second, the author-subject must be a real person.[9] Figured as a self-story, autobiography actively fosters the assimilation of author, narrator, and protagonist under the single pronoun 'I.' But, from the perspective of the autobiographical story as aesthetic creation, these three roles do not share equivalent ontological status; they reside instead in a series of nested worlds, which we can imagine as a set of concentric rings. The outermost ring comprises the actual world, and the autobiographical subject is an autonomous citizen of this world – designated world[a]. The narrator, albeit a mirror of the subject and voice for her thoughts, is her fictional creation. This narrative figure is a selective and not fully determinate doppelganger, residing in the inner circle of world[b]. Next, the protagonist is the narrator's character. Although the character is conjured in the first person as 'I,' this 'I' is subject to the descriptive control of the narrator. This 'I' is yet another layered persona-within, belonging properly to world[c]. By affirming the identity of these three roles, Lejeune's autobiographical pact emphasizes their congruence as aspects of the world[a] subject and minimizes their necessarily fictive separation arising out of the constructive act of writing a life. The novel form also conspires to elide this graphical difference by rendering subject, narrator, and character invisible, giving the reader the illusion of direct and unmediated intercourse with the authoring subject. The textual symbol 'I' speaks ambiguously for all three personae.

However, the dramatic form in performance, which replaces the printed 'I' with a fully determinate actor body, works in the opposite direction, tending to highlight the ontological separation of roles. In the theatre we are always confronted by the embodied actor who is ambivalently both an actual-world person and a fictional-world character. Embodied autobiographical performance fosters tension between the biological equivalency of the author-subject and the protagonist and the necessary ontological difference between creator and character. This situation further augments perceptual slippage between the fiction and the actual-world referent. Even in identity, both performer and audience still must engage with the multiple ontological roles of autobiography. Although Lejeune's pact fosters a unified view of the autobiographical 'I,' and the essential duality of theatre demands that these 'I's' be kept separate, the theatrical imperative need not nullify the autobiographical pact. Both these audience attitudes can be held in a productive tension.

Amnesia also problematizes the expected unity among these autobiographical roles. Not only are the roles of author-subject, narrator, and protagonist separated by ontology as shown above, they are also divided by time. Each role engages the narrative self from a different perspective and with different knowledge. Without memory, the bridge between the past subject and the present author breaks down. Self and narrative are interdependent, mediated by memory. Without memory there can be no narrative, but similarly, without memory there can be no self.

Another core feature of autobiography is that it is always relational. Whereas the autobiographical pact considers the vertical relation of subject-narrator-protagonist, there is also the horizontal relation to be accounted for. Even the self-story of a single individual includes the story of others – parents, children, spouses, friends, and acquaintances. And so, autobiography implies biography. Conversely, biography also entails autobiography. Focusing on the process of creating biography and autobiography, Susanna Egan targets this relational aspect of autobiography, which blurs the traditional distinction between biographer and subject. Invariably, in such narratives, the biographer himself becomes the subject as well. She identifies the graphic novel *Maus* by Art Spiegelman as a key example of this phenomenon. In *Maus*, the story is divided between the biography of the father Vladek and the shared experience of father and son in the recounting of that story, and so both men stand both inside and outside the narrative. Taking on the dual roles of autobiographer/biographer and biographical subject, these paired characters each straddle two worlds. Mirror talk, for Egan, then, is plainly 'the encounter of two lives in which the biographer is also an autobiographer.'[10] This is the reason for my use of the blended and/or construction 'auto/biography.' It is intended to denote the interdependent dialogue of the primary autobiographical subject and the biographer who finds her own life inextricably reflected and embedded in the shared process of creating a narrative self. 'Such collaborations seem far less concerned with mimesis, however, than with authenticating the processes of discovery and re-cognition.'[11] This focus on the processes of self-discovery and renewing cognition is especially relevant to the potential for auto/biography in *The Drawer Boy* and *Perfect Pie*, where characters suffer significant memory loss, making recovery of an objectively authenticated past difficult at a minimum, and in some important ways, impossible.

This chapter, then, explores how the intersubjective process of mirror talk functions as a kind of therapy to the injured extended self. Taking the two plays as parallel case studies, the narrative strategies whereby the dialogic auto/biographical pairs of Angus and Morgan and Patsy and Marie/Francesca exploit the tension between ambivalent theatrical duality and the expectation of unity to reconcile the tripartite roles of author-narrator-protagonist (discussed by Lejeune) will be compared. Although on one hand, Patsy and Angus's status as fictive characters leaves them vulnerable to the power of words to undermine the stability of a narratively generated self, on the other hand, their ontological situation as characters born in words also grants them significant power to wield that same performative power to write a self. Drawing on the cognitive pairing of procedural memory and episodic memory, Patsy and Angus use strengths in one to supplement faults in the other. Weaving across multiple ontological levels of nested fictional worlds, these characters are empowered by the world-building processes of performative narrative. It is through the combination of theatre-making and self-making that they move towards healing. Ultimately, the reflexive process of undertaking performative autobiography then becomes not simply self-discovery but a radical act of self-creation.

Arrested Narration (Angus)

Angus, in *The Drawer Boy*, is plagued by significant memory loss, resulting from a wartime head trauma. His procedural memory is intact but his episodic memory is almost nil. As Morgan says, 'He can run the tractor, he can use the stove. Knits. Does the accounts. You should see him with a bunch of figures. Only thing that makes Angus different is he can't remember from one minute to the next. He only knows right now. He won't remember you' (13). Each time Miles encounters Angus, he has to reintroduce himself:

ANGUS: Hullo. Hey. Get outta here.
MILES: Hello, Angus. My name is Miles and I'm staying with you and Morgan to
    learn about farming so I can write a play about it.
ANGUS: Hello, Miles. Okay. (15)

In terms of a narrative self engaged with worldmaking, Angus's world is a very young world, only a few minutes old and constantly being recreated. It is also a world full of gaps; although at least initially Angus seems unaware of them. This pathology precisely matches a condition Kay Young and Jeffrey L. Saver term 'Arrested Narration.'[12]

The central biography of *The Drawer Boy* is couched in the narrated story of the drawer boy and the farmer boy told daily by Morgan to Angus. Although recounted in the third person, a feature which endows the tale with a mythic quality, this is patently their own history. Angus is the one who draws, and Morgan is the farmer. The story traces some highlights of their youth: playing shinny and building a cabin, through their enlistment in the army and tour of duty in Europe. In England, they meet two girls and fall in love. The four friends are making plans to marry and return to Canada when Angus, the drawer boy, is injured in an air raid and 'before the doctor could close up the wound, the boy's memory escaped' (29). In the story, they all come home. There is a double wedding. They start to build a house. Then one day, the English girls are out driving and are both killed in a collision with an army transport. Morgan tells how they are buried at the highest point in the county. And then it was the two friends again. 'The farmer farms and tends to the place on the hill and keeps their memories safe, like a pail of raspberries between them' (30). This story is retold by various narrators four times over the course of the play. The first of these retellings appears to be the worn standby told yet again by Morgan to soothe Angus. Inhibited by his amnesia, Angus cannot have autobiography; the actual world[a] subject does not recognize Lejeune's projected equivalency to the story's world[c] protagonist. This disconnect also precludes successful mirror talk since Angus lacks autobiographical memory. Although he is ostensibly the subject, he cannot produce his own story; rather, it is given to him. Likewise, Morgan's participation in a shared mirror-talk relation is also reduced. Morgan is Angus's biographer and to a lesser extent his own autobiographer as he too appears in the history. But significantly, Morgan contributes to the subject-protagonist break because his choice to frame the story in the third person stylistically downplays the expected equation of auto/biographer to the story. Moreover, the dialogic interplay of biographical mirror talk is abridged to a rehearsed script with stock phrases and responses. When we first witness this storytelling in the play, there are two additional layered audiences – the actual-world audience and Miles, who overhears the story and records it in his notebook. The second version of Angus's biography is truncated, delivering just the beginning sections as Miles rehearses the story privately. The full performance of Miles's enactment of the story takes place offstage at a rehearsal.[13] In the third version, Angus asks Miles to enact the story. When he balks, Angus takes up the narration himself.

I want to pause here between the second and third retellings of the 'drawer boy' story to draw attention to a key relational shift with regard to Angus's position vis-à-vis his own obscured biography. After Miles performs the story for Angus and Morgan as part of an invited rehearsal, Angus not only remembers the performance that he has just witnessed, but he remembers Miles as well. It is significant that the catalyst to this breakthrough, this small repair to his extended self, seems to come out of performance.[14] He has listened to Morgan tell the story innumerable times without any effect on his memory; however, in seeing Miles as Morgan telling the story, the event becomes memorable and so does the performer. Faithful to the essential dually aware audience stance, Angus is not confused by the actorly embodiment that allows Miles to become Morgan. He reflexively traces his awareness of theatrical duality, walking through the process of theatrical embodiment and the resultant doubleness and comes to the correct perception of the event he just witnessed: 'D'you know for a long while there I thought she was Alison Lobb? I thought, good Lord, Alison Lobb's lost her senses and gone up there on the stage and was talking to us. It wasn't, you know. That was an actress. Acting' (32). Likewise, Angus marks the highly presentational style of a mimed tractor: 'Them two girls were the tires … That was exactly right' (32).[15] Taking note of the innate gap between theatre and (fictive) life, between world^c and world^b, emphasized in Miles's show through stylized mimicry, Angus revels in the process of the story, in the relational dialogue between the actress and 'Alison Lobb,' between actor bodies and a tractor. These pairs display as part of the theatrical embodiment convention an analogy to auto/biographical mirror talk. The actress is to 'Alison Lobb' as the auto/biographical narrator is to the protagonist, expressing simultaneously both unity and aesthetic separation as one creates the other. These relational pairs reach out in two directions: upward from the actress to the real Alison Lobb – Alison^b – and downward from the actress to the fictive character, Alison^d.[16] Bending across worlds, this performative triangle is closed on the third side, linking the two Alisons as an autobiographically congruent subject and protagonist. That Angus can remember the procedure for making a fictional person or object fits with the pathology of his amnesia – procedural or routine memory is intact. It is only episodic memory that is lacking. By apprehending theatre-making as similar to baking bread or doing accounts, Angus is able to absorb it. He recalls Miles, perhaps not in his own right as an autonomous person, but as an ingredient of that process. Also Miles's transformation into a second Morgan further cements this recollection, since Morgan is the one person that Angus does remember. Surprisingly, Angus also recalls the performance event itself, not just the procedure but also this particular instance of doing the procedure. Moving beyond the initial catalysing performance of Miles as Morgan, Angus begins to practise this process for making fictional worlds. Displaying that same critical awareness of theatrical duality, Angus and Miles work through the plot of *Hamlet* (37–9) and begin on James Reaney's *The Donnelly Trilogy* (39). Whether this is sound psychology or not, the play does suggest that apprehension of a new procedural memory makes possible retention of a related episodic memory. This is the first stage of Angus's cure.

The next step builds on this causal relation between procedural memory of theatrical embodiment as productive mirror talk showing how to tell a story and on the episodic content of the story itself. With the process now apparent, Angus desires to repeat Miles's impersonation, putting into practice the theatre-making/autobiography-making recipe. By doing so, he evolves from the passive subject of his own biography to take a hand in the telling of that story. Angus applies the distanced embodiment process of meta-auto/biography, repeating the performative structure that he witnessed with the actress as Alison and Miles as Morgan. Instead of taking on the role of Morgan directly, he creates two inset levels of framing. 'Okay. I'll pretend to be you pretending to be Morgan telling the story ... Now, would I be on a stage, or ... Okay then. (*he contorts himself, raises his voice an octave*) Now I'm you. (*he hunches over, drops his voice two octaves*) And now I'm you being Morgan. Any good?'(42). The careful procedural establishment of theatrical multiplicity is central. The effect is to create yet another Morgan and to push the story even deeper in terms of its ontological status as a multiply nested fiction. Telling the story, Angus makes a few small adjustments. His version is less elaborate with fewer details and some words are replaced, but he does not flip it around to his own perspective. At one point, the two even cite a little piece of stock banter with Miles as Angus and Angus as Morgan.

Out of this new cross-world mirror-talk play between Angus as narrator and Angus as biographical subject/protagonist, which aligns both the heightened aesthetic gap between these creative roles and their apparent autobiographical unity in one present body, two things happen. The first thing is that Angus becomes aware, seemingly for the first time, of specific gaps between the story and his experience. As Morgan, he repeats the statements: 'They went home. There was a double wedding, he said the stolen poem. They started the house, the two houses joined.' 'Right' says Miles, repeating Angus's usual response (29, 44). But then Angus asks, 'Where? … Where's the houses joined and separate.' Somehow by voicing this statement himself as an ontologically doubled subject/protagonist, it occurs to him that this statement, describing a 'fictional' world^d, does not accurately reflect his present experience in world^b. Miles deflects attention back to the telling of the story, deferring to Morgan as the authenticating author: 'Let's ask him later' (44). This works for a bit until Angus arrives at another inconsistency. He repeats that the girls were taken 'to the highest point in the county. Buried there' (44). He starts to continue but then stops, 'And now it's … I've never been there. The highest point in the county. Hey' (45). Twice, Miles tries to move past this to 'now it's the two friends again' (44, 45). Miles doesn't know that there is a problem with the story. He is committed to the script, and to the autobiographical pact embedded in the script, which promises fidelity between the life of the subject and its protagonist, bridged by narrative performance. But Angus gets stuck on this point. He can sense a rift opening in that triangular pact. For Miles, the pattern holds and this is an unproblematic autobiography. For Angus, however, his perceptual stance to the story to this point has not required him to consider the actual-world referent implied by autobiography. Now, by enacting the process of theatre-making/autobiography-making and taking on the performative role of narrator at the apex of the triangle, he comes to a new awareness of the expected, but here denied, conflation between life and story.

The second thing that happens as a result of Angus's performance of the story is that his narrative role does not hold. When naming his possessive relation to the girls, Angus gets himself tangled up in his performance of Morgan.

ANGUS: They bought a black car. Now, Angus, you say 'My Sally.'
MILES: My Sally. Your … ?
ANGUS: My Frances. Your Sally loved to drive the car, the black car. To where raspberries grew wild. A horse came the other way, and the army headed straight for my Frances, but my Sally – your Sally – Sally …
MILES: She turned her side into the truck, to save her friend, Angus. Your Sally tried to save Frances. (44)

Angus abandons his role as Miles-Morgan and Miles's clarification is directed to Angus as Angus. Starting as distanced narrative biographer, Angus momentarily becomes an autobiographer, and then quickly slides out of the story into his self as subject. The amnesiac disconnection between narrator and subject is revealed by Angus's immersion in the aesthetically distinct roles established by the theatrical frame. But the separation cannot be maintained and Angus seeks to renew the unity of roles promised by the autobiographical pact, restoring an integrated author/subject-narrator-protagonist. Enriched by new knowledge gained by these relational shifts and rifts, Angus is led 'by a memory so faint' to find under the floorboards the architectural drawings that he had made for the two houses joined but never built (45). A new memory surfaces and he can remember seeing Morgan hide them there. Ultimately, Angus's narrative agency, which is his own but which is also filtered through the persona of 'Miles-as-Morgan the biographer-narrator,' directly affects his subject memory of his own story. The shifting ground of this performance contrarily applies theatrical duality to align the unitary relational interactions of author-subject, narrator, and protagonist all in one person. In this interplay, Angus is able to change perspective among these roles, and through a meta-emphasis on the story of the story, is able to recover some of the original.

The fourth and last telling of the story is doubled. Overwhelmed by newly unearthed shards of memory and frustrated by the emerging inconsistencies between the story and his experience, Angus demands that Miles and Morgan both retell the story together:

ANGUS: Okay. Both of you. Tell it.
MORGAN: I will, but not with him here.
ANGUS: Yes, with him here. I'm scared. You're scaring me, yuh bastard. From
    the start. Both of you.
MORGAN: Angus, don't –
ANGUS: BOTH OF YOU. Please. So I can match them. Find me in them. I'm
    starved to know. (61)

Here, the concept of mirror talk is epitomized in performance in the twin biographers of Morgan and Miles as Morgan actually standing side by side, reflecting Angus's story back to him. Of course, auto/biography is as much about what is hidden as what is revealed. And in this case, Angus's amnesia abetted Morgan's own authorial omissions. This challenge to Morgan's biographical authority instigates a key shift bringing these auto/biographical deficiencies to the fore. Morgan has been the curator of the past. As he says himself, he 'keeps their memories safe, like a pail of raspberries between them' (30). It is ambiguous whether he is referring to the memory of the dead English girls or to the memories of himself and Angus. Comparing the first unaccountable telling of the story to the last version mirroring Miles against Morgan, there is a clear shift of causality relating to Morgan's fictive role-within. As Miles and Morgan square off, we read their narration in different modes – necessary theatrical duality against Lejeune's autobiographical unity. Whereas Miles performs the authoritative Morgan of version one, Morgan is compelled by Angus to speak as himself.

ANGUS: Right. Go. You start

...

But, as him

...

Like you did, on the ... thing.

MILES: I got it. (*as* MORGAN) A couple of boys played shinney, and went to
    school, and grew up.

ANGUS: Now you.

MORGAN: They built –

ANGUS: But, as you.

MORGAN: ... We built a cabin together. You dreamed it up, I did all the work. (61)

This shift from third person to the first person, from a theatrical performance of a scripted self to an integrated autobiographer-narrator-protagonist, marks a crucial change in the narrative relation between the two men. Events which Morgan formerly elided as passive events of unspecified causation are altered in the retelling to admit his influence; significantly, Morgan writes himself into the story. In the old version, Morgan says, 'And then they both got called up, both went off to Europe. No school for the one, no farm for the other' (28). In the last telling, 'You were about to go to university. I talked you out of it. The war started, and I talked you into volunteering with me ... We were so excited. No. I was excited, and you were – you were my friend. We joined up' (62). Similarly, in the recounting of Angus's accident, Miles performs the original detached narrative which is contrasted by Morgan's revision.

MILES: The drawer boy was standing down the street, looking at a large house.

MORGAN: You were running like hell down the street, trying to get back. Jesus.
    You were laughing.

MILES: The front door of the house flew off when the shell hit, and the drawer
    boy watched it come for him.

MORGAN: A piece of shrapnel caught you from behind. I watched you get carried through the air. You flew right at me. You nearly died. (62–3)

Not only does Miles mirror Morgan, but Morgan stages interior dialogic
reflections, reaching across time to rewrite his fictive autobiographical
protagonist. Morgan as biographer revises the story and begins to admit
his responsibility in Angus's injury, thus becoming an autobiographer.
And, while Morgan as protagonist is being written into the past, his subjectivity is being rewritten in the present. As a fictive character in world^b,
he actually changes. Paradoxically, he is recreated from the bottom up;
work done by the world^c narrator changes the world^d protagonist but
also by extension the world^b self. So, by the same cross-world process of
performative mirroring that allows Angus to access a new (possibly more
authentic) narrative past, Morgan too is reconfigured by the narrative
process, liberated into assuming an active role in their shared story. Significantly, after this point in the storytelling, Miles as second narrator
falls away and Morgan tells an entirely new story: All four friends did
return to Canada. But there was no wedding. Eventually Angus's injury-
altered personality made the situation untenable, and both girls left bro-
ken-hearted, returning to England. Clearly, the dialogic nature of auto/
biography is a transformative catalyst not only for the putative subject but
also for the narrator. Through this cross-world process of mirror talk, the
story that emerges is less idealized and heavily fragmented but assigns a
more balanced authorial agency to the players. Both Angus and Morgan
are held accountable for the past. This adoption of responsibility topples
the formerly monolithic fairytale, replacing the false object with a shared
creative process of discovery: 'MORGAN. We'll tell it to each other. Daily
… We'll fill it all in. If you can remember, we'll do that. / ANGUS. Even if
I don't. Let's do that' (65). This final agreement to continue the cyclical
narrative process of life-making through storytelling extends the restorative bridge by using procedural memory to feed episodic memory and so
rebuild a damaged extended self. But it is noteworthy that the emphasis
is on procedure. As Angus affirms, the 'cure' for both these friends lies
not in the revelation of a historical truth, which may lie permanently
out of reach, but in the continued reiterative exercise of creating a self
through stories.

Unbounded Narration (Patsy)

A similar cross-world strategy using procedural memory and theatre-making to rediscover or recreate particular episodic memory is also at work in *Perfect Pie*. Like Angus, Pasty also suffers from trauma-related memory loss that inhibits the realization of a full extended self, but in her case the pathology is more complex and the diagnosis, less straightforward. Patsy's memory loss manifests in disparate ways but all her symptoms originate with the last night she and Marie were together as teenagers. On that night of the Sadie Hawkins dance, while Patsy stays at home with a fever of 104°F, Marie is sexually assaulted by a gang of local boys. Later, the shell-shocked Marie and feverish Patsy cling together as they face an oncoming train. The resulting crash leaves Patsy in a coma. When she wakes up, her friend is gone. This is the primary loss; Patsy has an experiential rupture, commencing with the crash of the train and ending with her revival eight weeks later. During this missing time, Marie has disappeared and Patsy's ignorance (or traumatic repression) of her friend's fate troubles her. Moving backward chronologically from the crash, Patsy suffers other uncertainties and gaps. Neither Marie's account of her assault nor Patsy's witnessing to that account is very coherent. Caught between Marie who is rambling in her distress and Patsy, delirious with fever, even the audience receives only a fragmentary impressionistic sense of what happened. As Patsy says later, 'But I wasn't sure ... You know, you were talking so – so – fast ... And wild, you were turning in circles and ... you were, like, in a state of shock, I guess' (21–2). Arguably, Patsy shares in her friend's emotional trauma, which closes off access to those events. Trauma has a direct relation to memory, causing a violent experience to be effaced; that is, the emotional toll of the original experience overwhelms the subject, and to protect the vulnerable self, the traumatic experience is sequestered. And without the imprint of the original experience, that event cannot later be recalled as memory. 'What returns to haunt the victim ... is not only the reality of the violent event but also the reality of the way that its violence has not yet been fully known.'[17] One more lasting effect of Patsy's injuries is that she is now afflicted with epilepsy and experiences regular grand mal seizures. A mundane explanation for the onset of her seizures is that concussion can trigger epilepsy. The more magical explanation is that from the power of the train, Patsy and Marie have merged, and in the exchange Patsy has assumed Marie's condition. Epilepsy causes amnesia, not just in the duration of the seizure itself but repeated seizures inflict ever more damage to the brain, increasing memory faults. Linking her epileptic seizures to Marie's assault, Patsy describes one of her seizures in sexualized overtones as rape by a stalker (50–1). This too supports the hypothesis of transference of shared emotional trauma from Marie to Patsy in the moment of the crash.

If Angus's dysnarrativity can be diagnosed as Arrested Narration, I would argue that we might call Patsy's condition, according to Young and Saver's pathology, Unbounded Narration. Both characters share the primary symptom of amnesia, which divides the potential narrative autobiographer from his or her own lived subjectivity; however, secondary effects of that amnesia are virtual opposites. While Angus lacks basic narrative ability, Patsy exhibits an imaginatively rich and multifaceted capacity for storytelling. Those afflicted with Unbounded Narration 'develop confabulation, restlessly fabricating narratives that purport to describe recent events ... but actually hav[e] little or no relationship to genuine occurrences ... [Stories are told] not from a desire to impress, entertain, instruct or deceive, but simply from a desire to respond to another human being's query with a story.'[18]

The story of *Perfect Pie* proceeds along two parallel paths. One day, Patsy is visited by her estranged friend, Marie, renamed Francesca, and now a well-known actress. Interspersed with the conversation of the adult women are moments from their past, performed by a second set of younger actresses. As the play progresses, both timelines converge on a critical series of events – Marie's assault, the train crash, Patsy's coma, and Marie's disappearance. From one perspective, this arrangement seems like a straightforward use of memories or 'flashbacks' nested into a present-day main narrative.[19] However, the play subverts this simple understanding, suggesting quite strongly that Francesca is not real. Marie did not survive the train crash and the older version of Marie as Francesca has been conjured into existence by Patsy.[20] Drawing evidence from Patsy's opening monologue in which she declares, 'I know in my heart you did not survive' (4), several commentators acknowledge that 'the narrative line is ambiguous enough for the whole play to be read in retrospect as a story about Patsy keeping the precious gift of her dead friend alive in memory.'[21] However, this interpretation has significant repercussions for the play as auto/biography. Typically, mirror-talk pairs share an ontological equivalency, both inhabiting the same world and working interdependently to tell the story of two lives. This is the case in *The Drawer Boy* where the mirror-talk roles of auto/biographer, narrator, and protagonist are passed among Angus, Morgan, and Miles as they play a range of roles reciting the same story; in *Perfect Pie*, however, mirror-talk roles are radically blurred with these usually disparate perspectives housed within a single intra-dialogic person. Although the play is populated by four characters – Patsy and her friend Marie as children/ teenagers, the older Patsy, and an older Marie who has changed her name to Francesca – the geography of the narrative structure is such that they do not have equivalent status. In fact, as I will argue, Patsy is quite alone. Through the hierarchical organization of stories within stories and worlds within worlds, the adult Patsy is established as the pre-eminent playwright, ontologically superior to the others, who are her fictive creations.

If Marie's survival as Francesca has been authored by Patsy, then all the 'present day' scenes of the two women as adults are also a fictive creation. So, Patsy as playwright has given birth to the adult Francesca but also to a fictive version of herself. The borders between worlds have become permeable and Patsy of world[b] is talking to her own character born into world[c]. Thus, Francesca is Patsy's mirror-talk partner. Patsy has created her own mirror, bringing Marie into the present, reincarnated as Francesca. This scenario of cross-world mirror talk is further complicated by scene 2, which consists only of this stage direction: '*Light on MARIE/FRANCESCA, in her own dark apartment in the Big City, a great view of the city at night behind her. She remembers …*' (4). The illumination of Francesca marks her 'birth' into world[c] through Patsy's creation, yet critically, the stage direction '*She remembers …*' admits her as a co-creator of the past memories of world[d]. Just as Patsy is ontologically fragmented by her amnesia, the character of Francesca is not fully contiguous with Marie. Autobiography normally separates the narrator from her created protagonist in time, but here that gap is exacerbated by the ambiguity of Francesca's existence and Patsy's memorial control over both the historical Marie and the fictive Francesca. This persistent ambiguity regarding the genealogical links between author-subject, narrators, and protagonists precludes any possibility of accommodating Lejeune's expectation of a reliable unitary identity across roles.

Like Angus, Patsy applies procedural memory to compensate for a faulty episodic memory. Because Patsy is the primary playwright of *Perfect Pie* (we never hear anyone else's voice), all the stories she tells are reflections of her own creative process. Unlike Angus's resolutely linear story, Patsy's narrative is linked associatively. And instead of applying performance directly to repair a damaged self as Angus does, Patsy makes her lost friend as a pie. Her preoccupation with pie making and her thematic associations with pies embedded in her monologue and subsequent nested fictions are all part of her process of self-reconstruction. She metaphorically blends her use of performative language with her culinary art of assembling pastry and fillings to create both past Marie and present Francesca. During her opening monologue/letter to Francesca, Patsy makes a rhubarb pie and sends it in the mail to her friend. In the final framing speech of the play, Patsy begins to craft another pie and makes explicit the Francesca-as-pie metaphor: 'And I'll be looking at that snow ... and I will knead it and knead it until my hands they are aching and I think I'm like making you. I like...form you; right in front of my eyes, right here at my kitchen table into flesh' (91). It is noteworthy that the rhubarb pie filling of the play is substituted for steak and kidney in the pies Patsy makes in Thompson's 1994 monologue 'Perfect Pie,' which constitutes an urtext for the play. As in the play, Patsy's earlier monologue is underscored by actions of pie making. Images of internal organs and organ meats linked with Patsy's mother's cancer and the dead Marie permeate this monologue (167, 170). The plot of the monologue deviates from the play quite significantly in relation to Patsy's friendship with Marie. In the full-length play, Patsy is Marie's stalwart defender. She seems to hold her own against other kids at school, while maintaining a close friendship with the bullied Marie. In the monologue, however, Patsy buys her way into the dominant social circle by betraying her friend: 'I know I promised you, I swore on the lives of my future kids, I would never tell a soul as long as I lived and I never planned to tell at all, Marie, not at all. It just spilled out of my mouth. Like organ meats' (166). Organ meats are associated with Marie and also organ meats are the story, the telling of the secret spilling out. Patsy's crime then is the telling of Marie, Marie herself being a prohibited story. The parallel processes of Marie created by a story and Marie baked as a pie are much more clearly aligned in the earlier monologue; nevertheless, traces remain in the play. Since Patsy is the author (perhaps in combination with Francesca) of the past memories, the selection of these memories is significant. Many of the memories of the younger girls concern moments in which Patsy 'improves' Marie: Patsy gets rid of her lice, carefully picking out her nits and covering her hair with margarine (29–30). Patsy advises her that she needs to bathe more regularly (68–9). Patsy corrects her language (38). Finally, Patsy dresses her for the dance; she brushes her hair, she does her make-up, Patsy even sewed the dress (76–9). Marie is Patsy's art. In an act of projection, when Patsy imagines her lost friend into future existence, she calls her Francesca ('free') and makes her an actress, someone who makes new characters with her own voice and body.

If Francesca is a pie, is she perfect? Pies in *Perfect Pie* are prizewinning but are also burned and frozen. Leaving aside burning pies for the moment, ice images pervade the play. Virtually every nested narrative in the play is associated with ice or snow. More than once, the word 'Ice' is used with anomalous capitalization (7, 76, 79). 'Ice' seems to function as a trigger word, a key which opens up other memories. In addition to experiencing narrative disability stemming from basic memory faults, individuals with epilepsy also often have difficulty retrieving memories out of context. The memories have been correctly stored but access is blocked. Moreover, a distraction, in the form of a similar memory, can also become an obstacle to memory.[22] The seemingly random collection of stories told by Patsy and by her subordinate fictive personae appears to cohere in this way. They share similar associative elements, which may or may not be helpful, as Patsy circles to get closer to the hole at the centre. One therapeutic technique used with amnesiacs requires a psychologist to provide random words, attempting to draw up associated memories, as the afflicted person works gradually closer and closer to the temporal borders of the empty landscape of the post-traumatic amnesia period.[23] This seems to be what Patsy is doing.

The first image is ice, specifically the emotional impression that ice is beautiful and romantic. Young Patsy describes kissing as like making strawberry ice cream by hand: 'it's getting colder and churning and if you put your face in right into the churning ice cream at that moment when it's goin' pink with the red juice and turning from cream to ice cream ... THAT ... is the moment of a kiss' (74). The adult Francesca narrates in detail a dream of living alone in the Arctic 'near water, and giant shifting icebergs, surrounded only by violets and snowdrops and rough weeds, with the occasional hare racing by my little snow house' (59). Just as the red juice of the berries blends with the cold cream, and there are flowers in Francesca's arctic imaginings, quite a few of the ice and snow images combine some living thing covered over by snow, sometimes beautifully preserved in death by the cold. In their first meeting as children, Patsy invites Marie to her birthday party, 'We'll be going skating on the river' (14). Also, there will be a game of musical chairs using a 'really cool song about this pretty girl who is on her way to a party? And it's like really cold like a hundred below zero and so she like falls asleep in the snow and she freezes in her Sleighride thing?' (14). Later, there is a quite lengthy scene as the girls act out this song; Patsy calls herself Annabel Lee (a likely reference to the poem of the same name by Edgar Allan Poe)[24] and Marie becomes Bon Bon McFee (41–3). In act 2, scene 8, Marie rehearses an audition monologue. Patsy describes her audition rhyme saying, 'It was the one about these girls? Skating in the summer?

And falling through the ice' (62).[25] The name that Patsy gives herself, 'Annabel Lee,' connects to two other deaths in *Perfect Pie*. Annabel is also the name of Patsy's stillborn daughter: 'I kissed her sweet little face with the white down, her toes, like Lily Of the Valley ... But I did not cry' (54). She is not frozen, but the imagery of being covered in white down and white lilies is analogous. In this thematic rhizome, Patsy's narrative compounds the image of ice as a romantic kiss or utopian landscape with ice as a frozen, idealized, beautiful death.

As she continues to circle around the amnesiac block, she associates the baby Annabel with another 'Belle' – the lost dog of Patsy's childhood. In a non sequitur at the end of one scene, Patsy wishes for the return of her dog: 'She's been gone for so long' (57). In another scene a little later, she recounts unexpectedly discovering the dog tied to a tree, dead. The description of the rotting corpse of the dog is gruesome. This death with the flies and the smell and Patsy gagging is far from the bloodless perfectly preserved icy deaths of the first two Annabels. Following this thematic line still nearer to the amnesiac blank time, Patsy adds Marie to this catalogue of lost beloveds. Frequently, Marie in her tormented and scapegoat state is associated with dogs. Patsy brushes dog shit off Marie's coat. The boys call her 'You Dog' (84). She herself says 'I'm the town dog' (74). Francesca describes Marie as 'a weird sister I have dogchained in the attic' (6). As with Belle, Patsy yearns for Marie's return, made impossible by her death. And in contrast to the 'beautiful' deaths of Annabel Lee and the baby Annabel, the dog Belle's body in death is grotesque, and so we might imagine would be Marie's.[26] And with this, Patsy gets right to the edge of the blank space, almost to the brink of knowledge of the thing she cannot see.

Following this thematic spiral, I think the thing that floats just beyond Patsy's awareness is Marie's corpse. Already filthy and distressed from the boys' assault, Marie's body is crushed by the impact with the train. We can only imagine what Patsy saw. Although the play *Perfect Pie* progresses chronologically towards the dual trauma of sexual assault and the train crash, these are not the events that need memorial reconstruction. The thing Patsy does not remember is what happened to Marie after the train crash. This reading I am suggesting, in which Patsy's associations lead to this horrific image, opens up two possibilities: either Patsy did see the mangled corpse of Marie and has suppressed that traumatic image of her dead friend or she truly does not know and this traumatic image is one that she has conjured up but will not actively consider. There can be no definitive answer. Likewise, although this narrative cycle enacted in Thompson's *Perfect Pie* moves Patsy close to admitting this image, the amnesiac block is not removed. And yet, the cyclical structure of the play, beginning and ending with the same phrase and actions, implies that there will be other attempts, one of which may succeed.

These narrations, spiralling towards this blank at the centre, span several ontological levels: the fictive Francesca living in world^c tells her dreams creating a world^d, young Patsy – herself already several fictional worlds removed from Patsy the principal narrator – narrates her own past experience in discovering her dog, the girls assume the characters of Annabel Lee and Bon Bon McFee to perform the play-within of the sleigh ride, and so on. Patsy uses these stories-within to create a cross-world rhizomatic network in an effort to fill in the blank spaces of her own history. The self that emerges is not singular or necessarily coherent but rather takes its strength from its multiplicity of perspectives, putting down roots in multiple fictional worlds. Like Angus's meta-narration of himself as Miles-as-Morgan which brings him closer to building a subject-self through association with the fictional protagonist of his story, Patsy too makes deliberate use of explicit theatrical duality to build the bridge between subject and protagonist, finding herself in the stories of herself. There is for Angus some promise of equivalency between the present subject and the past protagonist as his recollections are supported and authenticated as 'true' by Morgan. For Patsy, as a solitary auto/biographer engaged in mirror talk with her own characters, authentication is beyond her reach. So rather than the one-to-one correspondence of protagonist to subject sought by Angus, Patsy develops a many-to-one web, feeding the creation of self from multiple possible protagonists.

The Extended Self as Artistic Endeavour

Ultimately, Patsy's diagnosis of Unbounded Narrative is also her therapeutic strategy. She expresses unbounded performative creation (in a way that might be perceived as excessive, or we might just call it art) as a way of dealing with her seizures. She reclaims space and opens up new spaces through the imaginative re-performance/reliving of those experiences stripped away by memory loss, caused by the entwined factors of epilepsy and emotional trauma. *Perfect Pie* therefore can be read as a *kunstlerroman* (artist-coming-of-age story) for Patsy. But the epilepsy challenges her bardic gift; she constantly needs to carve out space, to preserve the past with words.

As twelve-year-olds, Patsy and Marie are forced by Patsy's mother to hide in a closet until a lightning storm passes. But later in their lives, lightning represents power. The train is lightning, and the train is power:

'I stare out the window and I see – just the glimpse of it, of the train speeding on to Montreal, the crash … does flash out, in my mind; like a sheet; of lightning' (4). Thinking back to the way she was abused by local children, Francesca tells Patsy, 'You know its funny, I stand backstage sometimes and conjure … their faces and I am filled with a kind of electric energy, you know? And then I go out, like a lightning bolt; I guess it's revenge. I take my revenge on the stage somehow' (33). The lightning power absorbed in the crash is transmuted into an artistic power but it also flashes out in Patsy's seizures. The stage direction accompanying her entry into seizure instructs, 'the lights flicker as a lightning storm' (45). In June 1996, Judith Thompson spoke about her experiences with epilepsy and the relationship of fear to the creative process. When she describes her first grand mal seizure at the age of nine, the language she uses is very similar to that she gives to Patsy to describe her seizures. Both women identify the peak moment of fear as being pulled through the floor, out of the world, into invisibility. As mentioned earlier, for Patsy the fear is a sexual stalker:

> He is pulling and pullin' me closer … can't breathe … Can't breathe now and the people are so far away it's like he is moving me under the floor, the linoleum-marble floor and under the mall and the people and into the dark the pipes and the loneliness and they are all so far away and I will die under this floor like a cockroach all my life over, all over. (51)

In the next section of her speech, Thompson draws inspiration from a poem by Audre Lorde to assert that 'making theatre, or any kind of art, is taking up space.'[27] She connects the creation of art to epilepsy, presenting both as strategies for rebelling against a restrictive mask of imposed femininity; both are ways of taking up space. After writing her first play, *The Crackwalker*, she observed, 'not surprisingly, I am seizure free.'[28] For Thompson, art substitutes for the seizures as an alternate way of taking up space. It is noteworthy that both Thompson and her creation Patsy describe their seizures as being removed from the world, as not being allowed to take up space. So, paradoxically, whereas the inner imaginative experience of the seizure is to be without space, the outer experience of the seizure does take up physical and social space in a decidedly unfeminine way. Patsy draws power from her epilepsy and the lightning even as she creates stories to fill the void that lightning creates.

Patsy's nested stories about stories express a meta-auto/biographical awareness of process, each one meditating reflexively on the craft of performative storytelling, highlighting the distinct ontological status between the teller and the tale, between the artist and her art. In the early scenes of the play, woven into the conjuration of Francesca, the two women share a potent memory:

PATSY: And I think of the time.
FRANCESCA: that all but disappears
PATSY: We woke up.
FRANCESCA: when you wake up ...
PATSY: We were both in these softy soft flannel pajamees and you woke me up and you said, 'look' and I look out the window and I saw all this ...
FRANCESCA: Ice.
PATSY: Glistening, Shimmering, Crystalline –
FRANCESCA: Ice. (7)

The girls run outside in their nighties and slide all over laughing and shrieking – a joyful memory. After this, Francesca materializes in Patsy's kitchen. Out of the relived memory of the crash, Francesca realizes that in fact she saved Patsy's life. At some point, Marie recovered her senses and tried to get off the track. But the feverish Patsy became consumed with the idea of the power of the train: 'We are gonna die beautiful, we are gonna get crashed by the train and then fly through the sky' (88). Marie pulled her to safety. The adult Patsy says, 'You saved my life ... but you always had ... saved my life Marie. Ever since we were little girls ... Ever since you looked at me. With those eyes, like the bottom of Mud Lake. And spoke, with your mouth, all those thoughts. You will never ... know' (89). Patsy is saved by Marie, because it is Marie who makes Patsy into an artist. She is saved by her art. As she says, remembering Marie and the magical unexpected ice, 'you woke me up and you said, "look"' (7).

For Angus, too, the catalytic concatenation of theatre-making with self-making operates as a kind of *kunstlerroman*. Although for Angus it is not that he becomes an artist for the first time, but rather he recovers the artist that he used to be – the drawer boy reborn. As mentioned earlier, it is through cross-world dialogic auto/biographical performance that Angus is led to find under the floorboards the architectural drawings he made of the two houses joined. In the final image of the play, '*as the lights fade, ANGUS takes the drawings and holds them up where they used to live*' (66). Curiously, the drawings are not the only art object that is returned to Angus. In Morgan's fairy-tale version of their shared biography, he relates how Angus 'finished [school] easily, but never got his diploma because he wouldn't give back the poetry book' (28). Then, at the imagined double wedding of Morgan and Angus to the two English girls, Angus recited a poem from the stolen book. As the story is repeated, the poem from the stolen book morphs into simply 'the stolen poem' (44, 63). Ironically, the poem is not only stolen by Angus but also stolen from Angus by his amnesia. Through its shared association to the English girls and the wedding plans, the poem resurfaces with the drawings. Angus recites the poem 'At the Wedding March' by Gerard Manley Hopkins in full just before the lights begin to dim for the final blackout.

Like Angus at the end of *The Drawer Boy*, Patsy's potential cure lies not in the revelation of an objectively verifiable historical truth but rather in the pie making, theatre-making, self-making process of continued reiterative storytelling. For both characters, their location in an already fictive world precludes access to any kind of world[a] truth. And so this displacement of memory recovery shifts focus to the ongoing process of imaginative creation. 'Dysnarrativias highlight why narrative is the fundamental mode of organizing human experience … Narrative framing of the past allows predictions of the future; generating imaginary narratives allows the individual to safely (through internal fictions) explore the varied consequences of multitudinous response options.'[29] Performance is an external variation on this same kind of imaginative exploration of the 'what if?' Angus and Patsy cannot have auto/biography, for them it is not a noun. Rather, auto/biography describes the action of the story of the story. As an ongoing verb, it reaches into the future. Likewise, procedural memory is also future-oriented, as one follows the steps of a process moving forward to some end. At the end of both plays, the characters project this kind of future arising out of a repeated process of artistic creation and exploration. Angus and Morgan take on a shared commitment to tell the story every day: 'Let's do that' (65). Patsy also projects herself into the future: 'I'll be sitting here six months from now and making my pastry' (91) and making her friend once again. Through performative auto/biography, Patsy and Angus reconcile the present-tense and future-oriented author-subject of auto/biography with the creation of a historically limited protagonist, accepting both to be mutually contingent and fluid works in progress.

Chapter Two

Performative Witnessing to Autobiographies of Trauma: *Goodness*

'How does it feel?' 'How does it *feel?*' In an early scene of the play *Goodness* by playwright Michael Redhill,[1] one character asks, 'How does it feel?' to which another replies with the same question with a different intonation, 'How does it *feel?*' (11). In repetition, the question turns the object of interrogation from a direct experience ('How does it feel?') to a meta-experience of the experience: 'What does feeling feel like?' and 'What does it feel like to be asked the question how does it feel?' The main action of the play revolves around an encounter between a genocide survivor who tells her story and an initially reluctant listener who becomes a witness to that story. In that light, this question, 'How does it feel?' characterizes the play's central attitude towards storytelling and listening, an attitude which privileges affect over knowledge, and which employs a marked theatricality to translate that affective power of 'response-ability' generated by a survivor-storyteller into an engaged moral responsibility for that story taken up by a listening witness. As Kelly Oliver writes, 'Just as the various parts of the body cannot function without the circulation of blood and oxygen, the psyche cannot function without the circulation of affective energy ... We have an ethical and social responsibility to be vigilant in our attempts to open up the circulation and flow of affective energy in all of our relationships.'[2] In this chapter, I will demonstrate the way in which *Goodness* models the circulation of affect through dramatic creation. The play advocates for an active, ethically responsible audience-witness – what I am calling a performative witness – generating a hopeful witnessing strategy arising directly out of the play's looped metatheatrical structure of stories within stories.

When dealing with retelling significant traumatic events through drama, one approach is to adopt a style of documentary realism in the conviction that a strongly mimetic technique has the strongest claim to communicating truth. The more the presentation can deliver details, both factual and emotional, pertaining to the original event, the more convincing and moving it will be. Communicating the truth of an experience through an imitative imaginative re-enactment, however, can have a peculiar disconcerting effect. Julie Salverson, who writes extensively on the witnessing of trauma through drama and storytelling, recounts her audiencing[3] experience to one such retelling of a traumatic past: 'What disturbed me was a sense that [the performers] were not present in the performance, were not noticing themselves in the picture, and, consequently, that we as audience members were neither asked nor able to implicate ourselves. Audience and actors together were looking *out* at some exoticized and deliberately tragic other.'[4] Salverson argues that this emotionally submerged attitude and passive or effaced sense of self, which she names an 'erotics of injury,'[5] comes out of a naturalistic performance style and circumvents real engagement with the story at hand. Placing an emphasis on the obligation of the audience to become responsible witnesses to trauma, Salverson challenges us to find alternative performance modes and alternative dramatic styles and forms which promote active engagement for both performers and audience.

Considering the aesthetic component of art in relation to its content, Theodor Adorno famously condemned the writing of poetry in the aftermath of the Holocaust as 'barbaric' insofar as works of art generate aesthetic pleasure, and in this way they antithetically offer pain and horror clothed in beauty.[6] To see healing rather than horror in such art works, we might reread that word 'barbaric.' When we say something is barbaric, we mean that it is savage, cruel, or inhuman. However, this denotation of savagery comes out of a prior meaning: from the Greek word βάρβαρος (bárbaros), probably a reference to the stammering 'bar-bar' speech of foreigners, thus barbarians.[7] So, likewise, something barbaric is foreign or alien to civilization. In this second mode, poetry of the Holocaust is barbaric in the sense that it is unfamiliar or strange. Such an approach may remake an unspeakable history, rendering trauma again speakable through an aesthetic of strangeness or defamiliarization.[8]

Consistent with the search for an artistic form which captures this aesthetic barbarity, there has been a concerted move by trauma narratives in performance away from documentary realism and towards modes of heightened theatricality through the use of clown, melodrama, irony, and parody.[9] Operating within this tradition, *Goodness* also seeks to testify and recount a history of genocide using a heightened theatricality.

In this case, that theatricality is produced by metatheatrical play-within-a-play-type structures, relating to the creation of a multiplicity of nested fictional worlds and the solidity of the boundaries of those worlds. One way of arranging multiple worlds-within is to maintain world boundaries as solid, keeping each world ontologically distinct and producing 'neat' metatheatre.[10] In another pattern, the neat hierarchical arrangement of nested worlds is compromised though metalepsis as the barriers between the worlds are breached and characters from different worlds incongruously cross over and exert influence on the other play worlds in progress.[11] This is the 'messy' metatheatre produced by *Goodness*. This ontological messiness compromises potential access to any kind of authentic truth through its layered, looped narrative structure in two ways. First, the metatheatrical layering of worlds focuses awareness on the core process of engendering theatricality by reiterating the creation of fictional worlds. By drawing attention to the theatricality of the story being told, metatheatre serves to remind us that the act of telling history is just that; it is an act of telling. Any account of a past event lives at one remove from the original event, separated from it by time and inevitably tinted by an individual view. Distanced from the original event, history is necessarily a construction of the teller, and as such it offers no direct objective verification. Second, the persistent disruption of these looped worlds leads to competition between those sometimes divergent worlds for authenticity, resulting in a fundamental uncertainty about the story itself.

This ambiguity, the opening to doubt, introduced by metatheatrical and metaleptic structures, seems to pose a particular problem for a play concerned with genocide. A central feature of Holocaust narratives is the exhortation to listeners to remember the past. Desire to avoid the pain inherent in the retelling of horrific personal history is offset by a communal need to document that experience, to be fortified against deniers – accurate memory being a sure preventative measure against future horrors. As George Santayana said: 'Those who cannot remember the past are condemned to repeat it.'[12] Nevertheless, the recent and ongoing horrors of genocide in Cambodia, Bangladesh, East Timor, Bosnia-Herzegovina, Rwanda, and Darfur put the lie to this admonition. Simply remembering is not good enough. What is required is a move from an overwhelmed sympathetic passivity to a barbaric estranged engagement, from a concrete truth to an affective truth. Testimony to genocide lies at the core of *Goodness*. However, the play purposely dispenses with its duty to historical accuracy by sidestepping history altogether. Although one character presses for this information, he is continually deflected.

Beyond the reluctance of characters to divulge specific details, the play itself is silent, avoiding placing itself in time and space, but also purposely taking note of this silence. The worlds of *Goodness* are aggressively indeterminate in the way that Roman Ingarden reserves for fictional worlds, self-consciously contrasting these lacuna-riddled worlds with the fully determinate actual world.[13] *Goodness* is a play about an unnamed genocide, occurring in an unspecified county, which might be in Europe or it might be in Africa, at some time in the not-too-distant past. There is even disagreement between characters in different play worlds as to how many people were killed. In this way, *Goodness* overtly sheds its obligations to a rational objective truth of what happened, embracing rather a contingent affective truth, posed in the central question, 'How does it feel?'

Dr Dori Laub, a Holocaust survivor, a psychologist, and one of the founders of the Video Archive for Holocaust Testimonies at Yale University, tells this story about the importance of the affective aspect of bearing witness:

> A woman ... was relating her memories as an eyewitness of the Auschwitz uprising; a sudden intensity, passion and colour were infused into the narrative. She was fully there. 'All of a sudden,' she said, 'we saw four chimneys going up in flames, exploding. The flames shot into the sky, people were running. It was unbelievable.' There was a silence in the room, a fixed silence against which the woman's words reverberated loudly, as though carrying along an echo of the jubilant sounds exploding from behind barbed wires, a stampede of people breaking loose, screams, shots, battle cries, explosions ... The woman fell silent and the tumults of the moment faded. She became subdued again and her voice resumed the uneventful, almost monotonous and lamenting tone.[14]

Some time later, Dr Laub shared this woman's testimony at a conference with a group of historians. The historians claimed that this woman's memories were inaccurate – only one chimney had been destroyed in the uprising, not four. And because this detail was not accurate, the whole of her testimony must be discounted: 'It was utterly important to remain accurate, lest the revisionists in history discredit everything.'[15] Laub contests this dismissal, arguing that in fact this testimony offers a more potent truth beyond simple facts. He calls this affective shift in the tenor of the testimony 'breaking the frame.' Speaking about this experience is itself part of the experience. Laub writes, 'She was testifying not simply to empirical historical facts, but to the very secret of survival and of resistance to extermination ... The woman's testimony ... is breaking the frame of the concentration camp by and through her very testimony: she is breaking out of Auschwitz even by her very talking.'[16]

This temporal folding of the original event into its telling is a feature particular to trauma. With respect to how the past is retained and recalled, events marked by trauma are different from those which are simply remembered. Memories are narrative representations of past events. Memories repeat a previous lived experience. Trauma, on the other hand, causes the original experience to be effaced; that is, the emotional toll of the original experience overwhelms the subject and the experience cannot be fully experienced even as it is happening. And without the imprint of the original experience, that event cannot later be recalled as memory.[17] Thus, the telling of past trauma allows the event to come into being. Telling and living coincide. The representation is the event.[18] Testimony by a direct witness is not a reliving of the event but actually the original experience of the event for the first time. More than this, by recounting a strong affective truth, the testimony of this survivor has a real effect on her original experience. She breaks the frame of Auschwitz and performs her hope and freedom in the telling of this exceptional moment, coloured by the indelible emotional mark left by that moment. Thus, breaking the frame is not just a metaphor in the reliving of the experience, but actually in these particular moments when time folds in on itself, we see the performative power of language at work and present-day speech has the ability to rewrite past experience.

Theatre shares this seemingly paradoxical characteristic pattern of reiteration as creation. It is an innate feature of performance that stories rooted in the past – stories already written, already published, and already rehearsed – are (re)presented as spontaneous experience. Performance is a vehicle whereby the past is transmuted into the present. Theatre, like trauma, paradoxically generates primary experience through repetition of an obscured or missing past. This pattern of intrusion by present storytelling into a past story is the central feature of the metaleptic organization (or disorganization) of *Goodness*, which presents the same historical kernel in four distinct layers, ranging from world[a] – the actual world we now occupy – through a series of fictional worlds b, c, and d: Working from the inside out, world[d] contains the initial set of occurrences surrounding the incarceration of Mathias Todd. It is now ten years after the purges and Todd has been repatriated from Geneva as an accused instigator of the genocide in order that he may stand trial. However, rather than try him for genocide, the court decides instead to charge him with a single murder, the murder of a woman named Helena Sonnen, who belonged to the minority ethnic group and with whom Todd had had an affair. World^c consists of the telling of this story by Althea – Todd's prison guard – to Michael. In world^b, Michael, that is, Michael Redhill, the playwright, writes about his meeting with Althea. The product of his writing is the script for *Goodness*. And the outermost world, world^a, features the play *Goodness* as an immediate performance event, which stages within its frame each of these three repetitions.[19]

Typically, the layering of multiple worlds is figured as a spatial arrangement, described as worlds within worlds, or as nested boxes. The worlds of *Goodness*, however, are characterized primarily by time rather than space, as each layer repeats the same elemental story. Metalepsis, then, as it operates to breach the boundaries of these worlds, not only disrupts space allowing crossovers between here and there, but more disturbingly, time is disrupted and the past and sometimes the future merge in the ongoing immutable now of the performance in progress. By bringing two or more disparate times together into a shared now, this temporally blended metaleptic structure of the play repeats and complicates the relation between a play and its audience, between a story and its witness. Levinas describes witnessing in these terms as a feature of time: 'Witnessing is an event of two disjunctive temporalities, an event in which another's time disrupts mine. It is a new time, and interstitial time, neither mine or yours; an extraordinary disjuncture of I and other, an experience of proximity that initiates an "infinite distance without distance."'[20] In a small way, the dominant world of *Goodness* (world^c) is carved out from ordinary time in just this way. Michael enters into this interstitial time when he meets Althea, and bears witness to the story of her past. He is in London awaiting his flight back to Canada, held over in a third country which is neither destination nor home, when a man in a pub directs him to Althea. It is in this pause in his primary journey that Michael falls down the metaphorical rabbit hole. As he says: 'I had seven hours to catch my plane. I could have gone to a movie and had a nice long dinner somewhere, but ...' (22). The time spent with Althea in the isolation of her darkened apartment is very much a time out of the ordinary. As her dead are conjured and embodied in a ghostly performance which is past memory and present performance, the encounter between Michael's time and Althea's does initiate, through a disjunctive juxtaposition between these two temporal threads, a distance across time which cannot be bridged. But it is also a distance without distance as that past lives again in the present, close enough to touch. And Michael does interact with these apparitions: He grabs a deposition from Stephen and reads it. Julia argues with him. Todd drinks Michael's tea. The environment of Althea's apartment evokes the experience of theatre-going as also a similar interstitial time, in this respect creating infinite distance without distance, as we too sit in isolated darkness. Theatre augments this sense of the conflation of time as past events are re-enacted with seeming spontaneity. The impression of the story retold competes with the sense that we have been transported to bear invisible witness to the original event.

As a lived theatre event, *Goodness* fragments our phenomenological experience of time right from the outset. When the lights come up, we are surprised to find the playwright kneeling on the floor scratching down his thoughts in a notebook:

MICHAEL: That was it ... Sorry, I just have to get this down ... I'm trying to write a play ... although, if you can hear me, I guess it's finished. Even though right now I could throw it through a window. (*pause, realizing*) You're sitting in a theatre at this very moment, aren't you? Somewhere, in the future, you're in a dark room, and it just got quiet, and you have no idea what's going to happen to you. (9–10)

The notebook is the focal point for multiple synchronous interleaved timelines. In the present, Michael – Michael Redhill – is writing a play called *Goodness*. In his future (but our present), we are in a theatre watching the play that he has written. The play that the fictional Michael has written is autobiographical and so stands properly in the past, the foundation of the present writing experience. However, theatrical performance as a reifying of past experience, and also as an embodied creation from a text also fixed in the past, disrupts this orderly temporal relation. In the act of writing his past, a past which now includes the writing of this play, Michael casts himself forward into the future, where his past will unspool again. The notebook records Michael's experience in each of these timelines. It contains both a journal of Michael's encounter with Althea and it contains the doubled text of *Goodness*, running in parallel first as a printed pre-performance document and secondly as an underscore to its own performed repetition. Michael tells the audience, anticipating the play still to come, 'we have no idea what is going to happen to us.' In his capacity as the writer and narrator of that play, this Michael knows what will happen, but his temporal alter ego Michael – a character in this story – does not have that same omniscience.

Just as this device of staging of the playwright drives a wedge between the writer himself and his representation as a character, *Goodness* further fragments this persona again using metalepsis to detach the actor from the character, and present through this overt division alternate Michaels double-voiced with different levels of prescience and power. Michael continues: 'You're staring at the playwright. Although it's not me, I have to say. I'm being played tonight by Jordan Pettle. That's a little lie in the form of a person. You're in good hands with Jordan, by the way. He's an excellent actor … You probably saw him in *Waiting for Godot.* A Jewish Estragon – imagine. *For Godot, We're Waiting*' (10).[21] This confession exposes the primal theatrical lie – an actor speaks the playwright's words and both the actor and the playwright are pretending to voice a fictional third person. Here, the usual performative ventriloquism of the actor is brought to the fore with surreal effect as Pettle as Redhill speaks about himself in the third person. The result is a uniquely discomfiting blend, reminding us that the playwright, channelling the character, speaks in the actor's body. This 'lie in the form of person' is metalepsis personified, collapsing again the time of writing with the time of performance and letting both temporally absent Michaels speak to us simultaneously, channelled by the physically present actor.

By foregrounding the divisions and amalgamations between the playwright and his temporally distinct doppelganger within the play, *Goodness* underlines the causal relationships between lived time, knowledge gained from that experience, and the power that comes from that knowledge. As different retellings of the principal story repeat and overlap, what the characters and the various temporal incarnations of those characters know or do not know about how the story turns out has a significant impact on the capability of a character to be a responsible witness. On the most basic level, willingness to subject oneself to the experience of the story is connected to time via knowledge of the outcome, as the listener may quite naturally wish to resist exposure to the difficult re-experience of trauma. Laub asserts that 'the task of the listener is to be *unobtrusively present.*'[22] However, he notes that although the listener needs to fully partake in the experience of the trauma survivor, the listener is also a discrete individual who struggles with what he hears. The second witness faces the hazards of listening to horror, triggering his own existential worries, and opening himself to question his core beliefs and world view. Under these challenging conditions, listening witnesses may employ defensive strategies to protect themselves. Laub lists some of these usual defences, noting that these tendencies need to be controlled and overcome for authentic witnessing to occur. This question of how to be an authentic witness is central to *Goodness*. In this context, the question 'How does it feel?' is not primarily directed at Althea as a surviving witness but rather to Michael as a secondary, listening witness, emotionally exposed but also inevitably distanced and restricted in terms of his agency over the story.

However, significantly in *Goodness*, Michael in his capacity as a witness is not definitively restricted in this way. Because time is folded and characters live and interact across multiple iterations of the same story, knowledge can be carried across worlds. The looped temporal structure of the play permits characters to wield power over the story – both over its retelling and paradoxically over the original happenings. So, the defensive desire to avoid or deflect the story's emotional effects and moral reverberations can manifest in more than simple passive not listening. A witness can break through the world frames to exert performative agency and to change the story itself. Michael Redhill, in his trebled capacity as playwright, narrator, and character, is that performative witness.

The main action of the first act traces Michael's journey through various stages of resistance and avoidance as his defences are eroded and he learns to become the required witness without whom Althea's story and her truth cannot emerge. Michael's struggles with the witnessing stance become entangled with the normal prescience and performative power of being an author. At first, the writer in Michael inhibits his ability to give himself over to Althea's story, to be fully engaged with listening. Later, to become a morally responsible witness, Michael again takes up the power of words to exert agency. Through a key performative act, he moves beyond listening to accepting a certain culpability in the events he witnesses.

Even before one can be a witness, one must agree to enter into the contract of testimony.[23] Marital betrayal is the catalyst for Michael's first foray into witnessing. Wanting to gain access to his own family's historical trauma as Polish Jews murdered by the *Einstatzgruppen*, he travels to Poland in a misguided attempt to recover first-hand testimony from present-day Poles:

THERAPIST: You marry a non-Jew, she leaves you for a non-Jew. Any connection here to the sudden interest in the history of your people?
MICHAEL: Oh. You mean am I displacing my anger at my gentile ex-wife by trying to take it out on a bunch of Jew-killing Poles?

THERAPIST: Are you?
MICHAEL: I know what I'm doing, okay? (14)

Faced with this combination of righteousness and foreign naivety, the Poles he encounters are understandably not forthcoming. They are not hostile but are likewise not interested in Michael's 'quest,' and this preliminary and entirely wrong-headed gesture towards witnessing trauma is an unconditional failure. Significantly, Michael does not couch this endeavour as witnessing. His intent in going to Poland was not to truly listen. He arrived knowing the story already, seeking confirmation of the already known story.

After that debacle, when Michael again becomes aware of the audience, he exercises his authorial power to end the story: 'I took a train from Warsaw through the green green fields to Berlin, and from there went to London to wait for my plane home. Annnnd … you know what? That's the end of the play! Thank you for coming. Good night' (14). This closing declaration is followed by a blackout. When this first attempt at bearing witness fails, he takes action not as Michael[c] the character, but rather as Michael[b] the playwright-within. Defensively, he closes off that piece of his past experience and aborts the fictional world which housed its repetition. But in addition to his awkward experience in Poland, this is the narrative world that in his dual capacity as narrator of his own past and as playwright of *Goodness* he knows will lead to Althea and a second and more painful witnessing situation – a situation which he refuses. The story then starts again, seemingly without his permission: 'I said: good night' (15). In this moment, the temporal tensions between Michael[c]'s actual lived experience and the playwright Redhill's already-written drama bubble up. Although Michael[b] balks, godlike Michael[a] exerts his performative power and presses the story forward, compelling Michael to circle back into the past, to become again Michael[c] and accept the path which leads to a new contract of testimony. In performance, the music swells again 'Yonana, Yo,' and the other actors (characters?) take hold of Michael and force him into a chair, propelling him into the next scene. From one perspective it is the play *Goodness* and Michael[a] that restart the plot from their superior vantage. But from another not mutually exclusive perspective, it is the characters themselves from the inferior nested worlds that demand that their story be told. Michael does then capitulate and consents to participate, reactivating the story, addressing the audience, and introducing us to a man in a pub – the man who will send him to Althea.

The notebook is Michael's constant prop. It is rarely out of his hands. And following his nature as a writer, Michael initially performs witnessing as a writer and begins to take notes on what Althea is saying. When she sees him writing, she tells him to put the notebook away: 'You will not write about me' (28). Throughout the play, in the interplay between Althea and Michael, there are repeated contestations around his recording her words. In other moments, Althea uses the notebook as a way to affirm her authorial control over the story, saying to Michael, 'Why don't you take some notes ... Put this down' (40). Power inheres in writing through the possibility of mediation; as the story moves from the oral delivery by one person to the recording in writing by another, there is the opportunity and the threat of change, of editing, and of interpolation. Writing also exemplifies power as it facilitates the translation of story into property; the words of the story are now material objects, objects to be possessed and controlled through possession. Last, power is exercised through writing as it solidifies and fixes the fluid oral history. The story becomes fixed in the space of the page but also in time at the moment of its recording. In this way, the notebook seems to offer a certain kind of temporal security. All these characteristics associated with writing as a means of control are concretized by the key prop of Michael's notebook. However, the notebook itself, which at first seems to offer a bulwark against narrative instability in the looped worlds, is caught up in one of these paradoxical loops. Ultimately, at the very end – and I will discuss this important exchange in more detail later – Michael surrenders the notebook to Althea when he leaves her apartment, returning his knowledge of the story to her as a kind of property. However, this renunciation of the written narrative is problematic due to the plural ontology of the notebook and its contents. Although in one world the notebook contains Michael's recording of Althea's story, in another world it contains the script for *Goodness* – another iteration of Michael's recording of Althea's story. Watching the play, I am made aware of the play as a scripted object; holding the published text in my hands, the future iteration of the story is even more palpable. Further, the notebook is caught in a temporal paradox, appearing at the beginning of the play as the complete script but also travelling with Michael to meet Althea, a meeting in which Michael the playwright-narrator knows that the notebook will be relinquished. Yet, through the temporally folded structure of the play, the notebook is both lost and retained. Michael both surrenders control of the story to Althea and steals it back when he writes it again as *Goodness*.

When stripped of his notebook, and so unable to capture and control Althea's story that way, Michael tries to exert a different kind of control over Althea's story. Instead of pinning it down and gathering it to himself, he pushes and probes. He asks questions, presses for clarification of facts, and tries to interpose his own opinions and expertise. A skirmish occurs when Michael compares the moral question of trying Mathias Todd to the 1993 case of East German leader Erich Honecker who was already dying of liver cancer when he was indicted for treason. Objecting to this interpolation, Althea tries to regain control of her story: 'This has nothing to do with that' (35). When Michael continues to argue with her, she becomes defensive and threatens to discontinue the story:

ALTHEA: Would you like me to write this all down on the back of an envelope and then you can call me later if you have any questions?
MICHAEL: I'd just like to be completely clear about what it is you're telling me.
ALTHEA: Let's just say the situation was ambiguous. You do know what 'ambiguous' means?
MICHAEL: Fine. Go on, then. (33)

Althea forces Michael to accept a less than complete narrative. The ambiguity surrounding certain aspects of the story and the factual holes pertaining to experience beyond Althea's knowledge mark the story as distinctively hers, but also contest the omniscience of the playwright as God of this fictional world. In this move away from a need to confirm each detail and fill in every gap, Michael takes small steps towards accepting the story that Althea is telling.

Having been repulsed in world[c] by Althea the gatekeeper in the defence of her story, Michael goes around her and crosses into world[d]. Due to the metaleptic arrangement of these fictional worlds evinced by the other-worldly embodied presence of Todd, Julia, Stephen, and the young Althea, Michael is able to bypass the intermediary of the storyteller and engage the characters of Althea's past directly. At one point, Michael reaches in to take the coroner's report on Helena Sonnen out of Stephen's hands. Looking at it he muses, 'So this is the woman ... She probably betrayed him' (40). This personal interpolation, overlaying his own thoughts and feelings about his ex-wife Joanna onto Todd's mistress Helena, breaks communion with Althea's story world and the characters 'all back off, like an image fading' (40). This inappropriate imposition of his concerns onto the story is a kind of mutiny. He breaks faith as a witness and displaces Althea at the centre of her own story, substituting his own selfish and – from Althea's perspective – irrelevant concerns. Althea chastises him: 'Did I say that?' Michael: 'No, no. I'm sorry – please keep going' (40). In response to this first foray, the characters simply dissipate and retreat from Michael's interference. But the next time, with Michael again intruding into their world, the lower-order characters take action to protect their narrative interests in the story at this new inset level. There is a break in Althea's story when one thread pertaining to Julia and Stephen passes out of her direct experience. Michael tries to pursue this subplot: 'There's more here. Remember when she followed Stephen out of the room? You said you didn't know what happened next' (58). The stage directions indicate that Michael moves Stephen and Julia into the scene, writing dialogue for them, filling the gap in Althea's experience. In Michael's version, Julia negotiates with Stephen; she proposes that he let her father go and instead arrest her for sheltering a suspected war criminal. As this newly written scene develops, Althea interjects: 'Excuse me.' 'What are you doing?' (54). When Althea regains control of the dialogue, she uses it to mock Michael's imagined version of events, staging a scene in which Julia and Stephen fall in love (60). Julia, Young Althea, and Stephen then turn on Michael, accusing him of manipulating them: 'You don't get to reinvent your world using me'; 'Using us'; 'User' (61). Then on their own initiative, they perform a third even more exaggerated parodic version of the imagined scene, with Julia vampishly seducing Stephen, who agrees to let her father go in exchange for sex.

This final uprising in which the characters themselves not only refuse to be written but take up the authorial mantle themselves marks the lowest point of Michael's journey to becoming a responsible witness. Michael's efforts to control the story and to impose his own narrative organization on it are effectively countered by these other playwrights who apply the same strategy. To defend the story against elaboration and clarification, the characters exercise performative power to call into question the authenticity of any story. They offer a series of alternatives. By playfully tinkering with the story, these denizens of the primary core fictional world who embody the story itself teach Michael that this is a game he cannot win.

MICHAEL: All right, enough. Why don't you just cut to the chase then, okay? Todd stood trial or he didn't. He went to jail, he hanged, he's living in a condo in Argentina. I have a plane to catch.
ALTHEA: So go catch it ... You think it's easy for me to tell you this story?
MICHAEL: I know it isn't.

ALTHEA: I don't care if you want a tidy, happy ending.
MICHAEL: I'm not interested in an easy – (61–2)

Then Althea deliberately shocks him, telling him not what happens to
Todd, but that this story ends with the murder of Julia. This revelation
overwhelms him:

MICHAEL: My god ... Why does everything keep –
...
GOING TO HELL! GOING TO SHIT! I can't fucking stand it. I am *not* going to
    put myself through – This is not heading in any direction that interests me,
    okay? I'm sorry, I apologize, but I can't –
...
MICHAEL: Please. Let me go now. Okay?
ALTHEA: Touch me. (*Beat*) DO IT.
He begins to tentatively reach out to her. Althea grabs his hand and presses it to her face.
ALTHEA: Am I real?
MICHAEL: Yes.
ALTHEA: I live and breathe?
MICHAEL: Yes!
ALTHEA: Good
...
You sit down. And listen to my story. (63–4)

Helpless, he collapses into the only chair, and this is the end of the first
act. It is finally at this point that Michael abandons his defensive writerly
attempts to control the narrative. He surrenders to Althea's story. He is
ready to listen and to accept the story as her story.

Having brought Michael to this submissive position as a respectful
listener and setting up Althea's story as a privileged narrative, *Goodness*
challenges this relation by juxtaposing two timelines through its looped
structure. In each of the episodes outlined, Michael is progressively dis-
couraged from recording the story, from asking questions, from elab-
orating details. Under this construction, to be a good witness is to be
empathetic but inactive. However, the metatheatrical arrangement of
time in the play calls this view into question since although the earlier
Michael, Michael[c], is a witness in that way – at least initially – the later and
ontologically superior Michael, Michael[a] the playwright, takes a less def-
erential approach. Not only does the play as play explicitly run counter
to the lessons of the first act by retelling and reimagining Althea's story,

it goes further, repositioning her story in the overall narrative. *Goodness* decentres her story and reframes it through Michael's own experience of her story. Inside the fictional world, the play foregrounds Michael's questioning, manipulating, and interfering as he attempts to insert himself into the story, exercising his skills as writer. Outside in the actual world, Michael[a] succeeds where Michael[c] fails; the writing of *Goodness* itself permits him to insert himself into the story and to perform witnessing as an author. The paradox that allows these opposing strategies to coexist is elaborated in the second act and becomes central to the engendering of a performative witness. The second part of Michael's journey is a rebuilding process, bringing about responsibility and a renewed agency in the witness. Through metalepsis, Michael as witness will again be caught up in this productive paradox that enables both acceptance and action. From one angle, this is an agency that does not interfere or seek to reshape. But also through an engaged participation, by inserting oneself into the story, the performative witness comes to accept a moral responsibility for that story.

Even though the library catalogue lists *Goodness* under 'Genocide – drama,' a story about genocide is not the main narrative thread. Althea does tell Michael about the purges and the horrific story of the execution of her family – her sister, her brother-in-law, and particularly her young nephew, Domenic. She is spared by the murderous gangs, she thinks, to tell of their power. However, the principal story Althea tells is not about her experience of witnessing genocide as a survivor, but is instead about the culpability of being witness to a single murder and how one lives with the effects of one's choice to act or not to act, to speak or not to speak. It begins ostensibly as the story of the incarceration and the trial of Todd, but as she speaks, it becomes clear that the story she has chosen to tell Michael – the story that the man in the pub clearly intended her to tell – is the story of the murder of Todd's daughter, Julia. After some deliberation, the court declares Todd to be non compos mentis by virtue of Alzheimer's disease and so unfit to stand trial. As Todd and Julia are preparing for his release, Stephen Part enters the holding area with Todd's effects. Item by item, he hurls the mimed objects at Todd: 'Wallet,' 'Keys,' 'Lighter' (91). Then, in a display of pure performative power, Stephen says 'Pistol' (93). The gun is made of words, coming into being in the moment that it is spoken.

JULIA: He didn't have a gun!
STEPHEN: But he still has a mouth. (93)

The juxtaposition of gun with mouth bridges time to connect this moment of Julia's future murder to the past genocide. Todd was not a soldier or even a political leader in his country; rather, he was a professor, an intellectual. His role in the genocide is attributed directly to the power of speech, to incite hate through words. This moment then brings together Todd and Stephen as two men who exploit the performative power of language to effect real-world change. They are two men who kill with words. In another moment, in what I argue is the pivotal moment of the play, Michael will make a third.

In an impassioned attempt to shake Todd out of what he believes to be his amnesiac performance, Stephen grabs Julia, holding the gun to her head and demanding that Todd tell the truth. Here again the gun is connected with words, specifically to the concept of a narrative that is unspeakable. The story that Stephen wants to hear is unspeakable. Just as trauma manifests as a gap in experience, a hole in the middle of a larger narrative, Alzheimer's disease creates a similar kind of hole. Althea says, 'When the disease progresses, it is as if a sheet of paper with your life written on it has begun burning right in the middle. You are a baby at the top of the page and it is today at the bottom, and the flame is slowly eating everything in between –' (36). This image of an expanding burn hole in a sheet of paper appears on the cover of the published text of *Goodness*. Notably, the cover image diverges from Althea's description of Alzheimer's disease in one important way. In Althea's description, the burning text is the story of one's life, a complete biography from birth to the present. Specifically in that context, it is Todd's life story that is being destroyed by the flame of Alzheimer's. On the cover, however, the burning text is taken from Althea's testimony regarding the purges and murder of her family and her neighbours (66–7). This transfer of the point of reference speaks specifically to the destructive side effect of Todd's memory loss on Althea's story.

Looking at the cover, I am also struck by how the ragged hole looks like what I imagine a bullet hole might look like. Three characters in the play are shot in the head – Julia, but also in two other narrated histories: Todd's wife, Margaret, and Althea's nephew, Domenic. The thematic association arising out of the parallel damage to brain, memory, and story caused by Alzheimer's disease and a bullet in the head is inescapable. All these holes – suddenly violent or slowly degenerative – debilitate speech. But also, these attacks comment ironically on imperatives to speak. In each case, paradoxically, the silencing action itself is heavily invested in a desire for testimony. Like Julia, Margaret is killed to compel confession of a past truth. When Todd's affair with Helena Sonnen was discovered, her kinsmen invaded his house and threatened Margaret, forcing Todd to admit the affair. Even after evincing his anguished confession, they still kill her. In her story, Althea tells how during the purges, she, her sister, her brother-in-law, and their young son, Domenic, were rounded up with their neighbours. From fear and in the face of such surreal horror, Domenic began to laugh. 'They took him out of the line and put the gun in his mouth and told him to laugh some more and they would spare him. And out of him came this unworldly laughter, as if the sun and the moon were laughing at the stupidity of being human. It was a real laugh, a deep, deep, laugh. And they shot out the back of his head and he stopped' (67). For all three victims, the gun is aligned with forced speech. For Margaret and Domenic, the result is a truth brought to the surface. In Julia's case, the result is silence as two holes overlap. Despite this show of power, the unspeakable remains unspoken, because the truth is already gone. Her father cannot speak his lost past. Compounding this pervasive silence, yet another hole is created in the narrative when no witnesses come forward to fill that first hole with words. Stephen murders Julia and makes a hole in the world. Althea assents to this rent and adds another dimension of loss by not testifying. She fails to perform here as a responsible witness and fails to reify the lost event by becoming its storyteller. She is the only witness; and when her words do not materialize, Julia is erased.

Stephen begins to count to three: 'One –' (95). In shock, Michael turns to Althea watching Young Althea: 'What's wrong with you? You're just standing there … You didn't do anything?' To which Althea replies, 'I did. I watched' (95). Stephen continues counting: 'Two –' (95). Before he gets to three, Michael can no longer simply watch and he yells 'STOP!' The scene freezes and is silent (95). Julia steps out of the tableau to confront Michael. She is openly disdainful:

JULIA: Stop? Why? … Are you going to rescue me?
MICHAEL: He's going to –
JULIA: What, Michael? What's he going to do?
MICHAEL: You know what he's going to do.
…
JULIA: This is what happened.

Then the scene gradually starts into action again.

STEPHEN: SAY IT!

JULIA: (*to Todd*) Don't tell him anything. (*to Michael*) It's going to be such a relief to be free of you.

STEPHEN: Tell her the truth, or so help me –

MICHAEL: Three. (*Instant blackout, gunshot.*) (95–6)

This is the key moment which breaks the frame. It is Michael who says 'Three.' The consequences of this moment cannot be overstated. With this word, Michael fully accepts Althea's testimony. Earlier in the play when Michael stepped in to manipulate the imagined offstage scene between Julia and Stephen, he was motivated by curiosity, by a desire for a more complete and comprehensible story. Then, he exercised authorial power to tinker, to smooth out the wrinkles and fill in the holes. Here, he does not redirect the story so much as he actively chooses to accept the story on its own terms. He lets it simply be itself in all its ugliness, allowing the story to go forward to follow its original path unimpeded to its predetermined end. It is not a good ending, but it is Althea's ending.

Uttering that word 'Three,' Michael displays a marked passivity. He does not change the past. He does not move to stop Julia's murder, aligning himself with Althea: 'You didn't do anything.' 'I did. I watched' (95). To watch is to do something. Here, simply watching, simple witnessing, is an action of import, carrying a moral weight. The breaking of the frame, which allows Michael to witness at first hand Julia's murder, to stand there as someone with the potential to prevent that murder, also restricts that potential through temporal looping. It situates the tragedy both in the future where it can be deflected and in the past where it cannot. Like these doubled temporal streams, Michael's stance as a watcher is morally divided. As a past event, Julia's murder is inevitable. It must happen. To watch this event unfold in the past tense is to watch over it, somehow to sanctify the story and protect its coherence and continued existence as a story. However to watch the event in the present tense carries a different moral obligation. From this position, Michael, again aligned with Althea, tacitly sanctions the murder. He does not stop it. This later scene is contrasted by an earlier parallel; Julia visits her father in his cell. In his delusion, Todd seems to mistake his daughter for Helena Sonnen, shouting at her 'BLOODY PEOPLE! ... Swarming our ... the places we built! ... Get the fuck off my lake!' (54–5). He grabs her by the throat and tries to strangle her. Michael and Althea watch from the future. Young Althea watches from outside the cell.

MICHAEL: And you just watched? …
Young Althea remains inactive, watching.
ALTHEA: I stopped him. (*on Michael's look*) I did. (55)

This time, the watcher steps in to act and to change the course of events. Young Althea (possibly prompted by her older self in the future) moves from passive bystander to active participant, and this time she saves Julia's life. The moral burden to take action, to stop 'it,' connects Todd to Althea and Michael, binding together the perpetrator of genocide with those who listen to genocide's stories. Michael accuses Todd of just watching and doing nothing: 'It doesn't matter if he didn't actually do anything, he certainly didn't try to stop it … Your father either goaded a country of stupid farmers – … into murdering thousands of people, or he sat back and enjoyed watching it!' (70). Althea points the same accusation at Michael: 'Where were you with your notebook when we needed a witness? Bathing in milk and writing cheques for charity, that's where you were: one dollar a day – buy a village a goat' (99). Todd did nothing. Althea did nothing. Michael did nothing. The world stands by and does nothing.

Yet in speaking that word – 'Three' – Michael does do something. By voicing Stephen, caught in the temporal folds between worlds, Michael enters into that past. He acts and thus is doubly culpable in Julia's murder. Aligned with Althea, he is culpable as the witness who does nothing to stop the violence. But aligned with Stephen, he himself has killed Julia. Not only does Michael assent to the story, allowing it to move forward to its fixed end, but Michael actually causes it to happen. Just as Jordan Pettle, the actor, is an intermediary between Michael the character and Michael the playwright, the same kind of cross-world ventriloquism is at work here. Through Stephen, Michael bridges his roles as character-within and playwright-without. Stephen here is only the conduit and Michael is responsible for Julia's death as an author who has killed his own creation. He is a playwright who kills with a word. To protect the integrity of the story, the watching witness who becomes a storyteller sacrifices a character in that story.

When Michael meets the man in the pub, a man he realizes in retrospect was Stephen Part, the man challenges him to go to Althea to have his questions answered. 'Why do good people rush to do evil? And what do they become?' (21). This is what Stephen says, but Althea presses this further: 'He wanted you to see what you were going to turn into … A lonesome fuck-up who can't live with what he's done' (99). But, what has Michael done? What crimes has he committed? Reading Joanna's diary? Succumbing to a depression when she leaves him? Behaving like a rude foreigner and failing to make meaningful contact in Poland? No, these are the errors of the past. Stephen wanted to see what would become of Michael in the future, in light of his experience of (and *in*) Althea's story. His crime is that he has killed Julia. But it is his passivity that speaks to his larger crime. Julia's murder functions as a synecdoche to all the other murders ringing Todd's jail cell. Insofar as Michael did nothing to stop her murder, he is guilty by extension of doing nothing to stop the genocide. The folding of time which structures the worlds of the play makes this paradox of responsibility possible. He is guilty both for acting and for not acting. Nevertheless, in this ugly ending, there is, paradoxically, a strong sense that both by watching and by speaking, Michael has done the right thing. Michael has become a performative witness.

Struck by the epiphany that Stephen was the man in the pub, Michael also realizes what Stephen wants: 'Jesus, how long has he been sitting there? Waiting for someone to ... You still have it' (98). 'It' is the gun. Apart from Althea herself, it is the only other witness to Stephen's killing of Julia. Stephen may not actually need the gun per se. He only needs Althea to tell her story and he needs Michael to hear it. Through storytelling, the same performative power that is endowed in testimony – the power that reifies the past, actualizing it in the present – transforms the gun from a word to a thing, bringing it into the present.[24] Having finished her story, Althea unfolds the cloth where she has hidden Stephen's mimed gun to reveal a real gun. The play's central props, the notebook and the gun, come together at this point. Both the notebook and the gun perform as physical witness to the story, containing the story coded into the material object. As a result of being invested with the story, both objects also bring freedom through performative agency. Michael realizes that Stephen wants the gun so he can be free – free of the ghosts of his past. Julia, by her death, is free of the control of the playwright, the control of the story itself. As she says to Michael just before her death, 'It's going to be such a relief to be free of you' (96). Through testimony, she is freed again as the story fills in the hole generated by the lack of witnesses. In two iterations, first Althea and then Michael take up Julia's story. And although their testimony recaptures Julia through scripting and performance, it also brings her embodied into the present, and she can be released.

Fused by performative language, the gun created by words and the notebook with the power to kill share a chiastic relationship. Subject to the metaleptic structure of the worlds of *Goodness*, time folds to allow the notebook and the gun to be synchronously both the cause and the result of the story. In the moment I referred to earlier, Althea tries to reclaim control over her story. She gives the gun to Michael and wants his notebook in exchange, calling it 'spiritual collateral' (101). 'Now we're back where we started. I'm harmless and you know nothing. I've turned back time' (101). In this exchange, just as the gun came into being out of Althea's story, the notebook is reabsorbed, folded back into the story, lost in Althea's world. Yet, at the beginning of the play, Michael has it again in the future as he writes her story, carrying it with him as he circles back to their first meeting. The notebook, being made of words, transcends barriers between worlds to reify the story again in Michael's recording of it as the script for *Goodness*. Claiming the notebook, Althea tries to erase her telling of the story, reclaiming Michael's experience of the story. But as it slips between worlds, the notebook – and with it, Michael's version of the story – defies capture. In a note appended to the published text of *Goodness*, Redhill flags this moment for future productions. He states that he had originally written that Althea would destroy the notebook, observing that 'obviously, this changes the temperature of that scene significantly.' And he invites future productions to experiment with the alternate resolution (105).[25] Certainly, burning the notebook would create meaningful resonance with the image of Alzheimer's disease as a flame consuming biography.

When Michael walks away with the gun, the fate of the gun is also ambiguous. In the stage directions, Redhill presents several options: Michael throws it in the trash. He keeps it. He points it at other characters, at himself, at the audience. Or he just looks at it (102).[26] Among these printed alternatives, the gun also slips Althea's world and dissolves back into words. When she gives him the gun, Althea challenges Michael to pick up the gun any time he thinks he can make a better world, taunting him with the threnodic question, 'How does that feel?' (100). Michael's answer to that question, his gesture towards that better world, is through another exercise of performative language, through another cycle of storytelling – *Goodness* is his answer to that question. In this new alchemical iteration, the gun becomes the play, it is absorbed into the text as words, and the notebook re-emerges, taking material form.

Metalepsis blends borders between fictional worlds and allows Michael to fulfil his obligations as performative witness to Althea's story and to Julia. Michael[c] as a fictional character crosses the border into world[d] to exercise performative agency and influence the story of Julia's murder. Likewise, Michael[a] the playwright is a substitute divinity and shapes the fictional world[b] of *Goodness*. But the actual world is not permeable from a higher-order world in this same way. And so the potential for similar real-world interventions is negated. However, the metaphor of the *theatrum mundi* – the world as stage – offers an equivalent arrangement with regard to the actual world of world[a], positing God as a superior playwright-witness in world[0].[27] Although *Goodness* establishes the potential power of the divine performative witness, the play simultaneously figures this witness as markedly absent. In the closing lines, the characters reprise an earlier Zimbabwean song:

Horiyatsa (Look around / pay attention)
Hamuzani waka (To what is happening)
Tobela (Pray)
Ayitobela – (O pray to –). (103)

Having heard this song earlier, the audience is primed on this third repetition for the completion of the line with the word '*Murena*' – '*Ayitobela Murena*' (O pray to God) (9). When the music line is cut short, the expected but missing cadence fills the space, and the silence is pronounced. So although Michael becomes a performative witness through the metaleptic structures of looped theatricality, the play's ending reminds us that the same divine salvation is denied to us. We must find recourse in more human and necessarily more flawed alternatives.

Although the ontological terms have shifted from fictional worlds to the actual world, the play nevertheless does offer another path. Part of Michael's agency as a performative witness is to continue the chain of witnessing and to become the playwright-storyteller who passes that story on to us. But Michael is chastised by Todd who taunts him: 'All those people – real people – died for you, and the best you can manage is a little play?' (76). Even to the end, the act of witnessing is caught in a performative paradox, where the story is both preserved and threatened by metalepsis, and a character from deep within the fictional worlds over which Michael himself exercises dominion can rise up and criticize the vehicle of his own existence. Recovering the past and filling holes through storytelling is hopeful but morally insufficient. It is something, but it is not the right thing. The play does not suggest that simply watching is enough, but the play does recognize that it has no viable alternatives to offer. Even if there can be no moral absolution, we are called to enter into the story; through an engaged theatricality, we are called to become an affective witness, to feel, to become implicated as Michael is in the ugliness of Althea's story. *Goodness*, as part of the chain of witnessing, passes that question on to the audience: 'How does it feel to be out there in the dark? Just watching. Invisible, but still a part of everything. A part of *this*. How does that feel?' (102).

Chapter Three

Setting Free Silenced Autobiographical Voices: *Eternal Hydra* and *Shadows*

'God likes to own things. The very first and best of things ... And, as the Gospel of John attests, words are God's possessions. His proclamations and servants. His very life ... Words are His products above all others. They are flexible and violent and beautiful. The most useful things of all. And more fun than a bar of soap for the truly ambitious collector ... We are jealous creatures, aspiring divinities' (*Eternal Hydra*, 2003, 86). This is how Gordias Carbuncle, the author of the Joycean masterwork *Eternal Hydra*, characterizes the power of language exercised by those who create worlds – both real and fictional. That flexibility and violence of words is central both to Anton Piatigorsky's play *Eternal Hydra*,[1] which houses the character Carbuncle, and to Timothy Findley's play *Shadows*[2] – also home to several fictional creators.

In *Shadows*, a group of friends, lovers, ex-lovers, and strangers gather for a dinner party. There is Ben Singer, a professional playwright; his wife Shelagh; his former lovers Dan and Lily, who are actors; and Shelagh's former lover Kate, who is a theatre designer. Into this omnivorous theatrical group are thrown two seeming innocents, Owen, a photographer, and Meredith, a playwriting student. Between dinner and postprandial aperitifs, the guests begin a game called Storytime. To play, each person is required to tell a story: 'something personal they've never told before. Something absolutely fantastic. Something that really hurts to tell' (*Shadows*, 60). Shocking and cruel, these autobiographical confessions not only pain the teller but also inflict injury on others as autobiography intersects with biography. In this narrative web, everyone's deepest secrets are fodder for the storytelling game.

Eternal Hydra also takes up the theme of appropriating other people's life stories in pursuit of literary fame. Anton Piatigorsky's world[a] play shares its title with an imaginary world[b] novel by a fictional novelist, Gordias Carbuncle. Lost more than sixty years ago, Carbuncle's *Eternal Hydra* is purported to be the great modern novel. Publisher Randall Wellington summarizes it this way: 'There are ninety-nine distinct chapters. He [Carbuncle] intended one hundred, but it seems that the final chapter was never written. The novel's composed of a series of first-person monologues. Different voices, from every corner of the world' (*Eternal Hydra*, 2009, 9). To gather these stories, Carbuncle has not concerned himself with the niceties of who owns a particular story, depending on the labour of others to research and even write some of the tales. When the play begins, academic Vivian Ezra has recovered the manuscript and undertakes negotiations to get the novel published. In the offices of Wellington and Company, Ezra meets contemporary novelist Pauline Newberry. Newberry's latest book, *Scribbled Away*, is historical fiction based on the life of Selma Thomas, an African American expatriate writer living in Paris in the 1930s. (Thomas, it must be noted, is not a really real world[a] historical figure. She is 'real' only in relation to Newberry.) In addition to the 'real' Thomas, Newberry has included a biographical portrait of Gordias Carbuncle as a minor character. This is the beginning of a series of 'borrowings' as auto/biographical stories-within are lifted, adapted, and reframed.

In the field of auto/biography studies, the terms autobiography and biography are invariably integrated either with a slash, 'auto/biography,' or with double capitalization, 'AutoBiography,' paying homage to the almost inevitable recombination of these two complementary directions in life writing. Susanna Egan's concept of mirror talk begins with the interwoven stories of a biographer and her biographical subject, where the story of the process of research and writing of the biography is part of the resultant work, and so it is an autobiography of the writer as much as a biography of the subject. 'Narration then takes the form of dialogue; it becomes interactive, and (auto)biographical identification becomes reciprocal, adaptive, corrective, affirmative ... Such collaborations seem far less concerned with mimesis, however, than with authenticating the process of discovery and re-cognition.'[3] This is the main organizing motif of the relationships discussed in the previous two chapters, exemplified in the mirror-talk pairs of Morgan and Angus (*The Drawer Boy*), Patsy and Marie/Francesca (*Perfect Pie*), and Michael Redhill and Althea (*Goodness*). Clearly, the work of biography must always implicate the biographer to some extent, even if this involvement is suppressed below the surface of the text. The experience of the biographer rendered as autobiography permeates the work. The biographer's perspective informs the questions asked, the episodes selected, and the shaping of the subject's life into narrative. Likewise, a participatory subject is also an autobiographer as he spins out the stories of his life, making the same kinds of selections and omissions, forging associative sequences and connections. Thus, it is difficult to discuss biography without also delving into autobiography. And the inverse relation is also true – it is difficult to generate autobiography without also crossing into biography. Acknowledging the combination of two autonomous but interdependent narratives, Philippe Lejeune terms works in this blended genre of life writing 'heterobiography.'[4]

The actions and experiences of my life do not occur in isolation and so any performance of autobiography will necessarily include the biographies of other people whose lives intersect with my own – parents, children, spouse, friends, and so on. 'Because our own lives never stand free of the lives of others, we are faced with our responsibility to those others whenever we write [perform] about ourselves. There is no escaping this responsibility.'[5] Acutely aware of this obligation necessarily associated with the exercise of autobiography, Deirdre Heddon subtitles her chapter on ethics 'The Story of the Other.' Heddon wonders what such a 'responsibility' might mean in the field of autobiographical performance. If, as argued earlier with respect to *Perfect Pie* and *The Drawer Boy*, narrative is essential to the development of an individual's sense of self, how is this right to the expression of self-story to be accommodated with another person's right to privacy?[6] Among the interactions of the disparate subjects of auto/biography, privacy is not the only ethical issue arising out of the performance of autobiography. In *Vulnerable Subjects: Ethics and Life Writing*, G. Thomas Couser is particularly concerned with the relative balance of power between a biographer and her subject. Already, biography posits an unequal relationship, where only one person is holding the pen, that is, controlling the means of producing the work. This basic asymmetry can be augmented in situations where the biographical subject is vulnerable with regard to storytelling because of physical, emotional, or intellectual disability, or where the subject has been disempowered or marginalized by socio-economic, political, or cultural factors. Vulnerable subjects are rendered dependent on the biographer since they lack opportunity and resources to communicate their own story without mediation.[7]

Both *Eternal Hydra* and *Shadows* stage several biographer/subject pairs engaged in the process of collecting, crafting, and publishing life narratives.[8] It is through these performances-within that the plays engage with metacritical questions regarding the ethical aspects of auto/biographical authorship, asking: 'Whose story is this?' 'Who is able to tell it?' and 'Who will be hurt by it?' As demonstrated earlier, the ability to craft life narratives is central to the creation and maintenance of a comprehensive sense of self. For Angus (*The Drawer Boy*) and Patsy (*Perfect Pie*), the obstacle to autobiography was dysnarrativia arising from amnesia. For characters in *Shadows* and *Eternal Hydra*, the violence enacted on autobiography takes a different form. Here, stories are actively silenced through intimidation, lying, stealing, and plagiarism. These acts do not seem, on the surface, to be as harmful as other acts of physical violence like those experienced by characters in *Perfect Pie* and *The Drawer Boy* (wartime head injury, sexual assault, train crash). Nevertheless, for characters born of words rather than of flesh and blood, the consequences of undermining the fabric of their composition are serious. Whereas the physical and emotional traumas experienced by Patsy and Angus inhibit their narrative capacity, the verbal attacks in *Shadows* and *Eternal Hydra* cripple the corpus of the story directly. It is no longer the fault of memory loss, which cuts the story off at the root, but rather these stories are actively prevented from blossoming and bearing fruit – from being spoken aloud and being heard by an audience. For characters in these play worlds, the threat to the narrative self and its founding story comes, perhaps not surprisingly, from those who create these story-selves. Invested with the absolute performative ability to create worlds with words, the puissance of an author over his or her creations is without bounds. Carbuncle succinctly describes his role in this respect as a 'small god in the shallow heavens, hovering above *Eternal Hydra*'s pages' (90). Characters exist solely by the grace of their authors. But, naturally, with the power of creation also comes the power of alteration and annihilation. Fictional characters conjured out of the imagination are not owed any ethical consideration; they exist as the unencumbered dependents of their authorial masters. The ethical field shifts, however, when actual-world subjects are co-opted into fictional worlds.

Such is the case with biography. Although an actual-world person shares a name and experience with the protagonist of one's own biography, that subject has in fact been split into two ontologically distinct personae. The one who lives in the actual world (self[a]) is (or was) a flesh-and-blood person, living minute by minute in real time; the other one – the self in biography or autobiography – is a written or performed self, a fictional version (self[b]) of the original. Fictional is perhaps a poor word to describe the situation; it is not deployed here with connotations of being not real, feigned, or imaginatively invented (although this may sometimes be part of it), but rather it is intended to emphasize the constructedness of inset worlds. The fictive character of biography, although not deliberately unlike its actual-world counterpart, must inevitably be a thin doppelganger, always indeterminate. As compared with actual worlds which are fully determinate, fictional worlds are constitutionally indeterminate, being full of gaps and blank territory.[9] Spaces and events outside the scope of the work languish undescribed and unperformed and so do not come fully into phenomenological existence. For example, in *Shadows*, the action of the play is set in the dining room of Ben Singer. Apart from what we can see of the set and what is described in narration, nothing else exists. This fictional world is full of holes. Fictional characters are essentially indeterminate in the same way, generated by a series of schematized views. Taken as a series, each fractional view supplements the one before until we have the illusion of a complete representation.[10] So while purely fictional characters created in the imagination exist in a single world, the biographical subject is doubled, having both an actual self who exists on the same ontological plane as the author, and a fictive self subjugated to the narrative control of that author.[11] This bifurcated situation distinguishes these author-protagonist pairs from those discussed earlier. Whereas both Patsy and Angus each exist in two worlds as both author/narrator and protagonist of their own stories, here the author is non-congruent with the protagonist, who has invariably been fictionalized unwillingly. Threat to the integrality of the subject-self, then, arises in the 'graphical' process of biography, when life experience is selectively transposed into lower-order fictional strata. It is the performative power of the author to effect changes within subordinate fictional worlds that complicates the usual ethical issues associated with biography. The risk for the already fictive biographical subject is not merely misrepresentation; but, because the subject of these autobiographies-within is essentially a performative creation generated entirely by words, verbal manipulation or silencing can be catastrophic.

Borrowing the classical figure of the prolific many-headed Hydra, Gordias Carbuncle reiterates the potential threat in performative narration. He characterizes auto/biographical storytelling paradoxically as both a kind of killing theft and a life-granting freedom. He explains that in his work the human race is represented by the Hydra: 'eternal, ugly, mythic – and though each of our "unique" hydra heads may hold different thoughts, each with its own history and bitter will toward independence, we have just one body. The same coarse blood, the same molecules, the same stomach and heart and instinct within' (72). Upon hearing this, another character points out that the classical Hydra was not eternal. It was killed by Hercules. Musing aloud, the character asks, 'Who is Hercules in this equation?' She answers her own question: 'The superman who captures each of the hydra's heads. And how does he do it, this capturing? I think he does it in writing' (73). Later, Carbuncle tells his patron, Randall Wellington Sr, about the novel, touching again on the relation of Hercules to the Hydra: 'The protagonist is an interloper, a shape-shifter. He's the victor of history. A pseudo-Herculean figure, responsible for silencing the hundred voices, but also the one who speaks for them' (85). Hercules, then, is an author figure; Carbuncle, but not Carbuncle directly, a fictionalized narrator-avatar who lives inside the world of the book. The image of each severed Hydra head as a life captured in writing by a biographer neatly expresses the ethical dichotomy of biographical storytelling. In the act of writing, the author necessarily commits an act of betrayal that subdues the original subject. '"Getting" someone else's story is also a way of losing the person as "real," as "what he is"; it is a way of appropriating or allegorizing that endangers both intimacy and ethical duty.'[12] And yet, if the story languishes untold, then the writer is party to a different kind of sin. Without access to auto/biography, the subject remains totally invisible. Autobiographical scholar G. Thomas Couser sums up the dilemma this way: On the one hand, 'the art of writing another's life is inherently … inadequate, presumptuous and possibly transgressive'; on the other hand, there 'is the imperative to make something, through narrative, of the experience … with which we are entrusted.'[13]

This twin action of the betrayal of the subject-story and its simultaneous release into self-actualization and freedom is central to both *Eternal Hydra* and *Shadows*. In *Eternal Hydra*, Piatigorsky explores a daisy chain of linked stories. In support of his masterwork *Eternal Hydra*, Carbuncle buys one of his hundred stories from Selma Thomas. He is unabashedly candid about his plagiarism. He will use the story in a revised form as the basis for one of his chapters. During the negotiations for this transaction, Thomas herself admits that her story, which recounts in a first-person voice her grandmother's imagined autobiography, does not stand entirely free of the auto/biographical problem either:

THOMAS: You know what she wrote about that day? Nothing. No opinions for posterity. She never learned to write. Never had a chance to put her views to paper ... I took a year of my life. Gave her the public voice she was never able to claim for herself.

CARBUNCLE: That's very admirable. I mean that quite sincerely.

THOMAS: Is it admirable? I'm not so sure. I'm no more authentic than you. I'm not my grandmother, never been a slave, I hope never to be. I wasn't around New Orleans, 1866. I faked it. That's all. (79)

The grandmother – the unnamed Narrator of Carbuncle's Chapter 72 – has her story imagined by Thomas. Thomas relinquishes her story to Carbuncle, who reconfigures it for his own purposes. But Carbuncle too is subject to the manipulations of auto/biography. Pauline Newberry uses him as a character in her novel *Scribbled Away*. But more significantly, Carbuncle's own life writing comes under the control of Vivian Ezra, who found the lost manuscript of *Eternal Hydra*. Although she presses for publication, she also exercises control over the text. She has had the work in her secret possession for six years, deferring publication while she wrote an extensive introduction, notes, and commentary (12). Later in the play, she also becomes the editor of Carbuncle's diary, which she realizes is the lost monologue for the hundredth chapter of *Eternal Hydra*. In her own way, Ezra is another kind of inimical biographer, silencing Carbuncle's voice by her delay and reshaping the narrative with her editorial interjections and elaborations in the proposed published edition of *Eternal Hydra*.

Shadows also nests one story inside another; but in this case, the threat to the integrity of subject autobiographies comes from hostile interrogators of the nascent story worlds and from abrupt shifts in the landscape between what is 'real' and what is fiction instigated by a superior author. As the play reaches its final act, it emerges that Ben Singer is not only the host of the dinner party and Mephistophelian organizer of the Storytime game, but also the judge of a playwriting competition where the winner will receive a commission to write a play for the next season at the Stratford Festival. Rather than the neatly stacked arrangement of subjects and biographers in *Eternal Hydra*, with biographers residing in worlds that are clearly superior to those of their subjects, *Shadows* develops agonistic relationships among a web of storytellers who fabricate auto/biography from truths, partial truths, and outright lies about themselves and the other author-guests. Although Ben is nominally in control of this narrative bear pit, one storyteller rises above the fray to successfully challenge his performative authority. Meredith, the young playwriting student who at first appears naive and woefully out of her depth, emerges as a serious contender. Like Ben, she is capable of manipulating multiple levels of fictional worlds to break free and earn autonomous control over her own autobiography.

Auto/biography in these plays is not the private act that it is in *Perfect Pie* and *The Drawer Boy*. Even in the intimate duet of *Goodness*, which is later reframed by the immediate performance in progress, the inclusion of the audience stands outside the primary auto/biographical interview. By contrast, the central contest in *Eternal Hydra* and *Shadows* is for control over the means of production, those particular resources that enable the critical twofold act of voicing and disseminating the story. To operate as a felicitous performative act, auto/biography needs both a speaker and a listener. Identity constructed in narrative desires legitimation in the public sphere. Here, the fictional subjects wrestle with their authors to assert independent control over a biographical narrative, to overbalance the biographer/subject relationship and achieve narrative autonomy. Carbuncle, when he describes the godlike power of the writer, qualifies it with the adjectives 'jealous' and 'aspiring': 'We are jealous creatures, aspiring divinities' (*Eternal Hydra*, 86). Unlike a supreme biblical God, the authority of these minor creators is not secure or absolute; they strive and compete. After describing some basic principles of performative power and the creation of fictional worlds, this chapter will highlight and evaluate the effectiveness of four strategies for the control of auto/biography and the subjugation of fictional worlds. First, the generation of fictional worlds necessitates the erection of walls to keep the fiction in and to exclude undesirable elements. Even the primary act of creation is an act of control. Second, narrative discourse acts to protect those walls, reinforcing those containers by continual restatement. Third, competing authors attempt to open up holes in these walls by calling into question the authenticity of the fictional world, identifying potential inconsistencies which weaken the protective boundaries. Fourth, desperate creators may destroy their fictional domains rather than surrender control outright. In rebellion against their engendering author-biographers, disadvantaged or vulnerable would-be autobiographers struggle to compete on these terms and parry with these same aggressive tactics in an attempt to establish counternarratives. But there may be another way.

As Michael Redhill cleverly illustrates in *Goodness*, when he makes explicit the intermediary actor Jordan Pettle between the author and his character, ventriloquism is a basic situation of theatrical performance (*Goodness*, 10).[14] Ventriloquism is also the basic situation of auto/

biography, breaking the roles into author-subject, narrator, and protagonist. Ultimately, for the ventriloquized speakers identified here – the
anonymous Narrator of Chapter 72, Selma Thomas, and Meredith – the
question is to how to circumvent the core narrative structures mandated
by the biographical contract, that is, how to bend open the bars without
destroying the world wholesale. As I will show, although the bifurcation
of the biographical subject into actual and fictional personae subordi-
nates the subject to authorial control, this doubled situation both inside
and outside the fiction, straddling multiple worlds, can also be turned
to the subject's advantage. This ontological duality makes possible certain tricks using metatheatrical sleight of hand, which render the usually
rigid world layers permeable, allowing these suppressed stories to break
their bindings and take independent flight.

Let There Be Walls: World Creation as an Act of Exclusion

For writers, words – flexible, violent, and beautiful – are indeed the most
useful things of all. Words constitute the means and the materials whereby playwrights exercise godlike power to create new worlds. Generally, we
tend to think of performative language as creative and life-giving, engendering new entities and new arrangements. This is particularly true for
autobiography where performativity intersects with the psychological
self generated in narrative. As Deirdre Heddon writes, 'Autobiographical performance [serves] as a means to reveal otherwise invisible lives,
to resist marginalisation and objectification and to become, instead,
speaking subjects with self-agency; performance, then, as a way to bring
into being a self. Autobiographical performances provide a way to talk
out, talk back, talk otherwise.'[15] However, the act of creating fictional
worlds and their corresponding subject-citizens is a double-edged sword.
Naming what is necessarily excludes what is not. Judith Butler describes
this ambivalent process of becoming through language with regard to
gender. The process of assuming a gender is linked to discursive means
that enable certain gendered identifications and foreclose and/or disa-
vow other identifications: 'This delimitation ... marks a boundary that
includes and excludes, that decides, as it were, what will and will not be
the stuff of the object to which we then refer. This marking off will have
some normative force and, indeed, some violence, for it can construct
only through erasing; it can bound a thing only through enforcing certain criterion, a principle of selectivity.'[16] In the process of producing a
gender, or an identity, or a subject status, other alternatives are inevita-

bly closed off. Subject formation, then, is a normative and limiting act involving the marking off of boundaries, of setting up borders, and in this manner, operates to capture and to control. As discursive means are used to create new fictional subjects, this making of a world through division is the first violent act.

The book of Genesis describes the quintessential performative act. Here language is the divine vehicle for the creation of everything. But this language is significantly the language of division and exclusion. And this division and exclusion is central to the creation of identity. On the first day, 'God *divided* the light from the darkness' (Genesis 1:4; my emphasis). Then he declared, 'let there be a firmament in the midst of the waters, and let it *divide* the waters from the waters' (Genesis 1:6; my emphasis), and so created heaven and earth. Finally, 'let the waters under heaven *be gathered together* unto one place, and let the dry land appear (Genesis 1:9; my emphasis). Even in this last performative instruction, gathering together is also an act of division, setting up boundaries, separating land from water. This divine cosmological double act of constitution and exclusion through division is staged in *Shadows* at the outset. The play begins and the stage is empty except for Ben, who is surrounded by the detritus of a dinner party, when he is urgently summoned from offstage: 'Hurry up, Ben, it's about to happen' (55). He blows out the candles and dims the lights as he goes. The thing that is about to happen is a lunar eclipse. When the earth passes between the sun and the moon, it blocks the light from the sun. It acts as a wall or a border, casting a shadow on the moon. The shadow is brought into existence by virtue of the opaque boundary. Division is the means whereby light is excluded and the shadow is constituted. Significantly, the shape of the shadow is the negative image of the dividing wall itself. From this perspective, the eclipse is an embodiment of Butler's theory of performative subject formation.

Not only does the eclipse act as a visual metaphor for the act of exclusion inherent in subject creation, it also replicates a theatrical convention that is central to establishing boundaries between life and art. It is typical for indoor theatre in artificially lit venues to mark the transition into the world of the play with a dimming of the lights, commonly fading first to 'house to half' and then to 'house out.' Sometimes 'house out' occurs simultaneously with a blackout on the stage. Sometimes 'house out' is followed by another darkening step as the preshow stage lights fade out. In the only production to date of *Shadows*, the preshow lighting cue established the fictional room set for a candlelit dinner party.

The house lights dropped to half, and Ben entered onto the already lit stage. Then the house lights went out. Then Ben blew out the candles.[17] And the final step took the theatre space to full blackout to represent the eclipse. It is significant, therefore, in terms of setting up the layers of fictional worlds in *Shadows* that Ben's action of blowing out the candles and dimming the lights before going to the garden to view the eclipse repeats the usual pattern of dimming the house lights to half brightness in the theatre. Then the stage directions indicate a further dimming to complete darkness: '*The only light is now the shallow, diffused glow of the moon. Slowly, the moonlight begins to fade to complete darkness*' (55). This multistage fade to blackout marks the audience's entry into a play world. The effect is that the audience is now two 'levels' deep. At the top, the house lights mark the transition from world^a (the ostensible real world occupied by the audience) to world^b (the primary fictional world), and Ben's secondary dimming of the lights moves us from world^b to world^c. Although at this point in the play the audience is not yet aware of this additional world-creating act as such – an act that pushes the play world into yet another lower-order state. For us, the implications of this ontological move are still to be revealed.

One set of collectively acknowledged walls is necessary to theatricality; if actors and audience do not agree to perceptively carve out fictional space from mundane space, fictional worlds cannot exist. At its most elemental level, theatricality is made possible through a perceptual division between the actual world and the newly created fictional world.[18] When one of the characters in the play likens a play to a fortress, 'a hiding place for Ben Singer,' Ben agrees, 'Yes. You have to build walls to keep the play inside – where it belongs' (*Shadows*, 63). Maintenance of this first barrier is essential to the aesthetic detachment necessary for theatricality and, by extension, to the continued existence of the bounded fictional world. However, beyond this visible border, additional borders can sometimes be very subtle, as with the one created by Ben's dimming of the lights combined with the eclipse, or they may be created as a postscript, compelling the audience to retroactively realign their understanding of the ontological structure of the various play worlds. In *Shadows*, the eventual revelation that what we took to be 'truth' is actually another nested fiction is a startling coup de théâtre (more about this later). Yet, we would be a wise audience to suspect this turn of events given the title of the play and the location of its performance. The title *Shadows* refers probably most directly to the eclipse shadow of the earth across the moon, but given the play's origins as a commission for the Stratford Shakespeare

Festival, it points us too, I think, towards Puck's final speech in *A Midsummer Night's Dream*: 'If we shadows have offended, / Think but this, and all is mended, / That you have but slumb'red here / While these visions did appear' (5.1.423–6). When Puck steps forward, breaching the fourth wall, to address the audience, he acknowledges the play we have just witnessed is indeed a play. The ontological structure of the play is expanded in that moment to accommodate a new medial fictive world, containing a new Puck (or the actor playing Puck) as a self-aware narrator, distinct from his inset character. By complementing the unadorned strategy of direct address, the content of this speech also works to concretize the interstitial level. Casting the inhabitants of Athens and the magical forest as 'shadows' and 'visions,' and characterizing that world as a dream, Puck makes explicit their fictionality and thereby reiterates the boundary. The principal effect is disorientation and an awareness of ambiguity, followed by a readjustment in our understanding of the relative layers of actuality and fiction.

What Puck thinks about his double existence as both narrator of the story and character inside that story, we do not know; however, the biographical subjects of Ben's worlds are clearly not happy with their dual status: 'SHELAGH. Your fortress ... the unassailable symbol of Ben Singer's unassailable sovereignty over our lives ... Me – Dan – and Lily. God alone knows how many more. You're very quick to dismiss us when you think you don't need or want us any more – but the truth is, you can't live without us. Any of us. We are your bastion. And every one of us betrayed' (*Shadows*, 63). Shelagh describes herself and the other 'muses' as bastions (walls). In connection with the previously introduced image of the eclipse as a division or border, Ben inserts these three in front of the light to form a division. They constitute a wall used to create a fictional world, a world which is occupied by the shadows they cast of themselves. This is another representation of the violence of division inherent in subject formation. Ben, in his role as professional playwright, has become the biographer of his friends and lovers, writing their life stories into his plays. But as the group takes up the challenge of playing Storytime, Shelagh, Dan, and Lily are not the only characters transposed into fictional worlds, and Ben is not the only playwright in *Shadows*.

Because I Said So: Using Narration to Reinforce Fictional Boundaries

Talking about one of Ben's plays, *Revenge*, Shelagh recalls that the initial idea came out of the Storytime game. In this communal game of auto/biography, each guest must tell a personal story, the twist is that 'it can be something true, or it can be totally made up – but whatever it is, you have to get us to believe it' (*Shadows*, 60). Ben is nominated to begin. His story starts in the garden during the eclipse: 'In the garden just now ... dark of the moon ... someone came up behind me ... touched my shoulder and whispered something in my ear. Something private ... Something I wasn't prepared to hear. Or accept [...] *I ... want you*' (60). After several attempts to identify the whisperer, Ben turns the tables, challenging Lily: 'Yes. Tell them what I meant when I said that I don't like baby-killers' (61). The game at this point turns nasty – Ben and Lily argue about their previous affair, his infidelity, and her decision to abort his child. Lily then starts to catalogue Ben's lovers and the spiral of recrimination widens to include Dan and Shelagh. As Kate says, 'Here we go. Enjoy the ride' (63). The interpolation of the Storytime frame acts as yet another a wall, separating the pregame, post-eclipse characters of scenes 1 through 3 (world^c) from the self-narrating characters we meet in scenes 4 through 7 (world^d). Remaining mindful of this new fictionalizing border, a cautious audience should be wary of assuming that the relationships and experiences that are revealed in the Storytime worlds belong to their namesake precursors, meaning that, for example, Ben in world^c may or may not be congruent with Ben in world^b. Within world^d, the characters build on each other's stories, responding to accusations, cruelly scoring points, and embroidering the story as it passes from narrator to narrator. On the one hand, these narrators work cooperatively, insofar as they do not disagree about the facts of the story as it develops. This attitude to development is recognizable as a cornerstone technique of improvisation called 'Yes, and?' where participants accept without quibble all previous statements. Every new piece of information helps to refine the situation and move the action forward. On the other hand, via the content of the stories, each narrator takes a cut-throat approach, trying to inflict emotional damage on the other storytellers. In this way, the narrators compete for control over the interdependent fictional worlds, subduing other authors by rendering them mute. For example, this exchange between Ben and Lily ends in her retreat:

BEN: You're making this up.
LILY: Maybe. Maybe not ... But I've got you worried.
BEN: It was my child. Mine.
LILY: Could be. But you'll never know. I broke my promise – you broke yours.
 We're quits. *Leave me alone.*

SHELAGH: Yes, Ben. Leave her alone. (*She rises and goes into the garden*). (62)

Narration, in general, is another kind of wall or border, another strategy for the capture and control of fictional worlds and their citizens. At its most benign, we might view the narratorial stance as simply descriptive, the passive recounting of past events. However, as with all shifts from a relatively actual position to a relatively fictional position, the world becomes progressively more indeterminate. The view of the narrator as simply a neutral reporter is an illusion. Perched ontologically above the other characters, the narrator stands in as another author figure with full authorial performative power. Relative to the present-tense narrator, the characters caught up by narration exist in the past. This temporal disparity grants the narrator a superior viewpoint with knowledge of the whole and commutes the emphasis of a simple phrase like 'She said' from description to instruction. This shift in the performative frame is more pronounced in performance as a narrator conjures the enacted scene, standing apart from the characters in the play-within. The narrative voice not only creates fictional sub-worlds, bringing them to life through description, but it simultaneously promotes in the audience the continued consciousness of authorial mediation. Hearing the author function voiced by the narrator, we are reminded again that the scene that we are watching is a construction, crafted from an ontologically superior perspective. Thus, narration is a potent strategy for capture and control. For dramatic works, both *Shadows* and *Eternal Hydra* are unusually rife with narrative. *Eternal Hydra* is a play about books as literature. Its characters are writers of novels and short stories, editors, scholars, and publishers. Actual books as props abound. In *Shadows*, all the characters are ultimately outed as wannabe playwrights, but the storytelling game is explicitly narrative; the game is to tell (rather than to enact as embodied performance) the inset stories. They are all narrators in their turn. Where dramatic dialogue disperses its authenticating power among several characters, the monologic speech of narration recaptures that power and gathers it to one person.

Like *Shadows*, *Eternal Hydra* already begins two 'levels' down in terms of the ontological structure of the play worlds. Characters who reside in the primary play world – Vivian Ezra, Pauline Newberry, and Randall Wellington Jr – are themselves framed from the outset by narration and so rendered fictional. Rather than locating this predominating world as world^b, it is in fact world^c. From the very beginning of the play, Ezra addresses the audience directly and performs both as narrator of the whole and as her own fictional character. After describing Wellington's office in detail:

EZRA: Clutching the manuscript, I stood before Wellington.
WELLINGTON: Let's cut to the chase.
EZRA: (*out*) He said.
WELLINGTON: You've got Eternal Hydra?
EZRA: I do.
WELLINGTON: That's not possible. It's gone, lost, kaput.
EZRA: Not anymore, it's not.
(*out*) Then he looked at his watch.
(*Wellington is looking at his watch.*) (8)

From her superior ontological position, Ezra is in control of this scene, shaping and selecting those actions and details that become actualized for us. The other characters are under her control. Ezra is not the sole narrator however. When Pauline Newberry is invited to read aloud from her forthcoming book, she picks up the book and starts in a third-person narrative voice, but as the fictional world establishes, the characters and the world they inhabit become actualized through dramatic performance.

NEWBERRY: (*reading*) Three years she's lived in Paris, but still Selma warms with pride when a white man stands and bows as she enters a room.
  (*Newberry enters the world of the novel. She puts down the book. Her 'reading' is now a narration for Ezra and Wellington, with hints of a direct audience address. Her other lines are Selma Thomas's.*)
CARBUNCLE: Selma Thomas! What good fortune! A fresh Georgia peach falls right into my room!
NEWBERRY: I'm from Louisiana. (29)[19]

As the scene progresses, Newberry intersperses her performance of Thomas with word-painting descriptions 'out' to the audience. Gradually these interjections come less frequently until she is fully submerged into the inset world. This same technique is repeated as several characters read from and then 'fall into' several episodes from Carbuncle's diary. And, in the last act of the play, all the characters assume roles when Carbuncle's adaptation of Thomas's story, known as Chapter 72, is collectively read aloud.

Because she is the first narrator and because this first scene encompasses all the other characters, Ezra stakes her claim as the narrator of the whole.[20] This understanding is further supported by staging choices made in production.[21] During both Newberry's narrative in act 2, scene 2, and Wellington's narrative in act 2, scene 3, Ezra lingers on a downstage bench. Sitting there silently facing upstage, she is aligned with the audience as a higher-order observer of the dramatic action. She is a small god in the heavens, activating the Medieval-era metaphor of the *theatrum mundi* – the theatre of the world, where God is both galvanizing creator and distanced audience to his creation. The effect of this spatial organization is to rationalize the competing voices inside *Eternal Hydra*; everything we see and hear is managed by Ezra's point of view. Yet, this homogenizing frame at world[b] collates a disparate series of narratorial perspectives in world[c] as Newberry, Wellington, and Ezra again read aloud episodes from inset texts. Likewise, the various narrators of world[c] tell iterations of the same characters and events of world[d], generating equivalent but distinct worlds (world[d1], world[d2], and so on) stacked horizontally like the separate fictional worlds of a series of books on a shelf. This arrangement was concretized in performance as all the various text props – Newberry's novel *Scribbled Away*, the manuscript of *Eternal Hydra*, the diary, Jackson's research notes, Carbuncle's collected letters – accumulate anachronistically on the central table.[22] Carbuncle appears in different versions throughout as Ezra's imagined companion: in Wellington's office, in Newberry's novel, in episodes from his own diary, in a collection of his letters. The 'real' historical and unmediated Carbuncle remains inaccessible. Sentences migrate from one story to another. In Carbuncle's revised version of Thomas's story, renamed Chapter 72, Henry Warmoth offers to buy the shoes made by the unnamed Narrator, saying to her: 'For some reason, the U.S. bank at the end of Royal always has the freshest currency' (114). We have heard this line previously recorded in Carbuncle's diary when he offers to buy this story from Selma Thomas: 'For some reason, the American Express office over on Rue Scribe seems to have the freshest currency' (78). The incorporation of this line (and indeed the whole situation of buying the shoes/buying the story from a woman in desperate circumstances) displays the marks of Carbuncle's revising fingerprints on Thomas's story.

This blended structure reflects the play's dichotomous position on the issue of authorship. On the one hand, there is the solitary author, unassailable in his or her omnificence, and lauded like Carbuncle as a genius or recognized with honours like Newberry who, we are told, has been shortlisted for a Pulitzer. On the other hand, the play acknowledges the multiplicity of voices that impinge on the work of giving life to fictional worlds. This pattern of polyvocality encompassed by a single authority is typified by the split narrative introduction to the final scene-within. Newberry, Wellington, and Ezra conclude in their rehabilitation of the diary as the previously omitted final chapter of *Eternal Hydra* that Carbuncle was prepared to acknowledge Thomas's contribution:

NEWBERRY: He wanted his readers to know.
(*She looks at the galley copy of* Eternal Hydra.) Chapter seventy-two.
EZRA: Yes …
(*Wellington's office is fading away.*)
(*out*) Chapter seventy-two. New Orleans, Louisiana. 1866.
(*The scene has changed. Vivian has taken the book.*)
WELLINGTON: (*out*) By Gordias Carbuncle.
(*Wellington exits. Newberry has transformed into the Narrator from the chapter.*) (94–5)

As they begin to read the stolen chapter, the shared scene setting distributes the power of world creation among the three narrators. And yet, Wellington asserts the chapter to be 'by Gordias Carbuncle.' Writer Selma Thomas, researcher Gwendolyn Jackson, patron Randall Wellington Sr, scholar Vivian Ezra, and publisher Randall Wellington Jr are all subsumed back into the singular named author. This motif of shared authorship across multiple worlds persists even as the characters participate in the inset performances; the effect is to loosen the usually tight boundaries around each world and permit travel between fictional strata.

Each character who takes up the narrative mantle in *Eternal Hydra* also drops into that fictional world, newly read into existence, and participates as a character in that world. So for example, Pauline Newberry, when she reads aloud, is split, existing in two worlds in two separate but joined personae. As a narrator, she remains in world^c (the world of the offices of Wellington & Co. as narrated by Ezra from world^b), but as she reads, she assumes the character of Selma Thomas meeting Gordias Carbuncle (world^d). When Newberry and the other principal characters enter into these roles, it is not clear to what extent they are aware of their participation as actors in the inset performances. From the listing of dramatis personae, the multiple roles performed appear as simple doubling. For example, in both the Crow's Theatre and Stratford Festival productions, Karen Robinson played Pauline Newberry, Selma Thomas, and the Narrator of Chapter 72. But is Pauline Newberry the actress who plays the roles of Thomas and the Narrator or is it Karen Robinson? This is a significant distinction. None of the characters apart from Carbuncle acknowledge Newberry's (Robinson's?) performance at all.

It is significant that in every inset performance episode (with the exception of Chapter 72), each narrator enters the scene as a new character and meets Carbuncle: Newberry becomes Thomas, Ezra becomes Carbuncle's research assistant Gwendolyn Jackson, Wellington Jr becomes his own father, Wellington Sr, Carbuncle's publisher and patron. I want to deal with Carbuncle's fictional doubles first but will return to the fictional interpolations of these narrators. Carbuncle is also divided across worlds but his ontological situation is quite different from that of the narrator-performers of world^c. The historical figure of the author, that is, the (relatively) actual-world Carbuncle of world^b died in 1940. The Carbuncle that we meet in the opening scene haunts Ezra's imagination, existing like her other narrative vassals in world^c, distinct but ontologically equivalent to Ezra's narration of Newberry and Wellington. Ezra describes his emergence this way: 'Gordias Carbuncle lives with me at home. He first appeared in my dreams over five years ago, then extracted from my dreamscape and materialized in my life. Now, we walk together, talk together, jest and work and play, all our waking hours. Here he is, just now' (10). Although he does at times seem to be an autonomous spectre, there are textual traces, especially in early drafts of the play, that support this understanding that Ezra is his author. Although Ezra is now seeking publication for *Eternal Hydra*, we learn that before this she had stalled its release. Newberry accuses her of being overprotective to the point of obsession: 'Look at you. Been hoarding his great book. All to yourself. Pouring over it every night like some devout Talmud scholar. As if his words belonged to you and you alone' (41–2). Ultimately, Ezra is compelled to acknowledge the error of her grasping authorial act – keeping *Eternal Hydra* to herself, keeping Carbuncle as a private companion. With this new awareness, she frees her creations – letting the book go, letting him go. Inevitably, for the fictional Carbuncle, this act of release is also an act of dissolution; as Ezra renounces him, his world dissolves and he disappears. This Carbuncle ceases to exist but other Carbuncles remain at the level of world^d, appearing in the inset performances of the narrated texts (Newberry's novel, his letters, diary entries which may or may not be the same person in each). Unlike an actual-world (world^a) subject captured by biography, Carbuncle does not exist independently of language. Every version is someone's performative creation coming out of his own auto/biographical traces – already a self at one remove. Ezra tries to defend an 'authentic' Carbuncle, but there can be no access to that person. Ezra takes him to task for what she thinks is an unrealistic portrayal of the historical Carbuncle by Newberry:

EZRA: (*aside to Carbuncle*) You sounded like a racist.
...
CARBUNCLE: (*aside to Ezra*) She gave me the words. I felt compelled.
...
EZRA: (*aside to Carbuncle*) You embarrassed yourself with that display. You embarrassed me.
...
CARBUNCLE: (*aside to Ezra*) I'm sorry, Vivian. I let myself get carried away. It was beautifully read; she gave me lines. (38)

Describing himself as compelled and carried away, Carbuncle characterizes his performance as a kind of possession. The real target of Ezra's displeasure is not Carbuncle but Newberry's occupation of the outline of Carbuncle which she fills with new material. This Carbuncle is inconsistent with the one Ezra herself has created.

For the narrator-characters who also enter into inset worlds their genealogy is ambivalent because unlike Carbuncle they are rooted in a physical body. When they cross into fictional worlds, they become ventriloquists, presenting two distinct personae but occupying one body. Although they do not at any time in either the printed text or the premiere production betray any sense of awareness of their performance as such in the transition from narrators to characters, Ezra, Newberry, and Wellington Jr all serve as auto/biographers of these alternate selves, filling both roles as biographer and subject. This process of self-authorship or self-casting distanced at one remove breaks down the requisite barriers that typically restrict a fictionalized subject of biography. Newberry, then, steps into the role of Thomas whom she both controls as narrator and embodies in the inset world she is conjuring, thus spanning two worlds. In each case, the twinned roles not only share physical characteristics of age, gender, and race, which make this casting plausible in terms of a naturalistic verisimilitude, but they also share life circumstances, attitudes, and experiences. For example, Ezra performs as Gwendolyn Jackson. Like Ezra, Jackson is a scholar and researcher (and sometime love interest of Gordias Carbuncle). And where Jackson lobbies to provide an editorial introduction to *Eternal Hydra* and is harshly rebuffed by Carbuncle, Ezra manages to fulfil this ambition, complete with footnotes. Narrating/performing this scene of Jackson's rejection from Carbuncle's diary, Ezra reacts to it, fully cognizant of its personal resonance. Significantly, the transition from narrative to performance functions to realign the vertically stacked narrative structures, like a seismic shift realigning tectonic plates. In these narrative/performance shifts, two authorial forces are combined. Entries from Carbuncle's diary – written by a world[b] author now dead – are read by a world[c] narrator, but as the narrative slides into performance, both figures – Carbuncle and his narrator – are recast as world[d] characters. The two worlds are equalized. Unlike actual-world subjects, who are captured and rendered fictional in the biographical process, these authors enter into the fiction willingly. This realignment, which folds the overall structure of worlds, is collaborative rather than coercive and permits transit between worlds. As Newberry, Ezra, and Wellington Jr become incorporated in lower-order worlds, embodied performance offsets the purely linguistic control of narrative. These formal incursions across borders are reflected at the level of the story. In each inset scene, the narrators ventriloquize someone whose voice has been subsumed into the myth of genius and whose contributions to the work have been unrecognized. These performances, then, both at the level of the shared world[d] and in the superior frame of world[c], create fissures in the monolith of the singular, divinely created world. And so, this shift to performance is another strategy for mitigating the usually absolute power of the performative author.

Authenticity and the Security of Fictional Worlds

Like the declarations in Genesis that bring the world into being, naming is also a divine performative act. The grandiloquent and absurd 'Gordias Carbuncle' is a blatant pseudonym; Selma Thomas quizzes him on it and tries to decipher its meaning by tracing its literary and mythical allusions. Consistent with his authorial aspirations, Carbuncle has chosen his own name. Imitating godlike puissance, he tests his ability to give birth to himself. We can see this act of creating an identity that matches his self-image as another one of these ambivalently entwined acts of betrayal and freedom, since the birth of the ethnically effaced, free-floating signifier 'Carbuncle' also means the suppression of the culture and personal history tied up in his old identity of Jacob Figatner, an Irish Jew. When Carbuncle refuses to tell Thomas his real name, she replies that it is easier to change your name than the colour of your skin, 'which is a bit less susceptible to erasing and rewriting' (76). In this comment, the play recognizes the limit of the power of words.

The principal characteristic which distinguishes world^a from world^b (and subsequent inferior worlds) is that words in the actual world have markedly less performative range than words in fictional worlds because of the materiality of actual-world objects which precludes them from performative shaping. So when the sentries at Elsinore, Barnardo and Francisco, assert it to be midnight and bitter cold, it is (*Hamlet*, 1.1.7–8). By contrast, as a real-world person, I cannot step outside, speak the same words, and change the weather at all. Although there is no limit to the number of subordinate worlds within worlds that can be performatively generated, moving downward, there is a rigid upper limit which cannot be broached. To say that something is true in a fictional world depends on authentication.[23] In the case of a fictional world, since words create worlds, the source of those words is the source of existence. Because the source of fictional truth lies with the creator of the world, authenticity is generated in superior fictional worlds. Successful authentication is therefore the province of the narrator.[24] Where there is no narrator or where the narrator is unreliable, authenticity can be arrived at through internal consistency and consensus. This is why Barnardo is able to make his world in act 1, scene 1, of *Hamlet* a cold winter night; as long as Francisco does not disagree, this statement will stand as true. Authenticity not only distinguishes possible worlds from impossible worlds, bringing worlds into existence in the first place, it also contributes to the continued security of the world. If narration is a strategy for control of the story by a single, ontologically superior narrator, the introduction of multiple narrators subverts this authorial power. Challenges to coherence and unity of the story are challenges to authentication, and in this way the capture and control strategy of the single author comes under siege. Competing narrators try to recoup their autonomy and escape from narrative capture by a variety of strategies. One way is to compel the narrator to stop talking. This is the primary strategy described earlier when Ben attacks Lily and she backs down. Another way is to undermine the authentication of the fictional world being created, drawing attention to inconsistencies and untruths in an attempt to discredit the story.

Security of fictional worlds is dependent, then, on the solidity of the walls. Coloured by different voices, gaps in *Eternal Hydra* arise inevitably between texts. The multiplicity of perspectives is knitted together, assembling a mosaic of complementary and overlapping segments. It is notable, however, that in this particular arrangement, none of the inset episodes are mutually exclusive. One story does not contradict another; rather, they are juxtaposed as adjacent fragments differing only in tone or mood, according to their source. In *Shadows*, plausibility is the name of the game, and so as part of the contest, individual stories are questioned and tested. Some storytellers are more adept at building walls than others. Even though dinner is over, Meredith's friend Richard has not yet arrived. Meredith explains that his plane was delayed. When Owen asks where Richard was travelling from, Meredith says 'Vancouver,' while Ben says 'I thought you said Edmonton.' Shelagh says 'I thought she said Calgary.' Meredith responds, 'So – he's coming from somewhere out west. Stop picking on me' (57). With multiple versions of this story about Richard in circulation, each version progressively loses more and more credibility. Later Meredith tries to remember where she was when Ben's play premiered. 'Oh God – I missed that one, too. I was studying in New York ... Back at U of T ... Or maybe Queen's ... Or was it Ryerson ...? Gosh' (59). Meredith's inability to commit to the details of a story, here her own supposed autobiography, leaves her vulnerable as an author in the vicious game of Storytime.

Like Meredith, Owen is also struggling with the expectations of the storytelling game. His story begins when he was an instructor of photography at Ryerson University. A female student seeking extra help with her assignments makes false accusations about sexual harassment. These accusations are enough to destroy his career. Then when he next sees her, he loses control and assaults her sending her to the hospital. While she is rewarded, receiving a degree 'which her talent didn't merit,' he is ruined (68). Ben, as well as Dan and Kate, is quickly on to this story, and accusing Owen of plagiarism, they correctly identify this plot as David Mamet's *Oleanna*. Ben concludes cruelly, 'So. End of story. So much for Owen' and declares Storytime to be over (69). Whereas one can reach out horizontally to another equivalent fictional world as Owen does to furnish his own fiction, one can also borrow characters and events from superior worlds to help stabilize fictional worlds, creating authenticating bridges vertically between the two and binding the fiction to solid reality. Dan's story in *Shadows* is also plagiarized. Despite his homosexuality, Dan enters in to a marriage with a woman, Joanne. They both want children and decide to try. Tragedy strikes when the baby is stillborn, and their marriage collapses. The initial situation of this story has been gifted to Dan by his author. As William Whitehead writes in the introduction to the published text: 'He [Findley] built a lot from our own lives into the play ... One of the arguments in the play was almost a word-for-word duplication of an argument Tiff and I had on more than one occasion; the story of one character's marriage to an actress was remarkably similar to the story of Tiff's own brief foray into matrimony' (55).[25] Dan himself acknowledges this loan and admits later: 'My story was true, too. Only it wasn't mine. It happened to a friend … many years ago' (69).

Piatigorsky does something similar, borrowing real-world elements and pressing them into service of a fictional world. Although New Orleans citizens Léon LaBas, the cobbler, and Sarah Briggs, Henry Warmoth's fiancée, are fictional characters, Henry Warmoth is not.[26] Drawing down elements from the superior actual world and incorporating them into the fiction is a common method for increasing the plausibility and security of a fictional world.[27] Through this method, fictive authors imitate their creators. In support of her story, Meredith uses not only stories borrowed from superior worlds but employs props, co-opting actual-world objects to participate in her fictional creation. Although there are only seven at the dinner party, there are eight place settings; the extra having been laid for Meredith's friend Richard who is expected momentarily. Despite Meredith's initial floundering as an inconsistent storyteller, this strategy of incorporating actual-world elements serves her well in the competition. As demonstrated in the final section, this use of objects from a higher-order, relatively more actual world provides the model for a more nuanced cross-world narrative that allows Meredith, at the end, to transcend the limits of fictional world borders, achieve auto/biographical autonomy, and possibly even win the new play commission. However, in most cases, when the actual underpinnings of fictional worlds are exposed and objects try to move upward, straining against the containing and protecting world boundaries, those boundaries fracture and the resolute actuality of superior worlds becomes fatal.

Theatrical Terrorism and the Destruction of Fictional Worlds

Compelling a narrator to stop speaking is one successful strategy for halting the continued development of a fictional world. Rendering a fictional world unstable by drawing attention to inconsistencies and to the fictionalizing process and so undermining its authenticity is another strategy practised by jealous narrators. One more tactic remains for desperate authors to maintain control of their own fictional worlds or to escape the biographical control of another author. The reverse of creation is destruction. With the power to create fictional worlds with words also comes the power to destroy those worlds. The wall both makes their existence as fictional shadow beings possible and excludes them from the light. To destroy the wall would be to let the light flood in, and that fleeting moment of freedom would also bring instant extermination.[28]

In *Shadows*, despite her earlier missteps, Meredith's growing storytelling success causes tensions to escalate as Ben tries at first to discount her world by questioning its authenticity. When this strategy fails, he adopts the terrorizing tactics of a suicide bomber and decides to 'kill' everyone:

SHELAGH: Ben – it's only a game.
BEN: You think so? Ask *them*. (*The AUDIENCE*.) *Silence*.
LILY: (*Quietly*.) You said you wouldn't do that.
BEN: I lied.
LILY: Now, I feel as if you've tricked me into taking all my clothes off in front of strangers. (65)

In the performance I witnessed, the uncertainty and fear of the characters-now-actors was evident as they scattered off the stage and into the audience with some retreating into the vomitoria of the Studio Theatre or hovering skittishly in the neutral gutter between the stage and the house. Counter-intuitively, Ben asserts creative authorial puissance in the act of destroying his creations. Ben 'kills' everyone when he reveals the dinner party to be a fiction. He destroys world^c of the dinner party and eclipse, and by extension all the embedded story worlds told so far (world^d series). Ben takes his cue here from Prospero who abruptly ends the marriage masque, dissolving that world with a word (*Tempest*, 4.1.142–3).

Silvio Gaggi describes two modes of self-referentiality. Gaggi draws his examples from postmodern visual art, film, and novels, but he borrows the terminology for his taxonomy from drama, naming his two modes: 'Pirandellian' and 'Brechtian.' Pirandellian works of art present 'self-referential art works structured around the inclusion of one work inside another – plays-in-plays, narrations inside narrations, paintings inside paintings.'[29] The downward movement from world^a to world^b predicated on the creation of walls as previously described is very much a Pirandellian strategy, birthing new worlds by carving out space-within. Debra Malina picks up Butler's idea of walls as violent: 'if the erection of boundaries can be violent, their transgression may be more obviously so, despite or because of the fact that it sometimes serves paradoxically to reinforce the boundaries that have constructed the subjects to begin with.'[30] Gerard Genette calls this transgression of borders between worlds 'metalepsis.'[31] Metalepsis is another source of fictional violence which takes as its targets both the character-citizens of the fictional world under siege and the audience witness to those incursions. This breaching of the fictional world boundaries is figured as violent displacement, unwanted intrusion, or rape. For Malina, rape and torture are thematic representations of metalepsis and she tracks these fictional crimes in several postmodern novels, drawing parallels between fictional violence and the metaleptic assault on readers. Thinking about this second kind of authorial violence in terms of Gaggi's two metatheatrical modes, it becomes clear that whereas the Pirandellian mode moves downward and the violence of capture and abjection is a feature of the building of world borders, metaleptic intrusions of this kind fall into the Brechtian mode. When one knocks down the protective world border, as Ben does, it instigates an upward movement. The immediate fictional world is destroyed as it is assimilated into the realm of the world above. Gaggi describes works of art in the Brechtian mode as those which 'employ a variety of devices designed to foreground style and otherwise remind the audience that what it is experiencing is artifice. Style is "opaque"; it calls attention to itself and blatantly obtrudes itself between the viewer and the work's denotative content.'[32] So on the one hand, the descending Pirandellian mode of nesting worlds by creating walls is a life-creating 'push,' whereas on the other hand, the ascending Brechtian mode of exposing those creative walls is a destabilizing life-destroying 'pop.'[33]

Children, specifically babies, are markers of new life, of creation from the self, displaying the individual's godlike power to create life seemingly from nothing. Moving from biological creation to narrative creation is a small rhetorical step; it is a metaphorical commonplace to refer to a work of art as a child and the author as the engendering parent. *Shadows* is rife with talk of babies and the impulse to procreate; however, these babies are aborted or killed in infancy and fertility is persistently thwarted. These are failed Pirandellian inset worlds. As part of her vociferous attack on Ben, Shelagh condemns herself as infertile: 'No point having sex with me. I'm barren. Children? Never. Of course, Dan can't have your children, either, but I guess the thing was, it was easier to be with him than it was with me because I'm too demanding' (64). The failure is not simply romantic and the connection to the impossibility of children is made explicit. Later, Dan calls them 'genetic failures' (66). In the set-up to the game of Storytime, Shelagh points out the danger, remembering the time an earlier guest, Rosemary Neilson, let slip that she accidentally drowned her baby (60). Once the game is underway, Ben quickly passes off the storytelling responsibilities by labelling Lily as a baby killer. Confronted with this accusation, Lily claims that years earlier she aborted Ben's child: 'I did what had to be done [...] I chose abortion – in order to survive' (61–2). Yet another dead baby appears from an unexpected quarter. When pressed for a more believable story, Dan recounts his unhappy marriage to an actress. Artificial insemination produced for the couple a boy child who was tragically born without a brain. The mother Joanne 'never regained her ... self' (67), her own dependent subjectivity having been destroyed by the damaged child. Earlier, Lily, Shelagh, and Dan were all connected to Ben as his betrayed subject-creations. Through this cluster of stories, these three are again connected to Ben as his lovers; as such they enact revenge, refusing further fecundity – no children for Ben.[34] The dead babies are rejected, that is, they are cast out or, in Butler's terms, they are rendered abject: 'This exclusionary matrix by which subjects are formed thus requires the simultaneous production of a domain of abject beings, those who are not yet "subjects," but who form the constitutive outside to the domain of the subject.'[35] Through the subject-formation process, the child or the possibility of children is sacrificed to protect the survival of the self/world.

The babies, then, are stories, incipient fictional worlds, the offspring of creation. From these examples, the plays remind us that if you are the creator of a fictional world, you can also be its destroyer. Performative creation of a world is one strategy for capture and control; killing a fictional world and its inhabitants is another exercise in control. The viability of stories is also at risk in *Eternal Hydra*. In an episode enacted from the diary, Gwendolyn Jackson, Carbuncle's researcher, demands credit for her contributions. She wants to write an introduction: 'A glowing preface to help acquaint the reader' (56). Carbuncle is vehement in his rejection, arguing that this kind of contextualization is tantamount to thievery. His ultimate reaction to this contestation of his sole authority is to threaten to burn the *Hydra* manuscript.

CARBUNCLE: Let's burn it.
JACKSON: Oh God ... not again ...
CARBUNCLE: The whole thing. Come, let's do it [...] Rid the world of Gordias
    Carbuncle (59).

It is also significant in this context that he collapses the distinction between the material existence of the work and his own life. A threat to the work, especially a work of auto/biography, is also a threat to one's self.

Accounts of stories being destroyed or silenced in both of *Eternal*

Hydra's two historical settings are likewise characterized by censorship backed by physical threat to the author. The episodes coming from Carbuncle's diary are dated specifically as three days in June 1936. The characters in these Paris scenes are aware of the looming political menace. Wellington Sr asks Carbuncle where all the party boys have gone (81). Carbuncle tells Thomas that Paris is no place for an American woman 'with Spain escalating. Germans mixed up in it. I'm certain it won't be long before we're all again at war' (77). Ezra makes a point of telling us that Carbuncle died the day the Nazis invaded Paris, marking the parallel between the physical risk to an expatriate Jewish writer and the silencing of his writing. Similarly, in the contested Chapter 72, the violence of the New Orleans riot of 1866 forms a hinge. In the first part of the chapter, the anonymous Narrator acquires a job making shoes – a job which is explicitly linked to artistic creation and storytelling, even to autobiography. She is told: 'A great pair of shoes is much more than a thing of mere use. It's not so different from a painting by Michelangelo! It's an expression of yourself' (99). The state convention of July 1866 is called with the intent of granting 'the Negro his legal right to vote' (105). Murderous violence that disrupts the convention has two effects in the story. First, in the larger historical sweep, a collective political voice is silenced. Voting is also a kind of autobiographical statement, asserting individual beliefs and allowing people to speak. Second, in the smaller realm, the Creole cobbler Monsieur LaBas is killed in the riot, and the cobbler shop that employed the Narrator is sure to close, which would take away her livelihood and silence her artistic voice.

Just as creative opportunities for all three autobiographer-artists come under threat from these larger social forces, so too a similar threat emerges on a smaller scale from a more ambivalent source. Telling one's story is not simply a matter of opening one's mouth and shouting louder than everyone else. There are systemic barriers to speaking one's story and having it heard. Auto/biography is bound up with material conditions, which permit or deny authority and audience. Not only do *Shadows* and *Eternal Hydra* stage competing writers, they also stage the gatekeepers – the publishers who print and disseminate the physical text, producers who manage the resources to mount a theatrical performance, meticulous editors, possessive scholars, and cautious patrons. All of whom exert influence, for good or ill, to shape the path of the story. In the particular case of Carbuncle in the 1930s, he has to persuade his patron and publisher Randall Wellington Sr that *Eternal Hydra* is progressing well and is a project worthy of his investment: 'You know me. My reputation. I am very uncomfortable with this part of my profession. Please, Randall. Write me a cheque' (84). Wellington does give Carbuncle the money, and this is the money that Carbuncle uses to buy Thomas's story. Just before Wellington exits, there is a subtle suggestion of a sexual relationship, perhaps in the past, or perhaps just in unfulfilled desire between the two men.

WELLINGTON: I like you Carbuncle. Way more than my fancy factory guys. They don't have your blasphemous aspiration. I'd rather spend an evening with you.
CARBUNCLE: Would you?
WELLINGTON: Certainly.
CARBUNCLE: You can't stay. I have no food.
WELLINGTON: Who says I want to eat?
…
(*Wellington touches Carbuncle.*) (88–9)

Wellington Jr's comment after the enactment of this diary entry supports this interpretation. He says, 'To think that my infallible father could be charmed and seduced. And Carbuncle! Incredible' (91). In the parallel scene in Chapter 72, the Narrator also has a patron. As an audition for a job as a cobbler, LaBas asks the Narrator to make a trial pair of shoes. He lends her tools and materials: 'a hide of leather. Awls, clams, a jigger. Tranchet and cork. Good thread and shoemaker's wax. And a last the size of my foot' (96). After he has hired her to work in the shop, LaBas also offers to teach her to read.

LABAS: It's not your fault. I'll have to teach you.
NARRATOR: You'd do that?
LABAS: Absolutely. After work. (*He touches her.*) It would be my pleasure.
…
NARRATOR: (*out*) I felt stupid, all right, but what else am I gonna do? I got my own pair of shoes, then this here job with good pay, now a chance to learn to read! And he was kind, Monsieur LaBas. So much kinder than … (101–2)

Again, the implication of a sexual relationship is plain. Later he buys her a dress, and as she pulls it on, '*LaBas approaches and rubs his hand over her newly showing, pregnant belly*' (109). Although Wellington and LaBas are relatively kindly facilitators of the work of Carbuncle (and Thomas indirectly) and the Narrator, these essential materials come with strings attached. Both the necessity of these supplies and the threat of having them withdrawn are clearly depicted. If you can control the means of production, you can simply choose not to allow the world to live. In this way, other controllers enter into competition with the engendering artist; worlds may not be destroyed outright, but they can be 'lost' or 'silenced.'

The vulnerable situations of Selma Thomas, Carbuncle, and the anonymous Narrator are structured in tight parallel. Although the seed of the New Orleans autobiography comes from Selma Thomas's story, that is not the story that we hear. The only version to which we are witness is Carbuncle's rewrite. In the revised story, Carbuncle (presumably) integrates his own autobiography and that of Selma Thomas by putting the Narrator into a very similar situation or at least shaping the situation to underscore those points of connection. (It is impossible to speculate as to what Thomas's story was like before these radical revisions.) Just as Wellington Sr and Léon LaBas are played by the same actor, the double casting of Thomas/Narrator and Carbuncle/Warmoth reinforces this cross-pollination.[36] Due to the larger social circumstances – the impending war in 1936 and the death of LaBas in 1866, which means the loss of the Narrator's income – both women are blocked (at least temporarily) from creative work. Further, both Thomas's story and the Narrator's shoes are contextualized not only as art but as autobiography. Both women are then offered a chance to sell their work. In the case of Thomas, Carbuncle buys her story for one hundred dollars, planning to use it in his *Eternal Hydra*. As an act of betrayal, plagiarism silences her voice, disassociating the story from the original author. By contrast, it is also an act of generosity, because in Carbuncle's hands, the story will live. The selling of the shoes to Henry Warmoth reflects the same pattern of selling under straitened circumstances. The act of plagiarism is figured slightly differently, but the appropriation of autobiography still operates. Warmoth gives the shoes as a gift to his lady friend, Sarah Briggs. She promises to wear them to the governor's mansion when he is finally inaugurated. The Narrator reminisces about Governor Warmoth years later: 'NARRATOR. One time I took my daughter down to Jackson Square to hear that Henry Warmoth give a speech. "If you give the Negroes an opportunity," he said, "they can do almost anything. Like the Negress cobbler I met before the riot of '66, who made my wife a pair of shoes as beautiful as a painting on someone's wall." To hear him say that. Felt like me up there, onstage. Not him at all. You never know. Might just be my voice coming from his mouth' (116). This act of ventriloquism neatly summarizes the contrary tension of this motif where the autobiographical subject/story is set free only by stealing it. Although the act of auto/biography is fulfilled as it attains an audience, this freedom comes at a price.

Transcendent Objects of Autobiography

In contrast to these examples of appropriated narratives, detached from their originating subject and voiced by someone else, both plays stage key examples where autobiography attains an audience while still remaining under the control of the originating subject. There are three object-autobiographies in *Shadows* and *Eternal Hydra* that manage this transcendent journey: a glass of wine, Meredith's body, and the Narrator's shoes. These select metaleptic objects 'pop' out of the fictional world into the real world, that is, they are able to rise up to equivalent status with their creators, setting themselves free of authorial control.

First, the wine. In *Shadows*, at the revelatory moment when Ben explodes the world of the dinner party, he looks to a glass of wine for stability and truth, citing the wine as evidence that this is theatre. He argues that a mundane actual-world object – a glass of water – has been transformed by our belief into a glass of wine and when the fiction is destroyed it becomes water again. Certainly this is what we expect. When a fictional world dissolves, everything in it reverts to its prior status, revealing what it 'really' is. Characters become actors, the dining room becomes a stage, and the wine becomes water. Shelagh deflates this argument, however, telling him that he has chosen a bad example. The wine is real, that is, it is still wine. As a test, she offers it to an audience member who confirms that it is indeed real wine. Ben is surprised by this turn of events: 'Interesting. Not what I've been drinking all evening' (66).[37] In an earlier exchange, Ben and Dan assert the connection between wine and truth.

BEN: (*Pouring wine.*) In vino veritas. Right?
DAN: So they say.
BEN: (*Drinks.*) Well. The veritas is – I never loved you (63).

The expression 'in vino veritas' refers to the truth revealed in drunken declarations. Here, the core idea that the truth is in the wine is carried forward literally by Shelagh when she uses the wine to overturn Ben's challenge to change the world with words. He lauds the playwright's power: 'The ability to make whatever you imagine utterly believable. For example: that "wine" she's drinking ... Is it real – or just coloured water?' (66). Inside the theatrical frame, the liquid in the glass can be ambivalently both. In the actual world, wine is wine. Ben's Brechtian move nullifies the previous Pirandellian worlds, suggesting that this wholesale destruction is a superior strategy for continued subjugation and fictional control. Yet critically, the wine survives. It manages to make the upward shift between worlds; it transcends world^c and comes to rest intact in world^b. However, as discussed earlier, there is a limit to the destructive power of Brechtian revelation. The number of descending nested worlds is infinite, but of ascending nested worlds, there is an upper limit – the actual world – beyond which words no longer work. *Shadows* asks us to keep readjusting our assessment of where we think that hard wall is. But not only does the wine continue to exist in world^b, it makes that impossible jump and is consumed by a world^a audience member. We have been witness to a minor theatrical miracle, performing the usual theatrical transposition in reverse. Ben says, '[that's] not what I've been drinking' (66); in the world of the dinner party, Ben the actor has been drinking coloured water, juice, or tea, in compliance with the theatrical taboo against alcoholic props.[38] When that world disappears and the actual is revealed, the water becomes what we had believed it to be – wine. The transcendence of the wine suggests possibility and points the way for Meredith to make use of the same strategy to achieve the autonomous performance of autobiography and, by metatheatrical slippage, transcend her fictional trappings and set her 'self' free.

Like Carbuncle, Meredith has also shed an old identity and replaced it with a new one. After the exposure of the dinner party as a facade, Ben goes around the circle to each guest/playwright-competitor and asks for their truth. One by one, they confess their actual autobiographies. Shelagh is not Ben's wife: 'Last summer, I left my husband after fifteen years of married hell. My current partner is a theatre director some of you may know. I have two sons. And I write plays' (69). The others make similar revelations. Last, Ben turns to Meredith.

MEREDITH: My truth is [...] Richard. It's about him.
OWEN: You mean he's real? All that was true?
MEREDITH: Only part of that was true. But he did die. In Nevada. I killed him there. (69)

In the early part of the storytelling, the other guests, primed by the extra place setting, had been waiting for the arrival of Meredith's friend Richard. Later on, it is Meredith's claim that she has just received the news that Richard died in a plane crash that triggers Ben's outburst of scornful disbelief and his decision to collapse the primary fictional world. Despite the incredulity of the others, Meredith persists: 'Six years ago. And so ... since he can't be here tonight, I'll speak for him' (69). Her story begins as a biography of the deceased, as she claims the right to tell his story. Then the story takes a sharp turn to autobiography. When no one believes that she could kill a man, Meredith insists, 'I've told you that I killed him. Which I did. I unsexed him. He died on an operating table. In Nevada [...] I ... I ... am Richard Cassidy. Was ... Richard Cassidy' (70). Meredith's act of ventriloquism does exactly what Carbuncle thinks he is doing in cutting off the Hydra's heads, silencing a vulnerable voice to paradoxically set it free, detached but audible. The destruction of Richard's world is an act of creation as Meredith comes into existence. In her account, Meredith underscores this as an act of freedom: 'I wanted to live. I *wanted* to live [...] It's not a story, Mr. Singer. It's the truth. This has been the most important day of my life. I'm learning how to live again – to well and truly be here – and not to be afraid of who I am' (70). The public telling of the story is key, facilitating the release of 'I' through autobiography. On one hand, the theft of Richard's story (and his body/life) by Meredith is the same act of plagiaristic betrayal perpetrated by other controlling author-biographers. On the other hand, because Richard becomes Meredith, because they share one body, the story belongs to her too. Thus, the narrator and protagonist are folded into the same person, rendering this story a liberating act of performative auto/biography.

In *Shadows*, Ben still exerts control to the end, sending the six playwrights home with a promise to announce the winner the following day. The play hints that Meredith is the winner with the most persuasive story. After everyone else has left, Ben singles her out to say, 'Oh ... Richard ... (*MEREDITH stops and turns to BEN*) Good work' (70). Nevertheless, the fix is in. Ben's phone rings. It is one of the playwrights who just left. We only hear Ben's side of the conversation: 'No! I don't care how good she was ... Absolutely not. You're still going to win. No – he'll be no problem. Look, I'll take care of everything' (71). Even though the prize of a commission from the Stratford Festival is still under the control of gatekeepers like Ben and may still elude Meredith, we can still count Meredith's narrative as a 'win.' Taking what she says at face value, the act of telling her story this time (perhaps for the first time) is a seminal moment. The transformative journey from Richard to Meredith is completed by her autobiographical performance before a community of hearers.

To escape the performative control of words, Meredith uses material objects – the extra place at the table, the phone call announcing Richard's demise, and ultimately her own body – to make her story live in the actual world. By attaching the story to the body of the actor, Meredith's autobiography survives the dissolution of worlds and makes the transition upward to world[b] intact. Further, like the wine, Meredith's performed identity is tethered to a still higher-order object – the world[a] body of the decidedly female and feminine actor Kimwun Perehinec, who is the sole actor to perform this role to date. Meredith's story is the only one from all the Storytime playwrights to shed narration and become embodied performance. Like the doubled *Eternal Hydra* narrators who slip across boundaries between worlds to become protagonists in their own texts, Meredith takes advantage of the essential ventriloquism at the heart of theatrical performance to shift the frame and take control of her own narrative. In a less radical manner, Carbuncle too attempts to alter his physicality to match a performed identity. At one point, he talks about himself in the third person, analysing the face in the mirror: 'I know that face. I distinctly recognize that face. But the voice … and the clothes. Are you that Dublin Jewish boy who lived on St. Kevin's Parade? The one who never ate pig? Not possible. Not you. Now, I see you devour prosciutto. How good of you to eat prosciutto' (*Eternal Hydra*, 60). The act of eating pork, of course, informs the new, explicitly non-Jewish identity through a physical act, co-opting the body to participate in the performance of self. Like Selma Thomas, who can't change her skin colour as easily as her name, and Meredith, who undergoes sex reassignment surgery, Carbuncle is also exploring the transformative possibilities of a performative identity tied to a seemingly less malleable body.

Yet, although Meredith draws on the fixed materiality of a physical body to establish the credentials of her story in a superior, relatively more actual world, the success of this strategy depends on a body that persistently reads as ambivalent. Meredith's body, like the wine which still might be water, is uncertain. There is an underlying truth which we cannot access. There is an inherent materiality beyond the power of performative language. Meredith's story cannot be discounted, but neither can it be verified. She claims this as her truth after everyone else has revealed the gaps between world[a] and world[b]: Meredith insists that there is no gap. This dynamic interplay between a self-story as performed narrative and the self-story as marked on a material body is a principal crux of autobiographical performance. Like other world[a] autobiographers, such as Djanet Sears (*Afrika Solo*), George Seremba (*Come Good*

Rain), Guillermo Verdecchia (*Fronteras Americanas*), and Ken Garnhum (*Pants on Fire*), Meredith exploits the determined nature of the body as archive to lift her narrative out of the fictionalized theatrical frame and up into the actual world; however, it is precisely this ambiguity between performative identities in world[a] and world[b] that makes this transcendence possible.

Just as Meredith/Richard's body acts as an autobiographical archive pulling the performed fictive identity upward into a more relatively actual world in *Shadows*, so a pair of shoes makes the same journey in *Eternal Hydra*. The story that becomes Chapter 72 is the first-person monologue of a freed slave, Selma Thomas's grandmother, who comes to New Orleans around 1866. As Thomas says, her grandmother did not have the opportunity or the means to record the events of her life. This silence is filled by surrogate authors when first her biography is imagined by Thomas and then sold to Carbuncle who revises it further. Both Thomas and Carbuncle adopt the cloak of a first-person perspective, precisely reiterating the pattern of biographical ventriloquism. Yes, this auto/biography has found a voice and achieved a public, but only at two steps removed from the originating subject. Inside the fictional world created by these joint biographers, the unnamed Narrator performs her own act of autobiography – she makes herself a pair of shoes. The connection between the performative act of narrating a self into existence and this particular pair of shoes accrues through a developing series of analogies. First, the shoes are likened to a work of art. But significantly, it is not just that they are a work of art – additional import lies in the next thing that LaBas says: 'You think God looks askance at His own creations? A great pair of shoes is more than a thing of use ... It's an expression of yourself' (99). In this way, the shoes embody not only an act of performative creation but also an act that presents an autobiographical fragment or view. After this, the shoes are sold to Henry Warmoth in a scene that exactly parallels the sale of Thomas's story to Carbuncle. Again by analogy, the shoes are linked to a work of auto/biography. However, where Thomas's story becomes subsumed into Carbuncle's *Eternal Hydra*, the Narrator's shoes escape the confines of their fictional origins.

Instead of remaining in Henry Warmoth's possession, the shoes are passed on when Warmoth gives them as a gift to his lady friend (later his wife) Sarah Briggs. In the final moment of the play, as the Narrator is describing the ventriloquism of watching Warmoth speak, upstage Briggs puts the shoes on her feet and transforms back to Ezra. The stage directions sketch the action thus: '*Warmoth puts the shoes on Briggs' feet* ...

Warmoth exits. Briggs becomes Ezra. She listens to the Narrator' (116). In the moment when Briggs becomes Ezra, the shoes ride piggyback on that ascending transposition. When the actor body temporarily possessed by Sarah Briggs (of world[c]) is restored to its highest – most actual – level, becoming again Ezra (of world[b]), the shoes go too and make the transition intact. Magically and against sense, Erza is wearing the Narrator's shoes. Like the wine and like Meredith's body, the shoes take advantage of the metatheatrical ambiguity of fictionalized objects to slip through. It is the uncertain duality of the objects that renders the usually rigid world boundaries permeable and allows this transit. In the end, Ezra listens to the Narrator. She is hearing the story, but as the shoes are autobiography, she is also wearing it.

Reminiscing about Governor Warmoth's speech, the Narrator is acutely aware of her lesser voice in relation to Warmoth's; she is aware of his appropriation and grants it freely: ''Cause he's the reality of New Orleans. White man's the one who speaks, here. White man's the only one who gets heard. Better to give him my voice than keep it useless for myself' (116). But in this interrelation, the Narrator reverses the flow, changing the terms of the narrative chain. Instead of Warmoth telling her story and by doing so, capturing her in fiction, she imagines that her voice comes from his mouth, he is merely the conduit. More than imagination, she wonders if this is in fact so: 'To hear him say that. Felt like me up there, onstage. Not him at all. You never know. Might just be my voice coming from his mouth' (116). And of course this is what is happening in this section known as Chapter 72, the nameless cobbler is our narrator. This act of reverse ventriloquism extends to the highest stratum of the play. The voice issuing from the actor may indeed be that of the protagonist and not that of the author. The frame of the play is closed as we return to Ezra again, but now rather than positioning Ezra as a controlling narrative puppeteer, the sense is that Ezra is a vessel for the Narrator's voice, the vehicle for the telling of her shoes.

Chapter Four

The Autobiographical Body as a Site of Utopian Performativity: *Billy Twinkle*

Marionette virtuoso Ronnie Burkett is not shy about appearing onstage with his puppet creations. In defiance of the centuries-old principle that the puppeteer ought to remain invisible, Burkett has adopted a performance style called 'open manipulation.'[1] Fully visible to the audience, Burkett operates his marionettes. We see the handheld controllers, we see the strings, we see the marionettes hanging lifeless on their hooks as they await Burkett's animating movement and voice. In addition to performing 'through' his puppet actors, Burkett has also frequently appeared in various cameo roles alongside his miniature cast. In *Awful Manors*, a mock-Victorian melodrama, Burkett was the hectored butler at the beck and call of a dozen or more puppets, commenting ironically on his usual offstage duties controlling the puppets. Wearing a costume identical to that of his marionette protagonist Carl, Burkett doubled as Carl in the underground cabaret scenes in *Tinka's New Dress* (1994). Like Burkett, Carl is a puppeteer. And so when he takes the stage with his anti-authoritarian play-within featuring the cynical, controlling Franz and the elfin innocent Schnitzel, it is Burkett who manipulates their strings. In these scenes, the politically charged dialogue was improvised to comment on current political and social issues. Accordingly, Burkett acknowledges the ambivalent blending of himself with his character at this point as he voices his own critical opinions through Carl. He notes in the introduction to the play that these sections 'serve to illustrate that *Carl/Ronnie* is in constant danger of crossing the line' (*Tinka*, 3; my emphasis). In *Street of Blood* (1998), Burkett again enters the marionettes' playing space, this time to emphasize the difference of scale between his world and theirs. Relative size actualizes a metaphor for physical domination in two of Burkett's selected roles: the strict patriarch Stanley Rural, who hits his son when he finds him play-acting in his mother's wedding dress, and the rapist of Cora Jean Pickles.[2] In a more benign expression of this innate difference, Burkett also appears to his marionettes as Jesus. In his most recent play *Billy Twinkle: Requiem for a Golden Boy* (2008), Burkett moves to centre stage, taking on the title role.[3] Once again the poetics of the interaction and interdependence of human and puppet come to the fore in Burkett's work. Following in his creator's autobiographical footsteps, Billy is a professional puppeteer. When the dissolute, disenchanted, middling middle-aged Billy is abruptly fired from his job as a cruise ship entertainer, he contemplates suicide. He is interrupted in this act by the ghostly hand puppet of his dead mentor Sid Diamond. Compelled by supernatural forces to re-perform his life 'condensed and in miniature' using marionettes (*Billy Twinkle*, 20), the necessary autobiographical unity of subject, narrator, and protagonist housed in one body comes unglued.

It is Philippe Lejeune who first prescribed the principle of autobiographical unity in an effort to establish criteria for autobiography as a genre distinct from first-person novels. Principally, the author-subject, narrator, and protagonist must be identical and the subject must be a real person.[4] These two tenets address Lejeune's main concern with identifying and protecting the 'truth' of a life story. First, using a 'real person' as the subject effectively grounds the narrative in an actual-world truth; and second, identity between the elements of transmission – author, narrator, and protagonist – conserves that truth as it passes from role to role. The point made in chapter 1 with regard to the auto/biographical performer as distinct from the auto/biographical author of a printed text is that, relative to a printed text where the roles are amalgamated in the encompassing morpheme 'I,' performance tends to highlight and magnify the ontological separation of the narrative roles outlined by Lejeune. As one moves from author-subject (world[a]) to narrator (world[b]) to protagonist (world[c]), moving inevitably though increasingly fictional levels, the 'truth' undergoes a progressive process of construction, selection, and omission. In *Perfect Pie* and *The Drawer Boy*, the amnesiac characters of Patsy and Angus shift among these various roles to investigate gaps and to create new narrative material in the pursuit of auto/biography. These characters also make use of surrogates in some of the roles, allowing other characters (Francesca/Marie, Morgan, and Miles), through the use of mirror-talk strategies, to temporarily take up the narrative mantle. By contrast, in *Billy Twinkle*, the tripartite roles of author-subject, narrator, and protagonist are 'identical' in that they share a name and a life history in the person of Billy Twinkle; however, they are significantly non-identical in that the autobiographical roles are divided over different bodies. We might ask if the visual likeness of the puppet Billy protagonists to the human Billy subject is sufficient to save this performance, allowing it to continue to be classified as autobiography, or must it topple into biography? In a textual autobiography, the body is invisible – the author-subject body is absent and the narrator and protagonist bodies conjured up only in the imagination of the reader via print. Yet, in the context of performance, the palpable presence of the staged autobiographical body in each of its congruent roles is absolutely central to the process of autobiography. In consideration of the communicative weight invested in the autobiographical body, *Billy Twinkle* constitutes a valuable case study. The biological and material differences between human and puppet autobiographical elements, especially when married to already extant ontological differences, limn key areas of theoretical interest regarding the function of authentic or marked bodies in autobiographical performance. In other words: How are the central principles of Lejeune's autobiographical pact concerning authenticity and the identity of subject and protagonist to be upheld (or reconceived) when one role is occupied by an actual-world human subject and the other by a puppet doppelganger?

In conventional performance situations where an actual-world actor embodies an unrelated autonomous fictional-world character, as when Karen Robinson plays Pauline Newberry (*Eternal Hydra*), there is little or no concern about how the actions, emotions, or experiences of the fictional character might relate to those of its actual-world host body. However, when the actor becomes the autobiographical subject of her own performance, as when TJ Dawe declares in his autobiographical solo show *Totem Figures*, 'Hi! ... I'm TJ Dawe,' there arises in the audience a profound desire to square the circle and be able to equate the travails of the fictional protagonist definitively with those of his or her actual-world counterpart. As Susan Bennett writes, 'The singularity of autobiographical subject, author, and performer can hardly fail to create, as I have suggested, an over-investment of spectatorial response in corporeal evidence against which we might better understand the narrative, by sifting through its more or less fictive truths.'[5] Bennett goes on to describe the chiastic relationship of the subject body to the protagonist body rooted in time, reaching into the past but also into the future. Looking backward, in terms of its historical extension into the lived past, the body is an archive – 'the literal vessel of somatic history.'[6] In performance, as the protagonist-self relates and re-enacts the past experience of the autobiographical subject-self, these stories become doubled on the body. Experience is performed again in the present but also this same experience is rendered palpable through the presence of the historical subject body. The audience to such an autobiographical experience consumes the awareness that this staged body is a body that has already said those things, done those things, and had those things done to it. This body is a body that in turn has given birth, emigrated to Canada, undergone gender reassignment surgery, been raped, survived genocide. Invariably (and perhaps due to this intense body connection), the autobiographical solo show draws on significant body experiences. Looking forward, the performative bridge between the immediate protagonist of performance and the ongoing actual subject reaches into the future as well. Bennett describes this relationship as 'the signification of identity ... identity that is a production of the body's exteriority.'[7] Along this axis, the performative acts of the fictional protagonist are not merely flashbacks to an earlier self but are reinventions of a self under construction. Performance itself operates to actively shape the identity of the autobiographical subject, transforming it as it crosses out of the performance frame and returns to a singular existence in the actual world. The body, then, is altered not only by past experience but also by the performative repetition of this experience in the present. Emerging from this interwoven arrangement of the shared body of subject and protagonist, the hopeful transformation of identity is also a hallmark of autobiographical solo performance.

Picking up this idea of hope in autobiographical performance, Ric Knowles applies Jill Dolan's concept of the utopian performative to identify particular coup de théâtre moments where the subject body and protagonist body blend one into the other to open up gaps of signification. This assimilation generates a 'phenomenological frisson' for the audience as the fictional frame seems to dissolve and we are unexpectedly witness to something really real. These moments of communion with the authentic function as examples of the 'intersubjectivity between audience and stage.'[8] Knowles's opening example is perhaps the most potent. He describes his attendance at an autobiographical solo performance titled *Bathroom*, which deals with subject Emily Taylor's experience of bulimia. The play presents 'increasingly graphic first-person accounts of the obsessive ingestion and regurgitation of vast quantities of food; of a roller coaster of weight gain and loss over ten years ... of the ravages that the body we were watching had suffered and continued to be marked by.'[9] The conclusion of this performance featured Emily walking downstage, picking up a paper bag, pulling out a sticky, sugary apple fritter and 'devour[ing] it with what the stage directions call *"evident and uncouth enjoyment."*[10] One can imagine the shock of the audience witness to this transgressive act. Although Dolan and Knowles highlight intersubjectivity between the stage and the audience, I contend that the underlying cause of the frisson associated with this moment is the radical intersubjectivity between the two personae of Emily occupying a single body. The apple fritter consumed within the fictional frame by Emily in world[b] is also necessarily consumed by Emily in world[a] who is a recovering bulimic. An initially fictional act, the eating performed by Emily[b] crashes through the ontological border, overtakes Emily[a], and reveals the generally obscured authentic body. The world[a] audience connects with world[a] Emily and suddenly is lifted up out of the fiction, and as Dolan suggests, into a kind of utopian vision 'that lifts everyone slightly above the present, into a hopeful feeling of what the world might be like if every moment of our lives were as emotionally voluminous, generous, aesthetically striking, and intersubjectively intense.'[11] The efficacy of this example resides in two aspects: first, the act which crosses both bodies actually enters into the body, unequivocally affecting the actual body, and second, the act happens in the here and now, an integrated part of the performance.

Two other examples provided by Knowles highlight the significance of these qualities. George Seremba, in his solo autobiographical performance *Come Good Rain,* narrates the years of his youth in the Uganda of Idi Amin and Milton Obote. Amid the political turbulence, Seremba is abducted, shot, and left for dead. In performance, it is the moving display of his body marked by the scars of that murderous attack that bridges the fictional body to the actual body, creating that moment of phenomenological frisson. Shared by the fictional protagonist and the actual subject, the scars speak to the authenticity of the narrative. The main difference between Seremba's scars and Taylor's apple fritter as moments of intersubjectivity is that the apple fritter is consumed in the present tense whereas the scars also figure as visible evidence of the experience of the actual body but only in the past tense. Djanet Sears in her autobiographical play *Afrika Solo* also presents a moment of radical intersubjectivity where experience is shared by the two autobiographical selves. Sears's narrative documents her visit to Benin and Togo in West Africa where she discovers the faces of her family in those of locals in the marketplace. Here, Sears's intersubjective act involves changing her clothes; she sheds her Western clothing, donning instead a richly embroidered boubou and headwrap. As the stage directions indicate, 'wearing [these clothes] in some way transforms her' (65). In her transformation from Janet to Djanet, the act of dressing involved both the present-tense fictional character and the historical self represented by the actor-subject. Again, the manifestation of the cross-over action is slightly different; unlike the scars, the clothes are not the singular mark of past experience transmuted to the present, but rather a repetition – the double – of past experience re-performed in the present.

In each case, the moment of radical intersubjectivity ('the apple fritter moment') forms the nexus of the two axes of signification concerning the autobiographical body introduced by Bennett. First, these moments arise out of the experience of the body as archive in general, but also, more specifically, they demonstrate the personal historical crisis which motivated these autobiographical narratives. Second, these moments provide the performative catalyst for the transformative and future-oriented leap whereby the actual-world subject-self is changed by this cross-world act. These moments of utopian intersubjectivity located in the autobiographical body are comparable to similar moments of messy metatheatre discussed in previous chapters, those moments where the protective frame that enables fictionality parts to allow transit across worlds. Whenever the usual theatrical gap between worlds, here the actual world of the autobiographical subject and the fictional world of its protagonist, shrinks to a degree such that the distinction between them becomes ambiguous, we see the potential for fictional acts to have profound and almost magical actual-world effects.

Now, what about puppets? Can autobiographical performance where the human subject is physically divided from its puppet protagonist access this kind of utopian intersubjectivity which seems to depend on a unitary body? To begin to answer this question, we need to parse out how puppets augment or complicate the basic phenomenological situation of autobiographical performance. First, and this obvious point is what drew me to *Billy Twinkle* in the first place, puppets enable a spatialization of multiple worlds. Occasionally, theatre will present two or more worlds side by side; this is typically the case in formal plays-within, like *The Mousetrap* in *Hamlet* where we see both the fictional inset play and its relatively actual audience of Hamlet, Ophelia, and others. This is also the situation in *Goodness* where the ghostly characters of Althea's recounted past materialize in her apartment, audienced by Althea and Michael. More commonly, there is no explicit audience to frame the

fiction, and rather than share the scenic space, worlds shift wholesale
with one displacing another. One world comes to the fore, and prior
worlds remain as palimpsests – the actor underlying the character, the
set underlying the setting. By physically distancing the puppet-character from its motivating actor-puppeteer, the essential theatrical duality
becomes visible. Also in some performances, including those of Ronnie
Burkett, the puppets and their environment are crafted in a smaller scale
relative to human beings; the largest marionettes manipulated by Burkett in *Billy Twinkle* are twenty-seven inches tall.[12] Mind-bogglingly, some
of the marionettes in *Billy Twinkle* also manipulate their own 3:8 scale
fictional counterparts, standing approximately nine or ten inches tall.
Thus, the spatial metaphor of relatively actual and fictional worlds as
a series of nested boxes is realized with each respectively smaller world
simultaneously visible, connected by control strings.

Second, the puppets' strings and controllers span the borders between
these nested worlds, making manifest the authorial control exercised by
each successive creator in the generation of a fictional world. A corollary
to the emphasis on the fictional nature of the puppet and its world is
that we are reminded that these inset scenes are not flashbacks, that is,
they are not direct views into an authentic past. Rather, they are shaped,
inevitably coloured by a present-tense perspective as the puppeteer-
author creates them anew. Thus, the use of puppets severely undermines
issues around the perception of authenticity that permeate human autobiographical solo performance. Concern with the bridge of authenticity between subject and protagonist leads to a third phenomenological
characteristic of puppets that colours the autobiographical process. Puppets do not experience change over time.[13] Thus, as an inanimate object,
the puppet cannot be a vessel of somatic experience as a living person is.
Lookalike puppets can on the surface duplicate their originators. And
the growth, alteration, and decay of humanity can be mimicked to some
extent but only in disjunctive steps. Burkett, for example, commonly
uses multiple puppets of the same character in different clothes or holding different props, but also significantly at different ages or in the case
of Tinka #6, 'she is in the early, but obvious, stages of pregnancy' (*Tinka*,
71). Eden #4, likewise, appears with a bandage on his neck; he has been
wounded by vampire bite (*Street of Blood*, 134). Similarly, the puppets cannot express the future-oriented potential latent in the autobiographical process for performative transformation. Puppets are gifted with an
almost infinite capacity to adopt any shape. They can be highly naturalistic manikins or they can eschew the humanoid altogether and depict

anything the imagination can conjure. But once the puppet is fixed in a particular form, it is obdurately resistant to change. So, the same limitation of expressing past experience also applies to the pursuit of future transformation. Puppets, unlike their human counterparts, are trapped bodily in time. This fixity works against human performative potential. The puppet is a singular act of creation and does not easily evolve.

Despite whatever surface similarity a puppet may share with its manipulator, the division of the autobiographical self into two parts disrupts the bodily connection, which allowed the audience to trace authenticity back to an actual-world self. The apparent result of this disconnect is that both axes of signification identified by Bennett are nullified. Yet, although it is true that the puppet performs only the present-tense aspect of the relived experience, the past-tense subject is still very much here in the now and accessible to audience perception in the person of the puppeteer. The technical aspects of puppetry tend to obscure this role of the puppeteer as the narrator/controller function becomes dominant, especially when the puppeteer is hidden from view; however, one must remember that the autobiographical puppeteer, in addition to being creator and manipulator of the physical puppet, is also the subject source of its narrative. This interrelation between puppet self and the actual self is further highlighted in the style of puppetry practised by Burkett where the puppeteer is fully visible to the audience. Thus, although the puppet resides in the present tense, it is the puppeteer who houses both the bodily archive of the puppet and the potential for future transformation. Separating the protagonist from the subject in autobiographical puppetry seems to thwart the potential for an 'apple fritter moment,' eliminating the potential for a real act by the protagonist to flow back into the subject. And yet, in terms of this physical bridge, puppeteer and puppet are not really severed at all, but rather this connection is of a different quality – attenuated but not severed.

First, the puppeteer and puppet share a voice. The voice is being projected a little distance into an alternate figure, but essentially this is no different from a single-body autobiographical performance where one voice speaks for each of the ontological selves. Next, the puppeteer and puppet share movement. Unlike the voice, movements across ontological levels are not identical. Movement is indirect but parallel, since in order to make a puppet raise its hand the puppeteer may instead lift his finger to move one of the strings. The puppet moves its legs, the puppeteer moves his hands and arms. The movements are not precisely the same, yet they are synchronous and causally related. Last and most importantly, the puppeteer and puppet share an animating attention, a kind of psychological or spiritual sharing that quickens the puppet. Semotician Petr Bogatyrev calls it an 'organic bond.'[14] American Golden Age puppeteer Bil Baird describes this donation of consciousness as 'coming down the strings.'[15] Arguably, this is the same transference work that an actor brings to the creation of a character, or perhaps it is more like animating a mask. I want to suggest that this intentional work of characterization lies on a continuum that connects the character born out of one's own body to the worn and inhabited mask to the held and manipulated puppet.

Due to the particularly intimate interaction between puppeteer and puppet, the object animated becomes an extension of the puppeteer's actual body and a vibrant part of his self-image. Dependent on the puppeteer for existence, '[the puppet's] life is nothing more than a projection of the human imagination.'[16] 'And so the object offers itself to the individual as an extension of his being in the surrounding universe, an augmented affirmation of his total existence. The "I" duplicates itself in order to confirm its being.'[17] The puppet is precisely the kind of object that Elizabeth Grosz describes that becomes an extension of body image: 'External objects, implements, and instruments with which the subject continually interacts become, while they are being used, intimate, vital, even libidinally cathected parts of the body image ... The body image unifies and coordinates postural, tactile, kinesthetic, and visual sensations so that these are experienced as the sensations of a subject coordinated into a single space; they are the experiences of a single identity.'[18] Grosz gives the examples of pen, car, and scalpel. While sharing the intimacy of technical mastery apparent with the objects on this list, the autobiographical puppet has the added psychical magnetism of physical (and gestural) likeness to its handler, as well as the abiding affection of a creator for his creation. Taken together, these shared aspects between human subject and puppet protagonist replicate the bridge between fictional and actual roles that permits a flow of performative affect between them. Authenticity, perceived through communion with the real, may be read across the spatial gap, translated from the puppet figure back 'up the strings' to its origin.

So although there is not a singular body shared by subject and protagonist, nevertheless the divided autobiographical self in *Billy Twinkle* can and does experience a parallel moment of radical intersubjectivity involving cross-world blending and utopian ambiguity between differently constituted ontological selves. For Dolan, utopia at the theatre is mostly about the audience. Knowles, too, focuses primarily on the audience effect vis-à-vis the actor, on the perceived fellowship with an authentic actual-world autobiographical subject, which results in a moment of shared intersubjectivity. But autobiographical performance is, at that key moment, also an internal-actor effect. The revelation of the seminal action repeated in fictional re-performance propels the autobiographical subject forward into the future. The particular act of excessive reality which blends fictional- and actual-world selves is not an arbitrary one; rather, it is always specifically associated with the personal crisis at the heart of the autobiographical project. Susanna Egan posits that, fundamentally, autobiography emerges out of crisis.[19] This position is supported by Jean Starobinski, who writes, 'one would hardly have sufficient motive to write an autobiography had not some radical change occurred in his life.'[20] 'Much of our own narrating can be usefully seen as driven by some ... conflict, tension, or crisis in our own lives.'[21] Crisis thus constitutes not only the impetus to autobiography, but also structures the principal plot of autobiographical narrative. The reiterative performative enactment of personal history brings that crucial problem into the present, inviting a reflection, but also significantly instigating an embodied second experience of crisis. Emerging out of the catalysing crisis, the 'apple fritter moment' represents the turning point of the autobiographical performative journey, melding past with present to open a window into the future. Phenomenological frisson in Emily Taylor's performance arises out of the conjunction of her past-tense narrative of bulimia, the present-tense presence of her bulimic (or formerly bulimic) body, and the act of such voracious eating. Replacing the trinity of food, eating, and purging, in *Billy Twinkle*, the trio of elements that leads to radical intersubjectivity is puppets, the manipulation of puppets, and a debate concerning *puppenhaft* – or the true nature of the puppet.[22]

Burkett's autobiographical solo show, like all the other plays discussed in this study, takes as its autobiographical subject not an actual-world subject like Burkett himself but a fictional character, Billy Twinkle.[23] At the beginning of the play, Billy is a puppeteer on a cruise ship, performing a variety act with marionettes. Wearing a white jacket and a toothy smile, Billy entertains the ship's guests with classic 'trick' marionettes, displaying his virtuoso technique. The first marionette, Rusty Knockers, is particularly impressive as she performs a burlesque striptease, removing four layers of clothing – a fur cape, dress, corset, and bra.[24] Next is Bumblebear, whom the stage directions describe as '*a tired-looking, snaggle-toothed old bear wearing a tutu and roller skates*' (10). As designed by Burkett, the bear marionette also wears a small pink party hat with a pom-pom on top. While Bumblebear is skating through his routine, Billy, in internal monologue, starts to complain about the obliviously rude audience members who are talking through his show. Ultimately, Billy's aggravation breaks through and he audibly and pointedly shushes a member of the audience. For this inexcusable slip of showmanship, Billy is fired. Alone at the prow of the ship, Billy contemplates committing suicide by drowning. Kneeling to pray before jumping, he addresses God: 'Oh God, thank you for this day and all the blessings I have received … It's not been a bad life, God. It's been okay. So, thank you, Father in Heaven, for the bounty of thine okay. This isn't the worst time I've ever known, God, no … The worst is not liking puppets anymore. That's the worst, by far' (12). Mild by the standard of most autobiographical shows, this is the crux of Billy's crisis; Billy is stuck in the middle of his life, in the middle of his profession, and he has lost his sense of the way forward. 'And yes, thank you for the blessing of being one of the top-rated cruise-ship puppeteers in the world, dear Father; which, while not exactly the asshole of show business, is at least sort of the belly button, but I'm tired of being a bear in a tutu who dances in a floating cage for stupid people to poke at' (12). Having defined himself by this vocation of being a puppeteer for so long, when Billy experiences a loss of vocation, he also suffers a loss of self.

Just as Billy is on the verge of jumping from the ship, he hears the voice of his deceased mentor Sid Diamond: 'To be, or not to be, that is the question' (13). Billy is panicked to hear this ghostly soliloquy in Sid's voice. Billy becomes more alarmed as he realizes that Sid's voice is coming from his own mouth. Then *with a short, menacing musical sting, [SID] appears suddenly at BILLY's side* (15). This 'Sid,' however, is a hand puppet of Sid as an old man, surreally manipulated and voiced by Billy, and even more surreally wearing a pair of pink fabric bunny ears. Like Billy, Sid has become stuck. After Sid's death, Billy built a marionette of Sid wearing bunny ears to use in his cabaret act. Somehow the marionette has captured part of Sid's soul or spirit and prevents him from 'crossing over into the light' (17).

SID: Do you have any idea what it's like being stuck in the middle?
BILLY: Yes, Sid, I do! That's why I'm going to die.
SID: Oh no you're not! If anyone's dying around here, it's me!
BILLY: You're already dead!
SID: Half-dead!
BILLY: Whatever. (17)

In this way, the crises of the two characters are intertwined. Sid wants Billy to retire the Bunny marionette so that Sid can become unstuck and die. To do this, Sid needs to encourage Billy to see his marionettes in a different light, to regain his love for them, so Billy can become unstuck and live.[25]

The subtitle of *Billy Twinkle* is *Requiem for a Golden Boy*. If the play, then, is an act of remembrance and lamentation for the life of Billy Twinkle, is he in fact dead? The answer, I think, is both yes and no. One might argue that in fact Billy does jump from the ship to his watery death by drowning and that the rest of the play offers redemption through autobiography in the afterlife. This interpretation, however, does not square with several later scenes which happen in the present and are not flashbacks. And more significantly, it does not accommodate his ultimate return to the cruise ship and the resolutely upbeat ending featuring Billy very much alive. Instead, I contend that Billy's 'death' hinges on a shift of his ontological status. When Sid the hand puppet jumps from the ship, pulling Billy after him (naturally), Billy reacts as if he is in the water, '*writhing and gasping as if drowning in a pool of water. But there is no water, only stage*' (19). Confused, Billy realizes that he is not in the ocean. It is in fact, as Sid expected, a theatre. The cruise ship dissolves to become only a set of a cruise ship. The house lights come up to reveal the audience. Sid calls for the start of a new production: 'Starring ... you! The Billy Twinkle Show. Your life, condensed and in miniature!' (20). Clambering back up onto the stage, Billy and Sid find a finely detailed marionette theatre, equipped with marionettes of Billy at different ages and of significant people in his life:

BILLY: I don't know what we're doing.
SID: But you've already done it, Billy. So, get a hold of yourself and remember.
BILLY: Remember what, Sid?
SID: A real live boy who dreamed of being a puppeteer. (21)

When Billy jumps from the ship and finds that it is only a stage, Billy has in effect jumped through the border surrounding the world of the cruise ship. Like the destruction of the world of the dinner party in *Shadows*, this breach works the same way, eliminating a lower-order fictional world and compelling us to reconfigure our world schema by inserting a new intermediary world. The play begins with Billy on the cruise ship as world^b – our primary fictional world; Billy's puppets Rusty and Bumblebear inhabit world^c. Although, in general, borders between fictional worlds are somewhat permeable, allowing for migration between worlds, the border moving upward between world^b and world^a comprises a significant exception and is impervious. The effect of a successful move from world^b to world^a is to erase the primary play world and leave us all, actors and audience both, high and dry in world^a, the whole theatrical event having evaporated. Since this is not what happens, when we find Billy and Sid still fictional characters in a theatre, we insert a new world and rename the worlds we already know. Thus, Ronnie Burkett and the audience remain above the fray in world^a, the world of the theatre containing the cruise ship as a theatrical set is now world^b, Billy on the cruise ship is relegated to world^c, and his inset cabaret characters live in world^d. In this new configuration, cruise ship Billy (Billy^c) has equivalent ontological status to the marionettes that he will use to enact his life. In the series of Billys that we encounter – Billy at age eleven, Billy at fifteen, Billy at twenty-five, Billy at forty-five, and Billy at forty-seven – the Billy on the cruise ship (although embodied by Burkett) is simply the most recent incarnation. Thus, this Billy is a puppet too. As he says of himself, associating himself with Bumblebear: 'I'm tired of being a bear in a tutu' (12). As a puppet, he expresses similar qualities to a puppet, notably the puppet's duality between being and non-being. Like all staged phenomena (people, objects, lights, sounds), puppets are endowed with an innate theatrical duality. Subject to theatricalizing perception, the world^a actor becomes a world^b character. The world^a set of wood and paint becomes a world^b cruise ship. Puppets, perhaps not unexpectedly, combine characteristics of both actors and props in their theatricality. Inside a fictional world, puppets are characters – they are alive and express the same qualities as human-based characters, possessing a provisionally actual existence; that is, within the confines of the fictionalizing frame, their world is a real world – real to them. In this regard, they behave as actors. However, upon their reversion to the actual world, puppets behave more like props.[26] When the scene is over, actors cease to be their fictional characters, yet they still continue to live. Puppets, critically, lack this prior and ongoing autonomous existence, and so world^a puppets lapse into non-being. The theatrical dichotomy for puppets, then, has two components: oscillating between non-being/object and being/character. Thus, if a puppet jumps up a level, leaving an inset fictional world for a higher-order world, it turns off, becomes non-being, and returns to its status as a prop. This is what happens to Billy. So, in this respect, yes, Billy's suicide is successful and he is 'dead' inside the frame of the play.[27]

Sid's choice of phrasing to call Billy 'a real live boy who dreamed of being a puppeteer' (21), a phrase which is echoed in the title of this scene in the published play text, 'A Real Live Boy,' invokes Billy as a Pinocchio figure. In the story of Pinocchio by Carlo Collodi (*The Adventures of Pinocchio*, 1883), popularized in our cultural imagination by the frequently reissued Disney film of 1940, Pinocchio is a wooden marionette who is magically able to move and speak independently but still remains a puppet. His desire throughout is to transcend his puppet status and become a 'real boy.' This is precisely the challenge set for Billy. To become properly alive, to be more than simply an animated puppet, Billy as the autobiographical protagonist of his inset life needs to make the upward move to become the autonomous subject. Unlike that of humans, the puppet dichotomy is bidirectional, not life/death, but being/non-being/being. This ontological oscillation of puppets is an omnipresent effect in *Billy Twinkle*. A number of puppets in the play get this treatment. In general, we see this basic process in action each time the puppets are brought out or are put away. In scenes with multiple characters, Billy/Ronnie will hang one character on a static hanger while introducing the others. Also, the offstage racks holding the puppets not in use are fully visible. A puppet that has been quickly struck and stored will swing lifelessly on its hook. More specifically, Billy's cabaret puppets reveal this property of oscillation in his handling of them, alive in one scene and dead again in the next. For example, Billy, aged fifteen, performs his nightclub act with a miniature marionette he calls Randi Rivers. After her song ends, Billy is approached by a man from the audience; the once alive Randi now hangs inert, her feet dangling above the floor. Similarly, when Sid halts Billy's inset performance of 'The Taming of the Moo,' the stage directions note that Petrooster and Cowtrina '*droop lifelessly*' (58). It is also interesting to note that the theme of the teasing courtship of Petruchio and Katrina in this scene, as performed by Billy, concerns an extended play on words relating to the objectival nature of the puppet ('let him that mov'd you hither / Remove you hence') and featuring banter about being a 'moveable,' that is, a portable object or piece of property, or 'a join'd stool,' also an object (58; *The Taming of the Shrew*, 2.1.182–200). In this context of puppets that turn on and off and on again, Sid mocks Billy's pretensions to a human unidirectional suicide, possessing Billy's voice with Hamlet's vacillating 'To be or not to be' speech.[28] Rather than jumping into death, Billy jumps into a liminal state of non-being. As a puppet, Billy makes the transition from world[c] to world[b] when he jumps into the 'water,' and arrives in a theatre to find his own miniature marionette memory theatre. Later, when the frame of the play closes, he is returned to the cruise ship. Becoming human again in world^c, he gets another chance. He needs to recross that border, regaining his actual-world self, but this time without switching off like a puppet. In his farewell address to God before jumping off the ship, Billy complains, 'I'm invisible. Middle-aged and not even at a crossroads' (13). In an interview, Burkett elaborates Billy's malaise: 'Self-absorbed … and invisible. Just when we want the attention or really need it, we can't get it: we're not young, we're not the idle chic, we're not even cute elderly people, women in red hats, Winnebago-driving seniors. I could walk into a bar naked, and there wouldn't be a blink.'[29] Paradoxically, in his marionette cabaret act, Billy is very visible performing beside his puppets. Yet, he is disconnected from them in an important way. The attention that the middle-aged, mid-career Billy lacks, the attentive gaze that would render him truly visible and fully alive, is also significantly what Billy denies to his puppets.

After sketching out Billy's youthful obsession and early professional development as a puppeteer, the inset autobiographical performance arrives at the pivotal moment of Billy and Sid's estrangement. At a puppet festival, Billy, now aged twenty-five, performs a parody of *The Taming of the Shrew* retitled *The Taming of the Moo*. Petruchio is transmogrified into Petrooster – a marionette with the head of a rooster on a human body. Katrina likewise becomes Cowtrina – '*a cow, anthropomorphized to the point of standing on two legs in cloven high-heel hooves. A pink udder juts out from her faux Elizabethan gown*' (57). Sid Diamond, who has made his career performing marionette Shakespeare, is at first delighted by his protégé's proposed Shakespeare performance: 'Billy, I have waited years to hear you say this. At times, I thought I never would. There were moments when I despaired over having wasted my time on you. What took you so long to submit to my influence, to hear the Bard's whispers, to see the light? But now, at last. (*He hugs BILLY enthusiastically*)' (56–7). When Sid actually sees the animal-human hybrid characters, he is horrified.[30] This incident illuminates the basic philosophical difference between these two characters and opens the debate regarding their competing theories of what a puppet is and what its proper relation to the puppeteer ought to be. Sid believes in a profound personal connection between puppet and puppeteer such that every puppet constitutes an autobiographical reflection: 'Your puppets are supposed to be reinventions of self. To edify, to exalt, and yes, to mock and even condemn our graceless state. But is this how you want to be seen? As livestock?' (59). Billy denies this personal association, dismissing the puppets as 'characters, that's all

... They're not alive, Sid. They're puppets' (59). This disregard for the puppets as potential beings is the focus of Sid's criticism of Billy's performance style. Sid accuses him of leaving his puppets empty of any real emotion or thought, investing them only with 'cleverness and parody ....

Unless of course the point is not the text or the characters at all, Billy ... You're visible simply for the sake of being seen, pretty boy![31] Your focus is nowhere near the puppets at all; standing above them, mugging and posturing like a powdered vaudevillian playing God. We don't need you to be God ... There's already a God on the stage, and it's not you. It's the goddamn puppet!' (59).[32]

This disagreement between Sid and Billy regarding the basic nature of the puppet is more fully articulated by puppet theorist and historian Henryk Jurkowski. Jurkowski identifies two competing attitudes towards puppets, two distinct understandings of what a puppet is and how it lives: 'The characteristics and qualities of different kinds of puppet provoke me to think we are not at present within one cycle of the puppet's history but in two. They touch and even penetrate each other. The first is the cycle which deals with magic, rites, religious and similar sorts of puppets, all based on animism and the supernatural ... The second cycle is the one which deals with profane and secular puppets, wherein all the interest lies in the process of creation. Of course it is the actor who appears onstage as the "creator." The puppet is at most a participant of the actor's work.'[33] The puppet proper, then, is a citizen of this first cycle where the puppet possesses, a priori, a character. 'Each puppet embodies a programme of its acting self. It is its plastic expression, its technique of animation and its tradition of movement that give the impulse to the puppetplayer. If the player wants to realize this programme he has to submit to the puppet. And this is the model of the relationship between the "magic" puppet and its puppeteer. The puppeteer serves the puppet – that is, he serves its magic.'[34] This is the philosophy of puppets to which Sid subscribes when he argues that there is a kind of divinity in the puppet. In contrast to the puppet, 'the object holds no programme of acting: the performer must invent one from his own imagination. So he does not serve the object; it is the object which serves the imagination of the performer. That is why some contemporary puppeteers want to change their puppets into objects, depriving them of the remains of their ancient magic power and submitting them to the actor so that he may be the sole creator on the puppet stage.'[35] Having identified these competing views, Jurkowski notes sadly the contemporary preference for objects: 'The reason for this is not hard to discover. We have laid aside magic.'[36]

Burkett himself understands well the life-giving magic of the puppeteer's conscious focus on the puppet. Typically, the visible puppeteer
will look at the puppet that is talking, cueing the audience with his eyes
to understand that his voice is coming out of this puppet. In a lecture
for the Puppet Centre (London, UK), Burkett relates the history of an
insight into an alternate technique for keeping the marionettes 'alive'
when there is more than one talking in a scene: 'If I'm looking only at
the puppet that's talking, this thing (*gestures to other imaginary puppet over
there*) is pretty dead. So we know this thing is talking, so why doesn't it and
the performer look at the static one and imbue it with a little more life.'[37]
Rehearsing a scene from *Tinka's New Dress*, Burkett took this insight a
step further and animated the marionettes solely through gaze. Meeting
at a soirée hosted by arts patron Astrid Van Craig, Carl's sister Tinka and
Fipsi, Carl's former colleague but now a state-sponsored artist, exchange
archly veiled barbs. Tinka accuses Fipsi of selling out and betraying her
mentor Stephan; Fipsi criticizes Carl's political choices, hinting that
they might be actually dangerous. She invites Tinka to reconsider her
allegiances (50–1). Burkett himself characterizes this conversation as a
'bitch fight.'[38] Instead of jiggling both puppets, he broke a cardinal rule
of puppetry and stepped away from them. Normally this lack of movement, being disconnected from the puppeteer, would render a puppet
lifeless. As Burkett recounts, 'I actually just hung them up and I knelt
down and I just threw my focus to each of them back and forth.'[39] The
simple act of directing attentive focus towards the puppet seems to be
sufficient to make it come alive. Jurkowski calls this technique 'the ritual
way of making a figure live, which can be referred to as the "animisation" of the figure.'[40] He gives the example of a puppet-character called
Nadezhda. In the performance she was inanimate. But, 'in spite of that
she was "alive" because all the other characters, played by live actors
treated her as a live person.'[41] Something ineffable is given to the puppet in the act of 'ensouling' inanimate matter. John Cohen describes the
process this way, 'the human simulacrum [is] a projected double or *ka*
"that comes into being by the fission of its creator's personality."'[42]

Objects of puppetry can in general be household, non-purpose built
objects, but a lack of human resemblance does not constitute the limit
of classification for objects. Without that essential animising attention,
'puppets' too can be reduced to objects. Arguably, this is what Billy does
with his puppets. He does not treat his puppets as if they are alive. He
treats his puppets as props. In his 'Stars in Miniature' cabaret act, the
focus throughout is on the material qualities of the puppets, finding

humour in those instances where the object is at odds with its ensouled subjectivity. Not only can puppets assume any form imaginable, another essential feature of puppets is that they can easily do things that humans can't do. Puppets can fly. Puppets can breathe underwater. A puppet can remove its own head. Puppets can be disassembled and reassembled. Conversely, it is very hard for puppets, marionettes in this case, to do simple human things like blink their eyes, move their mouths, walk, eat or drink, take their clothes off, or play the piano. Attempts to surmount these two disparate classes of actions – those that are easy for puppets but hard for humans and, conversely, those that are easy for humans but hard for puppets – provide the raw material for much popular puppetry, especially in the variety/cabaret genre. Each of Billy's four cabaret marionettes works precisely this way. As described earlier, Rusty Knockers performs what the stage directions call '*a classic marionette stripper routine*' (7). The effect of this marionette is premised on the virtuosic mechanical ability realized both in puppet design and in manipulation to enable her to take her clothes off. Conversely, another aspect of this marionette's appeal comes from the opposite class of characteristics where she exhibits an uncanny sexuality. Removing her bra, Rusty reveals not just her breasts but her essentially objectival nature. We see the marionette joints (normally hidden by the puppets' clothing) attaching her arms to her torso and her upper body to her abdomen. Her breasts, instead of being soft and fleshy, are disconcertingly hard and, oddly, cone-shaped. Bumblebear's performance of roller skating is also premised on this human-puppet opposition. Being controlled from above and thus immune to the gravity which shapes human locomotion, the inclination of a marionette is to float. Skating is, like walking, running, or dancing, a relatively complicated action for a marionette to master, and thus having a marionette skate convincingly is a virtuosic trick. Drawing attention to the human-puppet gap from the opposite direction, Bumblebear is an animal and expresses uncanny animal behaviour. The third cabaret marionette, Biddy Bantam Brewster, is a 'strongly caricatured society dame' presenting her own salon show, 'Wine, Woman and Song' (47, 48). The trick here is that as Biddy talks to the audience she also 'drinks' through a straw from a glass set on the table in front of her. As she drinks more and more, she becomes progressively quite intoxicated and the song degenerates into a drunken comedy number. Again, this puppet pits a mechanical trick that allows the puppet to behave in a more human manner, against its innate puppet limitations, and also by doing so stages its objectival nature, underscoring that same human-puppet gap.[43] Like the display of Rusty's naked body, the performance of Biddy's drunkenness highlights the artificiality of her act since drunkenness is a biological state which she can imitate but not actually embody. The last of Billy's cabaret puppets is the Sid lookalike with bunny ears. Bunny is a shuffling old man wearing a hospital gown and slippers. In this routine, Bunny speaks directly to the audience: 'I like balloons. Do you like balloons? Would you like to see my balloon? It's a nice pink one. See? *He lifts up his hospital gown and reveals a balloon jutting out from his droopy underwear.* Would you like to blow it ... up?' (78). Plastic tubing runs from the balloon, up Bunny's back, and up to the marionette controller. Although Billy offers the tubing to an audience member to blow into, it seems that Billy will blow up the balloon himself. As he blows, the balloon-penis inflates. In production, the balloon is curiously spherical rather than sausage-shaped as one might expect from the phallic innuendo. As the balloon grows, Bunny begins to float off the ground as if he is being lifted by the balloon. '*Billy spins him round and round as the balloon slowly deflates and Bunny lands on the ground with a gentle thud*' (80). Again, the crux of this routine is the uncanny physicality of the puppet. Having a marionette float on a balloon and spin in the air is, like the stripper marionette, a decades-old classic cabaret trick, emphasizing the puppet's different relation to gravity from that of a person. Beyond this, the balloon-in-the-pants joke where the mechanism for inflating the balloon is entirely visible plays on the artificiality of the puppet body, and the sexual incongruity of a puppet with an erection. In every case, the charm of Billy's cabaret marionettes depends on an emphasis on their inert materiality at the expense of their incipient humanity.

This is the heart of the autobiographical crisis. The puppets don't live. Billy, having become a puppet-object, also does not live. Picking up the pervasive Pinocchio references in the play, Billy is cast as Pinocchio and the trajectory of Billy's journey takes its shape from that of Pinocchio.[44] Being initially stuck – a hollow puppet – Billy needs to see himself and his work in a new light. Like Pinocchio who is rewarded by the Fairy with the Turquoise Hair for his acts of goodness (specifically, taking care of his ailing father), Billy's ultimate redemption revolves around learning respect and love for those around him.

BILLY: So why are you here now? Oh yes, I remember. To fix your sad, dead, broken heart!
SID: No, to help you break yours.

BILLY: What kind of bullshit is that, Sid? Why would I want to break my own
   heart?
SID: So you can feel something again. (62)

Billy needs to relearn the innate magic of puppets, to be able to see
them as living beings, so that he too can be seen and live. There is a
congruence of inner and outer life in the puppeteer's relation to his
puppets; Billy's animisation is dependent on that of the puppets. As Kenneth Gross writes in *Love among the Puppets*, this intersubjective flow gives
rise to 'the paradox whereby manipulators, defrauding objects of their
right not to be alive, are themselves transformed by the life they invent'
(71). The puppets not only take the conscious spirit from the puppeteer
but they also give life in return: 'These small things measured the size of
souls. The life they offered was a peculiar gift, something wrought out of
the ambiguous exchange of the puppet and puppeteer.'[45]

As a work of autobiography-within, *Billy Twinkle* does not have a single
coup-de-théâtre moment, like the eating of an apple fritter or the display
of scars; instead, the radical intersubjectivity which moves the autobiographical performer into the realm of the real happens over a series of
cross-world interactions that gradually render Billy visible. Billy has three
encounters with puppets that express a split ontology. These are puppets that simultaneously present both actual and fictional selves; they
are puppets but they also live – really live. Breaking out of the autobiographical frame established by the memory theatre, the actions of Juliet,
Doreen, and Rocket are not scenes from the past. These three puppets
transcend their fictional status and actively enter into superior worlds.
But perhaps more importantly, Billy is able to move downward into their
worlds. By the time he meets Rocket, Billy no longer sees the puppets as
mere props. Parallel to the moments described by Knowles, the subject-
self and the protagonist-self merge to share an ambiguous ontology. The
shared experience precipitated by these dual ontological puppet-selves
is not quite the same as a 'body event' like the apple fritter, the scars, or
Djanet dressing, which are inscribed on a single body. Nevertheless, the
key feature of this radical subjectivity is an ontological blending, creating
an ambiguity of chronology such that the past event comes alive again in
the present. The opening sections of Billy's inset autobiographical puppet play show us his origins as a puppeteer between ages twelve and fifteen up until the central philosophical debate which marks Billy's break
with Sid at age twenty-five. Until this point, the marionettes of the supernatural puppet theatre have remained neatly and meekly inside their fic-

tional frame. But as Billy and Sid's reflections move closer to the present day, this safe border breaks down. Juliet of *Romeo and Juliet* participates in an alternate past, enacting her romantic suicide in a scene that never happened; Doreen collars Billy in the present tense; and a beautiful and audacious boy named Rocket prefigures Billy's future.[46] In each case, .these puppets escape from the memory confines of the marionette stage. The first of this trio of autonomous upward-looking puppets is Juliet.

After a twenty-year estrangement, Billy meets Sid again backstage at a puppetry festival gala event celebrating a 'Century of American Puppetry.' Billy with Biddy Bantam Brewster is slated as the opening act. Sid, now aged eighty-three, is prepared to do a scene from Shakespeare. When Billy identifies Sid's marionette as Juliet, he questions the appropriateness of Sid's choice:

BILLY: Sid, no. Why not Shylock? Or Prospero? Even Lear. Yes, Lear is perfect for your age.
SID: My age is irrelevant to my interpretation. Art is ageless.
BILLY: But you're not, Sid. Look at you. You're old. You're a little old man and you're going to go on stage and do Juliet. Sid, Juliet is a fourteen-year-old girl. You'll make a fool of yourself. Please, don't embarrass us this way. (66)

Billy's objections to Sid as Juliet emerge from his object-oriented theory of the puppet-performer relation. As a performer who places a premium on pure technical ability, Billy argues that Sid is too old to perform at all. 'Sid, please. You're great. You always were. They know. I know. But let it go ... You'll die out there' (66–7). Secondly, Billy objects to the connection of old Sid to young Juliet. He thinks it is unseemly. There is no fit between puppet and puppeteer. And yet, Billy's marionettes are women, an old man with bunny ears, and various animals. So this is not really the problem. Billy projects his own values onto Sid. Consistent with a performance style which puts him at the centre, Billy is concerned with his appearance, specifically with staying young. In his suicide tirade listing all the things that are 'the worst,' Billy complains that he is still using 'a headshot from nine years ago because [he hasn't] saved enough money for the facelift' (12). In the scene immediately following the one with Juliet, Billy discovers that his boyfriend Brian has spent his 'face money' on renovating the kitchen. For Billy, there is no need for the puppets to be self-reflections, to perform in his stead. This kind of connection is irrelevant because the puppets are merely props and he is the central performer. If the audience is watching him, then looking young is important. The emphasis is on him in the actual world and not at all on entering into the lower-order fictional worlds inhabited by the puppets. But as Sid (and Juliet) demonstrates here, the first step in bringing the puppets into visibility and life is for the puppeteer to become voluntarily self-effacing, redirecting his life force into the puppet.

In the end, so many years before, Sid never performed Juliet that night of the gala. While Billy was performing his act, Sid suffered a heart attack backstage. It is at this point that the inset marionette scenes first diverge from history and begin to embroider alternate stories in the present tense. To make up the gap, Billy suggests that Sid perform the scene now. '*BILLY reaches to the hanging puppets behind him and brings one out into the playing area below. It is a marionette of Juliet. She is identical to the one in the seated SID's hand on stage, although this Juliet is larger and in the same scale as the SID marionette*' (69). Enacting her death scene, the character of Juliet epitomizes the ability of puppets to oscillate between being and non-being. Waking from the feigned death of the sleeping potion, Juliet finds Romeo dead of poison. Desolate, she takes his dagger and kills herself. In Billy's marionette theatre, Juliet first appears as a prop marionette (world^d) held by the inset marionette Sid (world^c). She then becomes double, appearing as a larger version, now manipulated jointly by Sid and Billy from the bridge above. The larger Juliet is equivalent in size to all the other 'real' people in the inset scenes. This change of scale also constitutes an ontological split, with one Juliet in world^d (small Juliet) and one in world^c (large Juliet). As is the nature of puppets, there is no actor self behind the character, and so she *is* Juliet. Still holding the miniature prop Juliet, Sid assumes the role of Romeo. Doing so, he also experiences an ontological split. Juliet then plays this scene to the corpse of Romeo (world^d) and 'to the lifeless, seated SID marionette' (world^c) (69). For Sid, the change of scale allows him to become properly invisible and so enter into the lower-order fictional world. He participates in the scene with his own puppet as an ontological equal. Facilitated by this cross-world submersion, Sid treats Juliet as alive, and through his animating belief, she actually does become a real person.

After Juliet collapses dead on Romeo/Sid's lap, Sid says, 'See, Billy? That's the way to do it' (70). This conclusion reads ambiguously, depending on whose action Sid refers to. In reference to himself, 'That's the way to do it' is instructive to Billy, saying essentially, 'That's the way to do a proper scene,' this is the way to 'create something that breathes, that truly lives inside your audience long after the puppet stops twitching' (59). If Sid refers to Juliet, the message behind 'That's the way to do it' is 'That's the way to kill yourself,' commenting on Billy's earlier (failed?) attempt to commit suicide by jumping from the ship. Conversely, Sid's implied comment regarding killing oneself could also easily apply to Sid himself. Not only does Sid enter into the scene with Juliet to play the role of Romeo, thus assimilating himself into her fictional world, but Romeo is dead and Sid plays his corpse. As I've argued elsewhere, when a live human actor portrays a corpse on the stage, the distinction between the actual-world indisputably breathing body and the fictional corpse opens up a peculiar metatheatrical gap, underscoring the perceptual difficulty of effacing the actual and giving perceptual priority to the fictional.[47] When a puppet portrays a corpse, the phenomenological situation is just the opposite. Rather than facing a niggling irreconcilable gap, the audience perceives the actual and the fictional as identical. Unlike a living human actor, the puppet actor does switch off into non-being when the actual-world aspect comes to the foreground of perception. So on the one hand, we might read Sid's performance as similar to that of a human actor, that is, the puppet is still 'alive' but pretending to be 'dead' (and doing quite a good job). Or, the more likely reading, since the puppet does not show any traitorous outward signs of life, is that Sid as Romeo is indeed 'dead.' He is dead twice; once in the relatively actual world as an inert puppet and again in the fictional world as the poisoned Romeo. The language puppeteers use to describe the process of making a puppet live circles around an elusive, almost spiritual act. They talk about the gaze or giving attention to the puppet, directing one's focus towards the puppet, believing that the puppet is alive. In each of these acts, something flows from the puppeteer to the puppet. The puppet becomes not only a reflection of self or as Sid says 'reinventions of self' (59) but an extension of self as the puppeteer projects part of his or her consciousness, self, or soul into the puppet. Thus, in an extreme demonstration of the puppeteer's gift of self, the marionette version of Sid gives his life so that Juliet can live. So, when Sid says, 'That's the way to do it' he refers both to how to die and how to make the puppets live. Reflecting on our persistent fascination with 'the demiurgic infusion of soul into human simulacra,'[48] Victoria Nelson writes about the spiritual journey into the grotto: 'And for centuries it has been a secular society's only path back to the transcendent. We crawl into the hole – the grotto, ... the black hole of the cosmos, the hole in our own heads – in the unspoken and often unconscious hope of undergoing deep change ... We must instead try on the surprising premise that such a transformation is not metaphorical but real, a doorway not to the "primitive" but to a higher and more integrated mode of being ... To go higher, you must first go lower.'[49] This is precisely the trick of autobiographical performance. Temporarily submerging the higher-order actual self into a lower-order fictional self and then having travelled piggyback on the re-performance of crisis and its effects by that fictional self, the actual self re-emerges transformed and transcendent. Sid's literally self-effacing performance is a demonstration for Billy, showing him the path back to his life.

The second in the trio of autonomous puppets is Doreen Gray.[50] Doreen is an amateur puppet enthusiast, much derided and despised by both Sid and Billy. Sid colourfully calls her an 'obsequious hobbyist' (55) and an 'insufferable mitten-wiggling charlatan' (82). Doreen, with her green Muppet-like hand puppet of crucified Jesus and 'I ♥ Puppets' T-shirt, stands in opposition to Billy. Where Billy has lost his love for puppets, Doreen wears hers on her shirt. He has talent but no love. Doreen has no talent but lots of love. And despite her terrible technique, Doreen's puppet lives. She gives it her attention and treats it as if it is truly alive. Although Doreen is herself a puppet in the same scale as the inset autobiographical puppets, Billy's meeting with Doreen is not inspired by a memory. She exists very much in the immediate present, meeting Billy at a puppet festival. Also, despite her seeming status as a world[c] puppet, she behaves as an autonomous 'real' person and treats Billy as her ontological equal. She looks up, and looking through the fictional frame, she can see Billy standing on the control bridge above the miniature theatre:

BILLY: Doreen, how can you see me? I'm not a puppet.
DOREEN: Well of course you're not. You're a person. And you know why, Billy?
BILLY: Uh ... I don't know.
DOREEN: Oh you do too! Come on, Billy, it's inside your heart.
BILLY: Uh, because the Blue Fairy brought me back to Geppetto and turned me into a real live boy?
DOREEN: Oh silly Billy! No. It's because Jesus gave his life so you could have yours. Isn't that right, Jesus? *DOREEN lifts the puppet of JESUS up and converses with it. The mouth of the puppet moves when it speaks, although the lip-synch is dreadful.* (80–1)

Here Doreen folds Christian theology into puppet theory. Just as the ontologically doubled marionette/puppeteer Sid gave his life, submerging himself in a lower-order world so that his puppet Juliet can live, Jesus, shifting from supernatural to human form and back again, gives his life for Billy. Like the love of the Turquoise Fairy for Pinocchio, Jesus's love (Doreen's love) transforms Billy into a 'real boy.'

Despite their difference in size and ontology, it is paradoxically Doreen who is the puppeteer who animates the puppet Billy with her focus and her affectionate attention. From her Christian beliefs, Doreen already instinctively understands the process of imbuing the puppets with life. She is open to the flow of anima from fictional to actual worlds. Billy complains to God that he is invisible. Doreen renders him visible. She assumes that he is a person and that makes him a person. Rather than promoting Doreen up to world^b (where she would presumably switch off into non-being), she remains a puppet, and Billy's ontology splits. He straddles world^b and world^c, and like Sid with Juliet, Billy participates as an ontological equal with his own puppet. Billy, still, is not ready to shed his superior status and reach down into his own fictional world, so Doreen reaches up to him and pulls him in. Unexpectedly, it is Doreen who provides the model for Billy's rebirth into his love of puppets. With his undeniable talent, Billy thought that he had 'arrived' but instead he is stalled. Doreen, by contrast, knows that she is a terrible puppeteer, but is constantly seeking self-improvement:

DOREEN: I know. I suck! But even so, it makes me feel better. People laugh at
   me, Billy. I know that. But no one can doubt that I believe.
BILLY: In what, Doreen?
DOREEN: Tomorrow, and tomorrow, and tomorrow.
BILLY: You're a piece of work, Doreen Gray.
DOREEN: I'm a piece of work in progress, Billy. So I have to keep on moving,
   because in ten minutes there's a workshop on flocking foam-rubber puppet
   heads with dryer lint and I can't miss it, even though I'll probably suck at
   that too.
BILLY: Flock on, Doreen. (84–5)

In support of the interpretation that Billy is dead/a puppet, Doreen associates Billy with the biblical prodigal son (81). In this parable, the younger son of a loving father leaves home and 'wastes his substance with riotous living' (Luke 15:12–13). Reaching low ebb, working as a swine-herd and eating the same husks that the pigs eat, the son thinks it would be better to be a servant in his father's house than to live as a swineherd. Billy too is a kind of swineherd, often characterizing the patrons of his cruise ship puppet show as pigs. Upon his return, the prodigal son is embraced by his father. When the older son complains that the younger has been welcomed back so easily, the father says, 'My son, … you are always with me, and everything I have is yours. But we had to celebrate and be glad, because this brother of yours was dead and is alive again; he was lost and is found' (Luke 15:31–2). This oscillation between lost and found, between dead and reborn, precisely describes Billy's journey. Of course, *Pinocchio* too is a prodigal-son story.

The third and final autonomous puppet is Rocket. After Doreen exits, Billy looks for Sid, who has disappeared. '*BILLY looks under the stairs where he had last hung the SID handpuppet, but instead takes another marionette in his hand there.*' (85) This short-strung cabaret-style puppet is Rocket. In the transition, the lighting has shifted back to nighttime on the cruise ship, indicating that the world[b] frame of the memory theatre has dissolved and Billy has been restored to his world[c] status. Rocket is, according to Burkett's description, '*a slight teenage boy of fifteen, otherworldly in his beauty, and very androgynous*' (85–6). Dressed all in black, with longish black hair and long eyelashes, Rocket also wears a large set of blue-black sequined angel wings. In his hand, he holds 'a smaller marionette of a muscular man, naked save for a G-string and red stilettos' – a transvestite stripper puppet (86). Like that of the hand puppet Sid, the appearance and manipulation of this puppet seem entirely unintentional on Billy's part. Billy does not show any awareness that Rocket's movement is controlled by him or, in a significant departure from the Sid puppet, any awareness that Rocket's voice comes from his mouth. An aspiring young puppeteer, Rocket has persuaded his parents to take him on this cruise so that he can meet Billy. He has seen and heard Billy preparing to jump from the ship. Now, he wants to show Billy his puppet before Billy kills himself. As with the other cross-world pairs of Sid and Juliet and Doreen/Jesus and Billy, the relationship of Rocket and Billy is rendered ambivalent by the characters' fluid ontology. Rocket and Billy are dramaturgically of equivalent status, both being real people in world[c]. Apart from Billy, Rocket is the only other person we have met in this world of the cruise ship. The character of Rocket could well be played by a human actor and the scene would not require any adaptation. He is the only puppet in *Billy Twinkle* to be fully independent, not to be confined by any fictionalizing frame (apart from his own materiality). Rocket's materiality as a short-strung cabaret puppet, as one of Billy's fictional creations, is visually present since we can see that he is a puppet with strings but it is not acknowledged, and Billy treats him as a fully alive, wholly autonomous real person.

Dialogue between Billy and Rocket is lifted with only minor variations from an earlier scene where Billy, aged twelve, first meets Sid. In response to the defensive question asking why Sid/Billy should help the youngster, Billy/Rocket responds, 'Because I'm the next one. I'm gonna do it anyway ... And you could save me a lot of time if you just showed me how [...] if you just helped me' (33, 88). Both boys finagle invitations to visit their chosen mentors. Both are determined to come for an extended visit of several weeks at Easter break.[51] Both boys change their mundane names for showbiz names: Billy Ruggles casts himself into the future as Billy Twinkle; Rocket's real name is actually Kevin. (Rocket surpasses Billy here in his love of things sparkly with his blue-black sequined wings.) Whereas the first scene was framed by the marionette memory theatre, this second scene seems to be part of Billy's life. Yet the perfect iteration of the scene with Rocket as the young puppeteer and Billy in the role of senior mentor suggests that it too is a constructed narrative. Rocket is, finally, a puppet in adherence to Sid's autobiographical theory of puppets, a puppet that is a reinvention of Billy. He is himself but he is also Billy redux. In this moment of radical intersubjectivity, time folds over and this fictional performance of Rocket allows Billy to accept Sid's mentorship again in the present tense. Brought into visibility by Doreen, Billy now brings Rocket to life and so he himself also becomes properly real and alive. Only one more step remains as Billy moves to shed his world^c persona and return to the higher-order world of world^b.

As a eulogy for Sid, Billy declaims Prospero's epilogue from *The Tempest.*

BILLY: ... now, 'tis true,
I must be here confined by you,
Or sent to Naples: Let me not,
Since I have my dukedom got,
And pardoned the deceiver, dwell
In this bare island by your spell; But release me from my bands
With the help of your good hands (90; *Tempest*, Epilogue 3–10)

Like Sid and Billy, Prospero is also a character that is stuck. This speech is a plea to the audience to release Prospero from the island of his banishment. But on another level, the island also serves as a synecdoche for the entire fictional project of the play; and so, Prospero concurrently seeks freedom from the fictional world of the play and release back into the actual world as an actor. Dedicated to Sid, this speech recognizes Sid's release from ghostly puppet limbo, where he was trapped by the dual simulacra of the Sid hand puppet and the Bunny marionette. With the renunciation of Bunny and the disappearance of Sid the hand puppet, Sid supersedes these two ontologically divided doubles, and Sid is freed into the singularity of death. Reciting this speech for himself, Billy links Prospero's fortunes to his own. Not only has Prospero been stranded on this island, but like Pinocchio in the whale, the prodigal son, and Billy as puppet, he has been given up for dead; his release therefore – like that of these others – is figured as a rebirth. Prospero, in this speech, straddles two worlds, speaking both as a character aware of his situation as the restored Duke of Naples but also as an actor whose 'project ... was to please,' acknowledging the audience and their power to end the play. Taking on this role, Billy is also permitted to be both character and actor at the same time. Prospero is on the cusp of a geographical move from isolation on the island back to society in Naples, but he is also on the cusp of ontological change, ready to shed his character and return to the actual world. Prospero's island stands in for Billy's cruise ship; freedom lies on the land. Billy is also poised to make this journey, shifting into a superior ontological world. Billy ends his autobiographical project, and by shedding the split autobiographical roles of author-subject, narrator, and protagonist, he reverts to the singularity of the ongoing present-tense subject. Jumping again from the ship, Billy escapes upward from world[c] into his own relatively actual world – world[b], this time making a successful transition into his post-autobiographical life. With our applause, this Pinocchio's strings are cut and he becomes a 'real live boy.'

Chapter Five

Self-Authoring Characters in Recursive Autothanatography: *In On It*

Death is both promised by autobiography and explicitly excluded from it. As the writing (*graphy*) of life (*bios*), autobiography can never be fully synchronous with life itself, being necessarily limited in its scope of apprehension at the beginning of life and at the end. At both these extremes of the thread of life, there arises an inassimilable gap between the temporal position of the autobiographical author and that of herself as autobiographical subject. It is at these terminal points that the primary experience of life slips the grasp of the secondary recording of that experience. In the beginning, the earliest years of life are clouded by infantile amnesia, with reliable long-term memories only emerging between the ages of three and six.[1] Sifting the foggy landscape to identify and describe one's first memory is a potent cliché of the genre.[2] Likewise, the documentation of one's last moment is also elusive. Philippe Lejeune wonders about the last page of the thirty-five-year diary of French poet Jehan Rictus marked by 'black ink congealed at the bottom of the last page of [his] last notebook. Did he knock over his inkwell as he died? We will never know – the answer is drowned in the shadow of death.'[3] This is the problem of death and autobiography. Although one might continue to document one's life right until the very end, creative synthesis of that end into summary is impossible. One cannot encompass the experience of one's own death. 'There can be no phenomenology of death ... Death is radically resistant to the order of representation.'[4] And yet, in the face of this impossibility, autobiographers persist in attempting to write about death. For the autobiographer engaged in the work of sorting out a life, it is almost impossible to avoid consideration of death as the inevitable end of that life and of that work. Jeremy Tambling suggests that indeed death, rather than life, colours our understanding of selfhood and 'it might be better if we started with the assumption of death working through the living, and not dissociated, therefore, from our sense of the present.'[5] Nancy K. Miller sums up this perspective, asserting that 'every autobiography … is also an autothanatography.'[6]

Autothanatography, which replaces '*bios*' (life) with '*thanatos*' (death), manifests in two distinct modes, depending on how the topic of death is construed. In one mode, autothanatography traces the time up until death, engaging the subject in the process of dying. As Susanna Egan notes, quoting anthropologist Robert Murphy, 'the apprehension of mortality is a condition of our consciousness, a first premise of our sense of time, an axiom in our grasp of selfhood, a constant factor in all our plans, and a thread that is woven through the very fabric of our being.'[7] Apprehension of mortality, however, becomes acute when the autobiographical subject is terminally ill. Egan's examples of process-based autothanatography include Christina Middlebrook's *Seeing The Crab: A Memoir of Dying* (1996), Eric Michael's *Unbecoming* (1997), and Barbara Rosenblum and Sandra Butler's *Cancer in Two Voices* (1996). Switching from writing about death in the future tense to writing about it in the present or even past tense, that is, switching to writing which passes beyond the terminus of one's death, depends 'on the continued conceivability, to itself and to others *and after death*, of an authoring consciousness.'[8] Thus, true autothanatography, writing about the actual event of one's own death, is the sole realm of fictional characters. *The Lovely Bones* (2002) by Alice Sebold is a popular example of the genre. In the novel, the protagonist – fourteen-year-old Susie Salmon – posthumously narrates her own rape and murder, observing the effects of her death on her family, her friends, and her murderer. Able to transcend the absolute boundary between life and death, these ghostly autothanatographers take stock from beyond the terminus, fulfilling the projected trajectory of autobiography to encompass the whole of life to its very last moment and even to consider the continuing ripples of that life and death.

The autobiographical dramas discussed so far are rife with ghosts returned from the dead to participate in the crafting of their life stories. In *Perfect Pie*, Francesca appears in Patsy's kitchen one day. If, accepting the argument proffered in chapter 1, Marie is in fact dead, then the adult incarnation of Marie, now named Francesca, is a kind of a ghost. Although she is ostensibly a purely fictional character created by Patsy, Francesca's ghostliness comes from the taint of her imagined extrapolation from the dead girl. This sense of being both dead and alive renders her presence uncanny. Gordias Carbuncle (*Eternal Hydra*) is another ghostly character-within. Brought back from the dead and conjured out of his diary by Vivian Ezra, he is, like Francesca, a dependent fictional creation. Rather than acting as autonomous autothanatographers, both Francesca and Carbuncle are fictive participants cast in secondary roles in the autobiographical work of others. In *Goodness*, Althea's autobiographical history is populated by autothanatographical ghosts. Young Althea and Young Stephen are alternate versions of their older selves, selves who are still alive in the play's present-tense frame. But, Julia is dead, having been shot by Stephen, and given the decades that pass from then until the time of Michael's meeting with Althea, Todd is also likely to have died. These characters exist under Althea's authorial purview, but they are somewhat independent, expressing knowledge of their futures and taking the reins of authorship not only to contribute to their collective autobiography/autothanatography but also to embroider alternate storylines for themselves. Of all these, Sid (*Billy Twinkle*) comes the closest to being an autonomous autothanatographer. He has returned from the dead – a ghostly hand puppet – to oversee the performance of Billy's life 'in miniature.' He instigates the performance of autobiography to resolve, according to the cliché, some 'unfinished business': he wants Billy to recant his Sid-lookalike Bunny marionette so Sid does not have to spend the afterlife with pink fuzzy rabbit ears affixed to his head. His autobiography is linked to Billy's. As Billy's life story unfolds, we meet Sid at various points, tracing Sid's aging and his passage through life's landmarks. But even so, his life story is a sidebar to that of Billy as the main autobiographical subject.

Why is autobiographical performance haunted by ghosts? Why do ghosts tell stories? What do these dead characters want? As discussed previously, the usual trajectory of autobiography concerns identity construction and personal transformation arising out of crisis. For an already dead subject, presumably this avenue of development is closed. So what remains? These supernatural autobiographers are seeking what all autobiographers desire as writers; they want to resolve the shape of their lives, to see that the narrative of their lives has been given a proper ending. Autobiography, in general, has an underlying sense of quest as autobiographical author-subjects seek order and pattern in their lives. The work of autobiography is to organize the randomness of life and give it meaning through literary structure. This sense of life as a puzzle to be resolved or a mystery to be solved is heightened in fictional autothanatography. 'Stories told from the afterlife have the potential to reinforce this idea of meaning lying at the end by establishing themselves as the ideal form of narrating a life, of which all biography is an imitation.'[9] Someone has died. How did they die? In autothanatography, the murder mystery genre is overlaid on the usual autobiographical task of solving the mystery of my life. Now, I have the additional aim of explaining my death too.

The outermost frame of *In On It*[10] by Daniel MacIvor presents the story of This One and That One[11] who have rented a theatre and set out to stage a play about a terminally ill man named Ray. This play-within, designated by MacIvor as 'The PLAY,' is framed by 'The SHOW' where This One and That One speak directly to the audience and comment on the appropriateness of various dramaturgical and performance choices in their production of Ray's drama. In addition to these two worlds, there are also scenes, tagged as 'The PAST,' in which we witness episodes from the personal history of This One and That One – also known as Brad and Brian – tracing their first meeting, romantic partnership, and subsequent drift towards separation.[12] Linking these various worlds is a metatheatrically migratory car crash and a blue Mercedes. In his opening monologue, Brian envisions the scenario:

> The blue Mercedes. I can only imagine it but when I do, it's like this: You're on the road doing some errands; you've got to exchange some tickets, pick up a prescription for somebody's migraine, the usual. You pull out onto the highway to save some time, in your big powerful machine, being come at by a lot of other big powerful fast machines, driven by people about whose level of mental health or blood alcohol you know nothing. That's a sobering thought, you go for the radio … And in that tiny moment of taking your attention ever so briefly away from the big machine in your hands, the other guy veers into your lane and you look up just in time to see the headlights of the blue Mercedes. (155)[13]

Eventually, we come to understand that Brad has been killed in just such a car accident. In the theatre, Brian and Brad invent Ray as the fictional driver of the actual Mercedes. Through their play-within, they performatively imagine the circumstances that led him to steer the blue Mercedes across the median and into oncoming traffic. Two people die in the play: Ray and Brad. Brian's (and Brad's) ostensible motive, then, in presenting this play is to give meaning to Brad's sudden and random death. The inset play of Ray's fictive biography tries to do this by outlining the circumstances of Ray's situation that might bring him to crash the car in what is essentially a suicide. In the first scene featuring Ray and his doctor, Ray learns that 'it's not good news' (177). The rest of the play-within traces Ray's dissolving personal attachments to his wife, son, and father and his failure to make meaningful connections to two other characters – Pam and her son, Lloyd. Before Ray can tell his wife, Brenda, of his diagnosis, she declares that she has been having an affair and is leaving him. Ray's son, Miles, is entirely absorbed in the mundane trials of his own life. Suffering from senile dementia, Ray's father, Irving, doesn't recognize him. Isolated and set adrift, Ray opts to act:

RAY: And just a quick jerk of the wheel.
BRAD: And in that moment ...
RAY: Just like everything else.
BRAD: It's the headlights of the blue Mercedes.
RAY: Just another accident. (193)

Rather than wait for something to happen, for his life to stop, Ray takes a kind of authorial control and writes himself an ending. This distinction between things that stop and things that end is central to *In On It*.

In a pattern reminiscent of *Perfect Pie*, *In On It* is framed by a pair of monologues delivered by Brian. In the opening monologue, Brian considers the distinction between things that happen out of careful planning ('a wedding, someone builds a boat, a person writes a play. The things that happen around guest lists and blueprints and re-writes' [155]) and things that just happen ('The arbitrary optional life-changing things that seem to make no sense the things we have to invent sense for. Lots of things. Little things: the music our lover listens to; bigger things: the way our health can come out from under us like a carpet on a hardwood floor; huge things: the blue Mercedes' [155]). It is after this that Brad materializes out of the shadows to question the suitability of Brian's beginning. Then, later, after Brad has exited the theatre, Brian, alone again, closes the frame of the play, saying briefly, 'But why are we talking about endings anyway. Some things end. But some things just stop' (199). It is this 'some things' and the contrast of certain kinds of 'things' with other kinds of 'things' that suggest two correlated pairs, aligning things that require careful planning with things that end, and things that just happen with things that stop. Having classified both the loss of one's health and the blue Mercedes as things that just happen, Brian connects these events with things that stop. That is, the thing that stops as a result of these two arbitrary circumstances is life – a life cut short; two lives are cut short in the intersection of Ray's terminal illness and the fateful blue Mercedes. A play, however, by contrast, is a thing that is planned, controlled. It is a thing that ends. The ultimate goal then of Brian and the ghostly Brad in performing this autothanatography is not simply to understand Ray's motivations but instead to become authors too, as Ray does, and rewrite the story. Their goal is to transmute something that stopped into something that ends. The play is something that Brian can control, the blue Mercedes is not. So, by fictionalizing the blue Mercedes and shifting its ontological status so that it resides within the play on a subordinate fictional plane, Brian seeks to exert performative power over it.

As the creator of a world, the author wields total power over that world. As seen in chapter 3 with regard to Timothy Findley's play *Shadows*, this divine power extends even to the destruction of that world if desired. Such total control over fictional worlds is specifically called by Brian into contrast with life, where words do not have the same comprehensive performative sway. This, of course, is one of the key differences between life and art. Life is spontaneous, arbitrary, and chaotic. Art is not spontaneous. It is planned; it has a formal structure. And though it may work hard at presenting the illusion of lifelike spontaneity, especially in the theatre, even its improvisations are carefully planned. This innate opposition between life as lived and life as a performative creation influenced by the limits of performative power has been central to the discussion of performed autobiography so far. We use autobiography to shape our lives, to impose a pattern, to gain control. Autobiography, in other terms, assumes as its basic raison d'être the changing of life from a thing that stops to a thing that ends. Beyond this reshaping of experience, autobiography can also yield a second existence. In the second edition of a work, authors have the opportunity to review and correct the faults of the first. Applied to self-stories, the autobiographical work itself can offer a revised edition of a personal life. It is invested not just with the immortality arising out of people's remembrances, but with the possibility that one may actually live again. Famously, Benjamin Franklin's self-composed epitaph expresses this idea in a religious context: 'The Body of B. Franklin. Printer; Like the Cover of an Old Book, Its contents torn out, And stript of its Lettering and Gilding, Lies here, Food for Worms, But the Work shall not be wholly Lost: For it will, as he believ'd, appear once more, In a new and more perfect Edition, Corrected and amended by the Author.'[14] Here, Franklin imagines the soul as a kind of second edition, a new self authored by God, living again in Heaven. But in the case of the autobiographical author, a second self is also created – not in Heaven – but the second edition comes alive in the inset constructed

world of the book or performance. This is the prosopopoeical life given
to autothanatographical ghosts like Francesca, like Julia, and like Brad,
simulacra of their living selves. And yet, they are not fully bound to that
first life. Their fictive reincarnation seems to grant some autonomy from
their previous life narratives, allowing them to do as other characters do
and usurp authorial power to shift the game from biography to autobiography, and to participate in their own revision (as Francesca does) or
resist it (as Julia does). Brian, with Brad's collusion, invokes a second
fictional version of Brad (and the blue Mercedes) to attempt an alchemical transfiguration of the conceptual triumvirate of 'things that happen/
things that stop/life' into 'things that you plan/things that end/art.'

Since the two men – Brad and Ray – die together, Brian works both
ends against the middle to try to deflect the car crash, saving Brad by saving Ray. Brian begins with Ray's storyline to redirect the plot away from
the collision. Initially, the focus of Ray's auto/biography is to try and
understand Ray and the circumstances that bring about the crash. Brian
and Brad take turns assuming the role of Ray in the various two-handed
scenes of his life. As a result of the doubled world structure with Brian
and Brad in world^b, performing Ray in world^c, their understanding of
Ray as person becomes entangled with the question of how to perform
him as a character:

BRAD: How was that?
BRIAN: How was that how?
BRAD: How was I as Ray?
BRIAN: I don't think this is really the time to be talking about it.
BRAD: I'm just asking. Was the task fulfilled?
BRIAN: The task?
BRAD: Yeah.
BRIAN: Yes whatever.
BRAD: Okay then, I'll just keep doing what I'm doing. (160)

Auto/biographical performance of Ray is flexible, and the Ray we see is
a mosaic of Brian and Brad's different interpretations. The dramaturgical discussions about Ray as a character function as baby steps in the
direction of trying to shift Ray from world^c up into world^b. If Brian can
cut Ray free from the original story world, then perhaps he might have
a new ending.

As the play-within progresses, the plot inevitably approaches the point
of the car crash. Brian takes on the role of Ray, and Brad plays himself:

'And I'm me?' 'Yes' (192). Brian starts the sequence with an echo of his opening imagining of the accident: 'You've got to run some errands' (192). This becomes a cue line for Brad, a conjuration by switching the use of 'you' from an indefinite pronoun as in the opening monologue, using 'you' as 'one,' to a specific address to Brad. It is revealed to us in this moment that Brad is the previously unnamed person in the car crash imagined by Brian at the beginning. This puts him into the path of destiny. In interlocking monologues, Brad and Ray recount their thoughts as they drive, detailing the exact instant of the crash.

RAY *closes his eyes, seeing what BRAD is describing.*
BRAD: [...] The leaves the wires the trees the buildings. And you feel sad that
   it's going but at the same time you feel this blissful peace at being able to
   witness it go away. And you think: 'This is what it's like to die.' But no, then
   you realize; 'No ...
RAY *opens his eyes.*
No, this is what it's like to be alive.' And then ...
RAY: And then you're gone.
BRAD: ... you're gone. (193)

The lights slowly fade to black. In the moment just before the audience breaks the silence with applause, Brad interrupts, asking, 'Do you really find this a satisfying ending?' (194). In terms of Brian's plan to impose an ending on these events that just stop, he is successful. The accident is given a literary shape and Ray and Brad as fictional autobiographers-within are given the opportunity to articulate the exact moment of their shared death right up to the very last moment, describing being dead in the present tense: And then you *are* gone. In this inset fictional world, Ray and Brad[c] are gone. They die in their fictional world. But they also are simply gone; their story now complete, they dissolve as all fictional characters do who fall out of the sphere of attention of the narrative.

In an earlier scene, Brad and Brian imagine the effect of Brenda leaving Ray on the stepson of her new lover, Terry, a boy named Lloyd. The scene presents Terry and Lloyd playing catch, during which Terry explains that he won't be around anymore since he is leaving Lloyd's mother, Pam. Discussing the boy, Brad asks, 'What's going to happen to Lloyd?' (183). First, Brian invents a fictive future for him as a pseudo–Mark Zuckerberg figure: 'Oh he's going to grow up and become a computer geek and start an ingenious website and save the world and make a trillion dollars' (183). But then he recants:

BRIAN: I don't know. No. He just goes away when the play ends.
BRAD: That's sad.
BRIAN: That's life. (183)

This is indeed the fate of all fictional characters when the author's attention moves on; they are simply gone. MacIvor uses the same verb, 'to go' – he goes, you're gone – for both Lloyd's ending and that of Ray and Brad[c], eliminating the distinction between the death of actual people and the dissolving of a fictional character. Ray's father, Irving, who suffers from senile dementia, is very concerned by all the things that are 'gone.' He can't find his suitcase. At first, he can't find the word suitcase either, calling it a 'thingamajig,' a 'whatsit,' and a 'travelling box.' He hesitantly accepts the word 'suitcase' from Ray. Finally, it doesn't matter: 'I didn't bother with it since I couldn't find it. I won't be gone long anyway' (190). His hands are 'all gone funny' (190). The 'little skipping girls have all gone home' (191). And his uniform (presumably a military uniform) is gone. 'Took that too, the bastards. That was the thing. The uniforms. Because you just didn't think about it and you just put it on and that's what you wore and that's who you were and that was that' (191). As his memories degenerate and disappear, objects like the suitcase, the girls, and the uniform leave one's life, they are no longer part of the autobiographical construction. They don't 'die,' they just fall out of narrative awareness as Lloyd does. The uniform is a particularly potent memory object since Irving associates it tightly with identity; it is who you are. And without it, the answer to 'who am I?' is less clear. The effect of this associated cluster of departures around the verb 'to go' is that Brad, in Brian's play, does simply go. He dies a fictional-world death, and simply ceases to be. Thus, the re-performance of the car crash does not achieve the metatheatrical cross-world transfiguration that Brian hopes for. The essential story is not altered as the fictional world (world[c] of Ray) remains safely self-contained in its neat theatrical frame. No actual-world effects come to pass and Brad does as all actors do; after his fictive death, he pops back up again, alive and well in the higher-order world of world[b].

Two scenes later in the play, the dialogue between Brad and Brian circles around and picks up the thread that leads again to the car crash:

BRIAN: Where are you going?
BRAD: To pick up your prescription.
BRIAN pauses until:

BRIAN: Didn't you do that yet?
BRAD: I'm doing it now.
BRIAN: God. (196)

Brian's question ('Didn't you do that yet?') is intentionally double, read-ing both as 'Didn't you already pick up the prescription?' and also as 'Didn't you already die?' Likewise, his reaction, 'God,' voices frustration with Brad not picking up the prescription and distress, realizing that the car crash is looming. In this moment, Brian realizes what will happen; he sees the path ahead. Presented with another opportunity to try to change the outcome of Brad's encounter with the blue Mercedes, Brian again tries to use performative power to rewrite the scene.

BRAD: Prescription, toilet paper, tickets, and? ...
BRIAN: You've helped me to see the beauty in people and you've been a really
    good friend. ·
BRAD: (*mildly scolding*) That's not how it went.
BRIAN: Shampoo.
BRAD: Shampoo.
BRAD steps off the stage and walks through the audience toward the door of the theatre.
    (198)

But this time, the car crash will happen in a provisionally actual world where there is no recourse to performative power. This iteration of the car crash happens in world[b], in the world of the 'show.' Brad is no longer an actor playing a role who will revive after the blackout. And yet, as Brad acknowledges when he says 'That's not how it went,' this is still not a spontaneous, first-time around, actual-world event. The two enter into a mandated re-performance of the dialogue leading up to the crash and, inevitably, of the crash itself. The theatrical world splits, allowing Brian and Brad to exist in two states simultaneously. As the lighting suggests, '*Light slow fades through SHOW to PAST state, a hybrid*' (196). Beginning in the immediate now of world[b], a second layer is added which loops back to the past, bringing it into the present both as primary lived reality and as self-aware performance. By setting this outermost frame in a theatre, in the same theatre in which we are now seated, and by having Brad step off the stage and exit through the house, the play presses for the understanding that this is actually happening. The attempted sleight of hand to switch world[b] for world[a] adds significantly to the impression of life in progress. The conjunction of the present-tense unfolding outside any fictional frame and the strong teleology of recounted history conspire to protect the story and close off avenues for authorial intervention. This situation recalls the death of Julia in *Goodness*. Just before she is killed (again), Julia chastises Michael for attempting to alter her ending and save her from being shot by Stephen. She recognizes her ending as essentially hers, and as such it is valuable and inviolable. Likewise, when Brad and Brian reach that point of the story where it could diverge from its prior trajectory, Brian makes a bid to turn the narrative, Brad corrects him, and both assent to the inevitability of this conclusion.

After Brad exits the theatre, we hear the sounds of '*footsteps on a gravel driveway, a car door opening, a car door shutting, a car start, a car pull out of the driveway, driving, driving, driving*' (198). Having failed to deter Brad from driving the car, Brian urgently turns his performative attention to Ray. In a speech marked with ellipses and repetition as he thinks on his feet, Brian improvises another ending for Ray. Instead of Ray getting on the highway with the intention of committing vehicular suicide, Brian takes Ray back to the doctor: 'And Ray says: "Hey Doc." And the Doctor says: "How are you Ray." And … And then Ray says: "How long have I got Doc." No let's give him a name. Charlie. And Ray says: "How long have I got Charlie"' (198). Here Brian brings the full pressure of his powers of creation to bear. The Adamic naming of the doctor as 'Charlie' is a precise reminder of the divine performative power of the author. In response to Ray's question, the doctor prevaricates, telling him that it could happen at any time. It could be days or weeks or months, maybe even years – perhaps even thirty or forty years. Thirty or forty years is really all anyone in middle age might reasonably expect, and in that moment Ray realizes that his terminal illness is simply the teleology of life. As Lloyd says to him earlier, 'Everybody's dying' (183). Brian thus changes the ending of Ray's story and directs him away from the crash. This is more easily accomplished with Ray than with Brad because as an inset fictional character, Ray was always under his control. Brian's success is that this Ray is not driving the blue Mercedes. Since Ray was an invention from the outset, he can be saved, but tragically the blue Mercedes continues on with someone else at the wheel.

In addition to changing Ray's ending, Brian also changes Ray's ontological status and manages to set him free of the story altogether. Brad continues to narrate Ray: 'Ray looks out at the audience – almost smiling but still unsure. Then he steps off the stage, through the audience, out the door, into the world ready to begin his new life' (198). Ray follows Brad and exits the theatre, walking through the fourth wall to live a long and happy life. Brian transposes Ray into a higher-order world where the audience and the space of the theatre become visible to him. Narration shifts the space to create a virtual world of sound alone, where Ray can invisibly share our space and exit the theatre. He is a ghost walking through the theatre where we sit. We see him in our mind's eye. Breaking the boundary between world[c] and world[b] (paired with the persistent illusion of being in world[a]), Ray moves up a level into a 'new life.' Ray becomes 'real.' In this sense, he doesn't just go away when the play ends, in contradistinction to Lloyd and all the other things that go away. He becomes like an actor who sheds the theatrical duality of carrying a role and returns to his singular life outside the theatrical frame. More significantly, Ray is released from the suicidal drive of all narrative towards ending. His ending is simply that of life. So does Brian succeed in changing Brad's fate? In a word, no. Although Brian converts a thing that stops into a thing that ends, the outcome is the same. Caught up in the innate teleological drive of narrative, Brad still dies in the car crash.

Philippe Lejeune considers this pairing of the end of autobiography with death. He suggests that the diary genre manifests the ongoing promise of more writing connected to the promise of more life: 'All journal writing assumes the intention to write at least one more time, an entry that will call for yet another one, and so on without end ... It's an annual life insurance. The diarist is protected from death by the idea that the diary will continue. There is always writing to be done, for all eternity.'[15] Ending a diary, then, is a kind of suicide. Thinking about the nature of this inevitable ending, Lejeune makes a distinction between autobiography and the diary. Whereas the subject engaged with the production of autobiography is located (more or less) at a single point in time – now – and looks backward, the diarist produces her self-story from a series of multiple 'nows,' which are constantly moving forward. Lejeune describes the structure of the diary as a kind of 'shuttle,' 'an oscillation between the past and the future. They [the rituals of closure] partition off the past, like lowlands reclaimed from the sea and protected by dikes; and this structuring and protective operation that I undertake today with respect to yesterday seems to be the model of the operation that I will perform tomorrow on what I have written today.'[16] Conversely, 'an autobiography is virtually finished as soon as it begins, since the story that you begin must end at the moment you are writing it ... I am always at the endpoint of my story.'[17]

After considering four different alternative endings for diaries (voluntary stop, destruction of the diary, rereading, and publication), Lejeune hints that it might be possible to avoid all these options and stave off narrative death: 'Finally, though this is rare, there is writing that wants to balance itself at the centre of the system, trying to escape death by equalizing the oscillation. What a dizzying and chimerical effort! This assumes that we can neutralize or de-emphasize the story line. Story is undoubtedly necessary for constructing our identity, oriented towards the past, but its Aristotelian obsession with heading towards an ending is ... deadly.'[18] Writing in his diary on 26 September 1966, Michel Leiris imagined the contours of an evolving autobiography that might avoid the ragged edge of a work cut short by death – an immortal autoperformance: 'A book that would be neither an intimate diary nor a fully formed work, neither an autobiography nor a work of imagination, neither poetry nor prose, but all of them at once. A book conceived so as to be able to constitute an autonomous whole at whatever moment it is interrupted (by death, of course).'[19] To solve the problem of linear teleology he proposes changing the core assumptions around how we assess completeness, looking to music for a model: 'Whether or not the musical suite is interrupted here or there should only be of secondary importance, since there wouldn't be a progression toward a "conclusion," but merely proliferation.'[20] How is this to be achieved in writing? Lejeune suggests that 'perhaps the association can only be indirect, by recycling a past journal into a composition which is itself in the form of a current journal.'[21] He finds inspiration in the life writing of Claude Mariac, who 'reconstructed his journal into a gigantic accumulation of labyrinthine explorations, using a present which is itself subject to the flow of time [performance does this!], but which he integrates and disperses in his *montage.*'[22] In his autobiographical memoir, Vladimir Nabokov also sees the evasive possibilities in exchanging time for space: 'I confess I do not believe in time. I like to fold my magic carpet, after use, in such a way as to superimpose one part of the pattern upon another. Let visitors trip.'[23]

Susanna Egan identifies three tropes of autothanatography. First, autothanatography is a dialogic enterprise that invites the close involvement of fellow subjects. Sometimes these associates are even called upon to take up the pen for the completion of the task after the death of the primary 'I.'[24] Autothanatography that crosses the border between death and life makes even more demands on this dialogue since the ghostly subject possesses limited agency in the actual world. Focus shifts from the catalytic transformation of the (dead) subject to the effect of the event on those who remain. The second and third tropes noted by Egan are both concerned with how autothanatography manages time.

With regard to the chronological position of the autothanatographer, Egan notes that those confronting terminal illness invariably maintain narrative focus on the present moment. Journals or diaries are common forms, allowing the narrative to develop in short bursts. Autothanatography 'replaces chronology and teleology with a continuous present tense, which seems to be the true condition of dying.'[25] So instead of a line, we get a series of truncated dashes. Connected to this subjective location in the 'now,' the form of these narratives also pauses in the present by substituting space for time. Egan observes a move away from linear narrative to spatial forms, such as visual arts, installations, and quilting.[26] She gives the specific example of the comic/graphic-novel form, citing *Our Cancer Year* by Harvey Pekar, his wife Joyce Brabner, and the artist Frank Stack. This spatiality, which offers a simultaneity of multiple views, connects directly to Lejeune's musings about how to divert the teleological press towards death. Variation can flow sequentially like music, but nonending can also be staged through branching and reiteration.

Central to this arrangement in space of repeated elements is the flattening of ontological hierarchy, which encourages transfer from square to square. Douglas Hofstadter's book *Gödel, Escher, Bach* plays with this idea of repeated variations that jump across levels, tracing this pattern in mathematics, visual representation, and music. The patterns that he identifies are not simply random variation but cyclical repetition with a difference, a form he calls 'recursion': 'Recursion is based on the "same" thing happening on several different levels at once. But the events on different levels *aren't* exactly the same – rather, we find some invariant feature in them, despite many ways in which they differ.'[27] Hofstadter gives the example of a lithograph by graphic artist M.C. Escher titled 'Ascending and Descending.' The drawing depicts an architectural fantasy featuring a series of staircases arranged in a square. Approximately two dozen hooded figures march around this enclosed square, some ascending clockwise and some descending counterclockwise; paradoxically, they never reach either the bottom or top but go around and around ad infinitum. This scene is made possible through a compression of perspective called the Penrose stairs optical illusion.[28] The effect is a cyclical return but with a difference: the figures pass the same locations, traversing the same path over and over, but simultaneously they climb higher and higher or descend lower and lower. The 'Canon a 2, per Tonos'[29] in the *Musical Offering* by Johann Sebastian Bach applies the same principles to musical scales instead of staircases. Nicknamed by Hofstadter as the 'Endlessly Rising Canon,' this work employs Shepard

Scales, 'an acoustical illusion ... constructed by creating a series of over-lapping ascending or descending scales,'[30] beginning in C minor and modulating on each repetition through D minor, E minor, F-sharp minor, G-sharp minor, B-flat minor, and finally returning to C minor where it started, but an octave higher. But through the illusion of the Shepard Scales, the canon can be repeated without end, rising through the progressions but never leaving the same octave. Hofstadter calls these paradoxical iterations 'Strange Loops.'[31]

This is precisely the formal strategy adopted by *In On It*. The play is rife with strange loops. Brian wants to thwart death, to stave off the inev-itable. His initial auto/biographical strategy to transmute life into art and shift the blue Mercedes from a thing that stops to a thing that ends does not work. But the play offers another answer. Reversing the logic of stopping and ending, the play actually substitutes things that end with things that stop – more accurately, with things that pause. *In On It* takes up Lejeune and Egan's speculations for spatially oriented, branched autothanatography. The play does this primarily by introducing alterna-tive repetitions of key events, re-performing the same events but with a difference. Each new iteration brings us back to the same place, but like Escher's stairs and Bach's fugue, we have also changed levels. For Hofs-tadter, the gap between these identical yet different points is the cruci-ble for consciousness: 'My belief is that the explanations of "emergent" phenomena in our brains – for instance, ideas, hopes, images, analogies, and finally consciousness and free will – are based on a kind of Strange Loop, an interaction between levels in which the top level reaches back down towards the bottom level and influences it, while at the same time being itself determined by the bottom level ... The self comes into being at the moment it has the power to reflect itself.'[32]

Alice Rayner also identifies the creative potential in the self-reflexive gaps between repeated points, like a current jumping across two poles. She sees ghosts in these gaps. In *The Haunted Stage*, Marvin Carlson sees ghosts in the perception of an identical thing but in a new context that permits the recognition of that sameness. So for example, an actor in a repertory company whom we see as Hamlet at the matinee but returns as Mercutio in the evening performance of *Romeo and Juliet* is a ghost of this kind. However, Rayner argues that this similarity is not sufficient to trigger the uncanny. What is required is a return with a difference, a true revenant: 'The figure of the ghost accounts for a specific force in rep-etition and the double that cannot be identified simply as an imitation or representation.'[33] For Rayner, these strange loops in the theatre are encounters with ghosts that reveal the 'unconcealing of being.'[34] Theatre is already attuned towards ghosts. 'What sets a theater apart from other institutional spaces is not so much that it is haunted as that it produces ghosts by design.'[35] Theatre raises the dead through the repetition of sameness in a context of difference. The basic embodiment convention is a ghostly doubling that blends an animate actor with a non-living thing – the textual skeleton of the character – to produce uncanny spectacle.[36] '[The] whole is pointed at but not composed of the fragmentary pieces of writing called a dramatic text. That whole remains imaginary even in the concrete performance, which is itself made of fragments … Thus, theatre is the privileged arena where nonbeing – the absoluteness of absence – shows itself as being or, in Beckett's terms, is heard. It rustles, whispers, or murmurs across silences.'[37]

The first ghost in *In On It* is, of course, Brad. He is a ghost in the most conventional sense of a dead person returned to some kind of supernatural existence and able to interact with the living. He is a revenant returning over and over to the moment of his death. How to treat a ghost in terms of its ontological status in layered fictional worlds is not entirely straightforward because the basic ontology – the beingness – of a ghost is in question. Ghosts are, but also they are not. One way to understand a ghost would be to think of it as an extension of its previous living self and so according to this logic we might assign the ghost of Brad to a world^{b+}. He is no longer of the same world but is contiguous with it. Alternatively, ghosts may be comprehended as a performed version of the original self, based upon it but entirely separate. This model relegates the ghost of Brad to world^{c}, subordinate to his former existence in world^{b} with Brian. Framed by Brian's monologue, Brad is conjured by it. It is arguably Brian's evocation (invocation?) of the car crash that releases Brad into the world, a fictional denizen of his imaginings. Yet, since Brian in world^{b} is unable to rewrite Brad's life history, this suggests that Brad is ontologically equivalent to Brian and sharing a world which is 'real' to both and thus beyond the scope of authorial performative intervention. Between these two positions, Brad's status is undecidable. As a ghost, he occupies a liminal space between worlds, unable to be either fully alive or fully dead, but able to jump back and forth between covalent points in the loop.

There is, in *In On It*, a set of props that expresses this pattern of covalent bonds, highlighting the invisible yet powerful gap between paired atoms. In an inset scene between Terry (Brenda's new lover) and his stepson, Lloyd, the two play catch with a baseball. In performance, rather than face one another, Brian and Brad both face the audience and mime throwing and catching the ball. These actions are underscored with the sounds of the ball slapping into a baseball glove and when Lloyd misses the ball we hear it drop and skitter across the gravel. The ball is invisible and even the trajectory of the ball is not a straight line, and yet we follow it without effort. The effect of this arrangement is to draw our attention to the gap, to emphasize the thing we do not see and the experience of not seeing it. The ball, then, is another ghost. Three other objects are passed between the two actors that are shared and yet not shared. When Ray and his adult son Miles meet for lunch, Ray becomes teary over his diagnosis. To console his father, Miles gives him a tissue. Consistent with the style of blocking for the inset play, both Brad as Miles and Brian as Ray sit facing the audience rather than each other. So in order to pass the tissue, '*MILES raises his empty left hand toward the audience. RAY raises his left hand toward the audience and reveals the tissue he has been palming – the effect being that MILES has handed RAY a tissue*' (163). A similar trick is performed when Brenda 'hands' Ray his jacket (178) and remarkably, in the higher-order world of the 'show,' when Brian 'throws' his car keys to Brad (198). Like the mimed baseball, the trick of not passing these objects emphasizes the empty space they both do and do not traverse. The way these props are handled renders them ghosts in Rayner's sense of the word in that they exemplify the incompleteness of theatre and the uncanny sense of simultaneously both existing and not existing.

These moments of incompleteness, these ghosts, register, in Rayner's words, 'the presence of an absence.'[38] It is in these ghosted spaces that we become aware of what is missing. It is here that the play opens possibilities for mourning. Rayner contrasts the theatre with the permanent monument. Whereas 'the public monument is the vehicle for forgetting, for getting on with what Freud calls real and immediate,'[39] the theatre 'cryptlike, stands apart from the solid monument; its hollowness both preserves and empties itself through performance, allows remembering and forgetting to be simultaneous instead of sequential, because they are what is "being done." In other words, its haunted space reflects the therapeutic space of exchange both between the encrypted past and the present intersubjective space and between living and dead.'[40] Thus, the principal driving mechanism of the play changes. Brian's initial plan is to use performance to change the story and to save Brad's life, but Brad's dramaturgical interventions, which persistently introduce variation and multiplicity, offer another possibility. Theatre generates this duality of things that are both present and simultaneously absent, granting Brian (and the audience) opportunity to consider through these performances both what is theatrically (re)presented before us and the lacunae of the missing actuality behind these dramatic facades. Out of the strange loops of *In On It*, in the gaps inhabited by ghosts, the play becomes an occasion for mourning: an occasion not for averting tragedy and saving Brad's life, but rather for coming to accept his death and for memorializing his life.[41]

The presence of absence realized in the looped structure of the play to manufacture an occasion for mourning is further developed in an interrelated pair of elements – a grey lambswool jacket and a concrete boat. At the beginning of the play, a jacket lies on the floor at centre stage. Before beginning his framing monologue, Brian picks up the jacket and puts it on. During the rest of the play, the jacket is passed back and forth between Brian and Brad, changing characters and crossing fictional worlds. In world^{c1} of Ray's life, the jacket is usually worn by whoever is Ray. In world^{c2}, presenting scenes from Brad and Brian's past, the jacket initially belongs to Brad. Brian admires it the first time they meet.[42] When they are dating, Brian borrows it semi-permanently. Eventually, Brian's 'claiming' of the jacket touches off an argument between the two, ending with Brad shouting 'Fuck you!' and throwing the jacket to the floor (180–1). In the second scene between Ray and Brenda, she finally hears his prognosis but still insists that she is leaving him. Brenda begins the scene holding the jacket: 'I brought you back your jacket. I took it with me when I left, I thought I might want something to remind me of you ... But I don't' (178). Then in a liminal scene, which is neither properly in world^c nor in world^b, Brenda (performed by Brian) addresses the audience with 'a word in [her] own defense' (178). She attempts to describe 'the sensation of something suddenly going out. Not like a candle – not like a short sharp breeze and a pop and a slow glow down to nothing and then smoke. This is more like a shutter slamming or a cover closing – but not like that ... This is the kind of going out where something collapses into itself and without a flutter turns into air. It is the feeling of something suddenly going out which is forever strangely linked to the image of a lambswool jacket lying on the floor' (178). Brad is not impressed with the 'Jacket Thing' and insists that Brian try it again. 'Defend yourself now. Go on' (181). In the repetition of this speech, Brian again begins as Brenda, covering his tie with his crossed arms. Brad calls him on this, 'What are you doing with your hands? ... So she's wearing a tie' (181). When Brian resumes the monologue, the speech header in the printed text has switched from BRENDA to BRIAN. Retaining the general sense of the original and repeating some key phrases, Brian's version, nevertheless, elaborates the central sense of emptiness and loss: 'And it leaves no trace. Just an un-nameable emptiness – a name would give it too much weight – caused by something suddenly going out – and leaving behind nothing. Nothing not even a nothing to hold up the nothing. And a grey lambswool jacket lying on the floor' (181). Shifting speakers from Brenda/Brian to just Brian, the speech also shifts listeners. After the blackout, Brad replies, 'Is that how you felt about me? Empty? Not even a nothing to hold up a nothing? Is that why we were going to split up?' (182). This ghost begins in world^c, but when Brian repeats the speech, it returns with a difference, looping around in world^b. We are back in the same place but one level up. In this gap, Brad translates Brian/Brenda's statement from a comment on Brenda's loss of love for Ray to commentary on Brian's loss of love for Brad himself. For Brian, however, the mourning for the nothing that is left applies not only to the lost relationship, but also to that loss filtered through the loss of Brad himself in the car accident. Strongly associated with Ray and with Brad, the jacket is an object of remembrance that at first both Brenda and Brian think they want to keep, but later both, in a gesture associated with the rejection of their relationships, return the jacket to its original owner (178, 180). The jacket, then, spans worlds, illustrating the presence of absence in the missing body that should fill out its fabric. Even lying crumpled on the floor, the empty jacket predicates the missing body of its past wearer. We can see what is uncannily both there and not there – what is not holding up the jacket. It is a garment for ghosts.

Associated with the empty grey lambswool jacket is Ray's recurring dream of a concrete boat. He describes this image in the doctor's office: 'It's floating on like a kind of canal and it's made of concrete. Concrete blocks, concrete slabs. I keep thinking it should sink – but it doesn't. It's vaguely unnerving' (157). The doctor tells Ray that he doesn't know about concrete boats, but he offers that in general boats in dreams represent rebirth. Using the language of dream interpretation, a boat in a clear stream means happiness; to see a boat sink means disappointment. A concrete boat is definitely ambivalent in these terms. Correspondingly, Ray's primary concern with the boat is why it floats when to his mind a boat made from concrete should certainly sink. As Brad assures Brian later on, 'You know there is such a thing as a concrete boat. People race them on a river in Missouri … Lots of people go to watch' (182). The physical principle behind the flotation of concrete boats is that they work by displacement. Archimedes's principle dictates that in order for something to float it has to displace more water than it weighs. So, therefore, a two-ton boat must displace at minimum two tons of water. In practice, for a boat made of concrete, that amount of water is going to take up a lot more space than the concrete shell and so the effect is that of a large, empty space. Like the trick of passing the tissue, the perceptual emphasis is on the mystery of how it's done. And then this attention on technique leads to the consideration, again like the tissue, of empty space, of the void carved out by the displacement of so much water.[43] In this way, the concrete boat also carries a sense of nothingness. Like the jacket, the boat is a ghost that invites mourning.

Consistent with the play's attempt to pause time and escape the inevitable conclusion, the ending fractures into several different options. After Brad revives, following the inset performance of the crash featuring Brian as Ray and Brad as himself, Brad asks, 'Do you really find this a satisfying ending?' He continues:

BRAD: I just think there are probably a few more options.
BRIAN: For God's sake.
BRAD: Do you mind?
BRIAN: Whatever.
BRAD: First date. My idea. We go to a play. (194)

Brian and Brad begin jointly to narrate the action and then they '*find themselves back in the strange, uncomfortable moment*' (195). They go to a performance event staged by their friend Kate. Arriving at the venue, they find it empty. They find two chairs and they sit in them. As they describe the empty warehouse, the stage directions specify that they should briefly describe the set for this production, that is, the space for Kate's performance piece is identical to that of Brad and Brian's show (world[b]) and *In On It* (world[a]). Sitting in the two chairs in the middle of the space, they gradually come to see that in the darkness beyond the central circle of illumination is an audience. 'And you know first it's like "What the hell is going on?" and then it's like "Oh my God they think we're the show!"' (195). Sitting there awkwardly, Brad takes Brian's hand. Remembering and re-enacting this moment, both agree that it was 'nice' (195). By doubling the auto/biographical account of this event through backward-looking narration and present-tense re-performance, the moment is revived not just as memory but also as relived experience. This looping structure, which brings the past full-fleshed into the present, distinguishes performed autobiography from other printed or recorded forms. The opportunity afforded to the autobiographical subject who is doubled in the embodiment of his or her own protagonist-self opens up a performative gap between these two selves as the historical recounted experience (world^c) is juxtaposed with the immediacy of that experience relived on the stage (world^b). In *In On It*, the performative possibility in the gap gives birth to a new experience; a choice foreclosed in the past is opened up here and comes into being straddling both worlds.

As depicted in the scenes of Brad and Brian's past, the two men, then strangers, are thrown together and given the task of performing a dance for the wedding of their mutual friend, Kate. Kate has chosen for them the frothy 1965 song 'Sunshine, Lollipops and Rainbows' by Lesley Gore.[44] Brad figures that if he creates a truly ridiculous dance, Brian will balk and he will be off the hook. Brian hesitantly agrees at first to participate, but ultimately he bails out at the last minute, and Brad ends up performing solo. He is understandably quite irked (although Brad's intended angry confrontation of Brian ends in seduction). It is this 'lost' dance that resurfaces when the events of the two autobiographical worlds – that of the past subject in the theatre and that of the present narrator-cum-protagonist in the same theatre space – fold over, creating a bridge between the two and facilitating cross-world transfer. Thinking that they are done with the scene in the warehouse/theatre, Brian comments, 'Well, I guess it's an option for an ending, but it's a bit sentimental.' To which Brad replies, 'You ain't seen nothing yet. Hit it Kate!' (195). At this point, the invisible Kate (Where did she come from? Is she in the world^c warehouse or is she in world^b helping out with the present show? Or both?) presses play on a recording of 'Sunshine, Lollipops and Rainbows.' At first Brian is horrified, but then gradually he joins in, and by the end both Brad and Brian are dancing the ridiculous dance, '*laughing and loving it*' (195). In the context of Brad's past/future death and the crumbling fragility of their relationship, reviewer Peter Birnie captures the mood of this moment, writing that watching the goofy dance, 'it's tough to know whether to laugh or cry.'[45]

Earlier in the 'show' frame of the play, This One (Brad) and That One (Brian) argue about the image on the show's poster. Brian confronts Brad with the poster depicting the two of them. They are side by side, wearing the same clothes that they are currently wearing. '*BRAD has his head thrown back laughing, BRIAN looks very uptight*' (187).[46] Brian insists that this image is not acceptable. He presses Brad to explain what it means. 'Look at me! I look like I wouldn't know fun if it bit me.' To which Brad replies, 'Well if the shoe fits ...' (188). This triggers a slide into the 'past' and an exchange of blunt but scathing observations by each about the other ends with a near break-up of the couple:

BRIAN: I don't think we're working. I don't think we care anymore.
BRAD: What are you waiting for?
BRIAN: Exactly.
BRAD: No. What are you waiting for?
BRIAN: For something to happen. (189)

When the lights snap back to the 'show' state, Brad parses the image as follows: 'That One, the laughing one, represents something happening, and This One, the serious-looking one, represents waiting for something to happen. And it sort of means that, if you don't think about it too much, you'll realize, it's probably already happening' (189).

The dance then is something that is actually already happening. The re-performance by Brad and Brian of their first date in a space (world^c) that is identical to the spaces we currently occupy (world^b [Brian and Brad's 'show'] and world^a [our actual attendance at *In On It* in the Vancouver East Cultural Centre]) brings that moment intact, up through several ontological levels, into the present. Until this point, the dance has been ghosting the play. In the first 'past' scene, revisiting how they met, Brad finishes showing the dance to Brian and all we see are the last few seconds. Then, as mentioned earlier, the dance at the wedding is performed solo by Brad when Brian backs out. The audience again misses the performance as Brad skips that part in his narration of the event. Additionally, all the past scenes are underscored specifically with '*distant Lesley Gore*' (179). The dance duet to 'Sunshine, Lollipops and Rainbows,' then, haunts the fringes of the play, always imminent, yet flaunting its absence. At the point where it jumps across worlds to be really here and really now, it escapes its frame and becomes the opposite of a ghost. Rather than something that collapses into nothingness, the dance is born out of this nothingness. The opposite of mourning, which looks to the past, the dance is fully alive in the present moment. It is a vibrant, crazy celebration of being in love. For Brian, whom Brad accuses of always hanging back and waiting for something to happen, this 'happening,' this thing that is happening now, is a transformative moment.

The ghosts of *In On It* enable for Brian 'experience itself as a form of knowing the trauma of the impossible present as it passes, of *being there* when it passes, if it passes, and when love occurs, if it occurs.'[47] The gaps created by the cross-world loops and branches of the play open him up to the impossible present. 'The past is created because the present needs it; the past is needed because the present is dependent upon finding something which is other *within itself*, without which it would be, as the present, nothing but a necropolis. Its afterlife is dependent upon the creation of a past, which means that where the historical past seems to have failed, the present needs to revisit it and to double its own space.'[48] In the end, Brian is not able to change the course of Brad's life/death through pure performative power. Death is always the end of life. And yet, for Brian the experience of the performance of these intertwined cross-world stories is transformative. Caught between the moment of autobiographical articulation and death itself, the things that cannot be apprehended manifest here as ghosts. The purpose of the encounter with the ghost is to 'feel and recognize and remember life.'[49] Mourning, then, is not a static state, keeping the mourner trapped in the past. Rather, through performative autobiography, the recursive ghosts of *In On It* reincarnate the past, showing to us the lost past in the performed present. Mourning restores, at least temporarily, things that are 'gone,' revivifying them in the theatrical moment. In the final moments of the play, we hear again the car crash and the music of a Maria Callas aria. '*A long sustained note over tires squealing. A huge explosive impact. Accident scene sounds. Female voices shrieking: ... "The blue Mercedes swerved right into him" ... Finally the aria alone*' (199). Brian takes off the jacket, waiting for the aria to end. But it does not end, it stops in a pause. Concluding that 'some things end. But some things just stop,' Brian drops the jacket on the floor, returning it to its initial position from the start of the show (199). Although the play ends as it begins, with the grey jacket lying rejected in a pile on the stage, much has changed. Despite the illusion of circularity, we are, like Escher's stair-climbing monks or the musical progressions of Bach's canon, not in fact in exactly the same place where we started. Having travelled around the larger strange loop that encompasses the whole of Brian's play (and the whole of *In On It*) and the dozen or so smaller loops contained within it, we (and Brian) have been afforded a slice of time out of time to experience the ghostly uncanny and to remember the dead through the second life of auto/ biographical performance. After Brian exits, the paused aria starts again, and unspools to its poignant end. We are released from the paused time between, from this liminal in-between world of ghosts. We are released from mourning and back into life.

Coda

As these fictional autobiographers engaged in remaking worlds and selves have consistently demonstrated, autobiography is a uniquely powerful political act. Writing about actual-world autobiographers, Deirdre Heddon is a believer in the hopeful potential of autobiography. These are 'performances of aspiration and possibility, creative acts that have the potential to contribute to ongoing cultural transformations. Looking at the past through the present, we are urged to consider the future and what we might choose to make there.'[1] Through the performance of self-stories, previously marginalized or invisible identities are brought into visibility. A single story takes the stage and holds the attention of the audience. The encounter between the performing subject and the audience is rife with possibility – for understanding, for insight, and for tolerance and acceptance. Being an audience to an autobiographical performance gets me out of myself and allows me to spend time in the intimate company of another. Seeing the world through another's eyes can be a deeply humbling and enriching experience. But autobiography is not entirely without its dangers – 'dangers that include problematic essentialising gestures; the construction of limiting identities; the reiteration of normative narratives; the erasure of "difference" and issues of structural inequality, ownership, appropriation and exploitation.'[2] Hand in hand with the potential for positive change comes the risk of failure to change. Also, it is important to remember that autobiographical performance is itself a neutral tool – neither essentially positive nor negative. Autobiography may be used to bring insight, affectionate connection, and hope, or conversely it may radiate hostility, reinforce negative stereotypes, and alienate its audience.[3] For fully fictional protagonists, as the potential for change is expanded, so are the potential pitfalls. Detached from an actual-world body, and existing only in words/performance, the autobiographical subject grounded in world[b] is more malleable, more open to the influence of performative power than a world[a] subject. This flexibility is the basis for their heightened potential, for good or ill.

For the most part, the autobiographers discussed here have been reasonably successful in the end. Patsy and Angus are at first not very promising autobiographers. Given Angus's inability to remember anything that happened more than five minutes ago, his self-story must be seriously limited. Likewise, Patsy is also inhibited by amnesia. In her case, the blank space encircles the moment of the train crash that put her in a coma and (possibly) killed her friend Marie. The blank space tracks into Patsy's present-day wool-gathering as she continues to wonder what happened to Marie. Ultimately, both Patsy and Angus take up autobiographical storytelling as a healing process. With the help of their mirror-talk partners – Angus has Morgan and Miles, Patsy has her fictional character of Francesca (Marie) – they take up a theraputic program of auto/biographical story creation. Although they may never have full access to a verifiable authentic history, the ongoing project of incrementally generating autobiography fills their need. In this way, a self, albeit provisional and fictionalized, is brought into being. Both *Perfect Pie* and *The Drawer Boy* demonstrate the strong need for a self grounded in story. The plays advocate for shared autobiography and biography, promoting the benefits of intertwined narrative relationships. No autobiography can stand alone. We are, each one of us, bound up in the stories of others. When I hear my own experience reflected in the self-stories of other people – my family, old friends, my community, or my nation – highlighting those moments where our stories touch, my own autobiographical self is affirmed and stabilized.

Michael Redhill goes looking for this shared autobiography when he misguidedly travels to Poland, seeking to confront those he feels were responsible for the murder of his extended family in the Holocaust. What inhibits Michael from making a successful connection is that he is not ready to listen. Self-stories are performed, but they also need to be witnessed. Through the metatheatrical folding of one world into another, Michael becomes implicated in Althea's autobiographical account of past genocide in her country and the murder of Julia Todd. Insofar as Althea's story lives in the past, Michael is obligated to listen respectfully to Althea's account, accepting her history as it stands. But insofar as the story is relived in the present, he is equally obligated to step in and try to save Julia from being killed again. Michael turns the question back to us in the audience and so his dilemma becomes ours. What are our obligations as witnesses to stories of genocide and other abuses? What ought I to do when I encounter stories of trauma when I read about them in the newspaper? Recognizing that my actual ability to intervene directly – to make a real difference – is limited, the play asks me to consider what remains. There is a suggestion that simply participating in the chain of storytelling is a beneficial act. This is what Michael does; he hears Althea's story and re-performs it for us, as *Goodness*. As audience members, we validate Althea's story. Even so, the play undercuts this position, reminding us of the helpless passivity of our silence, as we sit invisible in the darkness, and diminishing the power of storytelling. It is Todd who chastises Michael: 'All those people – real people – died for you, and the best you can manage is a little play?' (76). Recognizing both its concomitant power and futility, the play does not offer an easy answer for the audience-witness.

For the vulnerable autobiographers in *Eternal Hydra* and *Shadows*, their difficult choice lies between keeping their stories to themselves – safe and intact but silent – or releasing the stories to someone else who may make insertions, cut, rewrite, or steal a story outright, claiming it as his own, but who will also ensure that the story is heard. In *Shadows*, six playwrights compete for access to the means of production, the prize is a commission from the Stratford Festival. But as we discover in the end, the game is rigged. Only Meredith successfully manipulates the multiple ontological levels of worlds within worlds to transmute fictional performance into a higher-order existence, shifting from subordinate fictional worlds into reality. *Eternal Hydra*'s Selma Thomas and the Narrator of Chapter 72, who even lacks the autobiographical marker of a name, are able to set their stories free only by selling them and allowing others to ventriloquize their voices. As the Narrator notes while watching Henry Warmoth give a speech, 'Better to give him my voice than keep it useless for myself' (116). And yet, she is able to pass her autobiography embedded in a pair of shoes upward out of her narrative frame to Ezra who, wearing the shoes, hears the Narrator's story directly from her own mouth. Despite the increasing democratization of autobiography through various innovations in communication technology, as noted in the introduction, there remain barriers to the performance of the autobiographies of vulnerable individuals. Attention must be paid to these stories and the mediated ways in which they are brought into view. Canadians are currently participating in just such a fraught narrative journey as the work of the Truth and Reconciliation Commission of Canada (TRC), the judicial commission charged with remembering the legacy of Indian residential schools, proceeds. Autobiographical storytelling in this context is intended to serve a healing purpose, and yet the structure of speaking and witnessing testimony in this context can itself be problematic. As Paulette Regan observes, the process as it stands 'focuses on individuals and cannot address the collective and intergenerational harms such as loss of language and culture.'[4] Moreover, in terms of how these stories are 'performed,' there is a legitimate 'fear that survivors' truth telling or public testimony about very personal experiences of abuse, trauma, and grief will simply be consumed by the public as spectacle.'[5]

Just as autobiographically invested objects migrate upward from fictional worlds into increasingly actual worlds, dragging autobiographical stories with them, the physical body of the storytelling subject also straddles distinct ontological worlds and acts as a cross-world conduit of experience. The body of an autobiographical performer houses the world^a actual somatic experience of the subject and also is 'possessed' by its self-identical fictional protagonist. This duality opens a pathway to experiential interchange as world^a experiences are relived in world^b re-enactment, but also the secondary world^b repetition feeds back into the world^a body. In *Billy Twinkle*, these paired characteristics of unity and separation in the performed autobiographical body are raised to our attention when one of those selves is housed in a puppet body. At the outset, Billy rejects Sid's philosophy that the puppets ought to be an autobiographical expression of self. Through his encounters with metatheatrically fluid puppets like Juliet, Doreen Gray, and Rocket, Billy himself embraces the connection between the world^a puppeteer self and the world^b puppet as another self. Building on Billy's own restorative epiphany, significant implications for real-world autobiography pertain to this bodily bridge. It would be interesting to collect more examples of cases where autobiographical re-performance of a historical event is reinscribed again on the body to see what the effects of such transference may be. Likewise, the opposite situation involves stretching the dual body connection to its limits. If the autobiographical story is housed in a completely separate body, is it still autobiography or does it devolve to biography? Are there, like the case of superficially self-similar puppets, other intermediary cases?

Brian (*In On It*) tries, through a series of nested stories, to change the course of the past. With the help of the ghostly Brad, the two perform new histories in an effort to redirect Brad away from his fatal car crash with the fateful blue Mercedes. In the end, pure performative power is not sufficient to shift the past. Brian does not realize his primary goal, and yet, a series of encounters with ghosts caught in that space between the end of autobiography and death allows him to recognize and to remember life and also love. One of these ghostly objects is a dance, which haunts the inset autobiographical performances by Brian and Brad as they discuss their past together. They talk about the dance, at one point we see the final pose, and Brad narrates why it never happened. Looping across worlds, Brad and the chagrined Brian do ultimately perform this crazy silly dance, filling a past gap, and converting the ghostly dance into a living monument. For these two, mourning restores the things that are gone, allowing them to momentarily live again.

Autobiography is a kind of time machine. That is, time is the main element that is manipulated by the act of autobiography. By doubling the thread of time, autobiography brings past into present through re-performance. This is the heart of the transformative potential of autobiography as the relived past changes the present. But, critically, it is imperative that linear present-flowing time be restored at the conclusion of autobiography. The thread needs to be untangled. The subject, multiplied into author, narrator, and protagonist, needs to become singular again, dissolving these concomitant fictional selves. World[b] selves, although provisionally real in their way, are only shadow selves. Autobiography must end, so that the subject can live again in single forward motion, drawing his life thread into the future.

How does one conclude an autobiography? As the previous chapter on autothanatography demonstrated, even death is not always the end. Nevertheless, autobiographies do end. Among the plays treated here, *Billy Twinkle* stages the clearest instance of the culmination of an autobiographical project and the return of the subject to life. As Billy returns to world[b], becoming a 'real live boy,' the scene abandons the performance frame of the supernatural marionette theatre, returning to the relatively actual world of the cruise ship. Beyond this first ontological shift, Billy makes one more move. As argued previously, Billy's use of the epilogue from *The Tempest* to eulogize Sid associates Billy with Prospero and the ship with Prospero's island. Prospero is released from his island prison back to Naples and from the play as a character back to his actual existence as an actor. Billy makes a similar move with his final declaration, 'Land ho!' Some autobiographical projects are terminated more suddenly and sometimes against the will of some of the characters. This is what happens in *Shadows*, of course, when Ben abruptly explodes the storytelling game. He effectively ejects Shelagh, Dan, Meredith, Owen, and the others from their fictional constructions. Ben compels them to another level of autobiography, insisting they declare 'who they really are,' and then sends them home. Both *Perfect Pie* and *The Drawer Boy*, with their promise of daily storytelling, suggest a cyclical return to the auto-biographical project within the larger scope of life, oscillating between the duality of telling and the singularity of living. *In On It*'s Brian also traces a circular pattern. Although his recursive loops initially seem to be static, ultimately, through his encounter with various ghosts, he does not end exactly where he started. He is released from mourning back into life. However, not all autobiographical characters are able to make this necessary return.

The same systematizing properties of autobiography, which give structure to life, creating stability and securing understanding, can also become a trap or a refuge. Applying narrative schemas to the chaotic and arbitrary events of a life is beneficial insofar as they create impressions of coherence on a chaotic life. But life *is* chaotic and arbitrary. Life is not a well-made play. The imposition of a too-rigid order or the bending of life to fit these schemes creates its own problems. Instead of opening an autobiographer to the fresh possibilities of a new narrative, these stories become limiting. One can get boxed in. And far from the promised freedom of self-invention, the security and stability of conforming to established patterns and genres turns out to be a prison. Paul John Eakin recognizes this danger. He writes, we are 'conditioned through social accountibility to think of narrative's contribution to identity as life-enhancing in these ways, we may find it hard to accept that narrative capacity is, in fact, value neutral, for there is evidence that narrative can warp or even destroy identity.'[6] Eakin finds this threat not in the content of narrative but in the act of narrative making itself. The risk resides in the potential for too much concern with reading experience as if it were itself a storybook. Eakin calls this attitude 'hypernarrativity.'[7] For autobiographers who become consumed by hypernarrativity, meaning is construed exclusively as narrative meaning. Eakin presents the example of a literary autobiography in which the best friend of the author-subject has been murdered, possibly by a boyfriend. In *The Dead Girl: A True Story*, the autobiographer Melanie Thernstrom 'overdoses on story thinking,'[8] projecting the conventions of a murder mystery, police procedural, and courtroom drama onto her own life. She begins to see herself as a victim, 'the kind of girl that those kinds of things happen to.' Reading her autobiography, one gets the strong sense that things may indeed turn out as she expects simply because she expects it. Ultimately, the autobiographer from Eakin's example frees herself not by shedding the story frame altogether but rather by converting her narrative to a new story, one that is not so burdened with strong genre conventions. At this point, I want to explore a counterpoint to this book's main thesis concerning the imperative to autobiography and the profound positive potential for significant real-world change emerging from autobiographical self-storying. I propose to do this by (perversely, perhaps) adopting the opposite view and examining this scenario for the failure of politically transformative autobiography by briefly considering two more plays: *Scorched* (*Incendies*)[9] by Wajdi Mouawad and translated into English by Linda Gaboriau and *Written on Water* (*Les Manuscrits du déluge*)[10] by Michel Marc Bouchard, also translated by Gaboriau.

The setting of *Written on Water* is a small rural town now populated almost entirely by elderly people, their children having left many years before, as children will, in search of greater opportunities in the wider world. After the departure of the children, the school gymnasium was converted to the 'Writing Room' – an archive storing the collective autobiography of this community. Samuel, a retired teacher, serves as the Keeper of the Writing Room. Following the typical structure of autobiography, it is the departure of the children that serves as the crisis that catalyses the collective autobiographical project. The elderly writers memorialize communal life with literary vignettes: 'The Municipal Elections,' 'The Arrival of the First Colour TV,' 'The History of the Choir,' and 'The Exodus of the Children.' At first, autobiography is a panacea to this community. As one of the women says to Samuel, 'when our children left, you saved us from sadness' (34).

When the play begins, the town has experienced a second crisis. A catastrophic flood has overtaken the town, rendering everyone – both living and dead – homeless as it has washed away the houses and uprooted the occupants of the cemetery. The flood has destroyed the archival autobiography housed in the Writing Room. In one sense, the destruction of the Writing Room is a kind of silencing of storytelling akin to amnesia (as discussed in chapter 1) or the intentional theft of stories by plagiarism, lying, or the suppression of vulnerable storytellers (as discussed in chapter 3). Here the flow of narrative is disrupted by a natural disaster, an act of God. It is true that the stories are gone, but in this loss, the play reverses our expected valuation of autobiography. It is Claire who describes the era of the Writing Room as a time of silence: 'If I could rewrite my life, I'd find the courage to tell you that this flood of ours isn't so awful. A village where you never hear a child laugh, isn't normal.

There was too much silence. Too much silence isn't good. It's like a fore-taste of death. And God takes advantage of it. Silence encourages Him to talk to us all the time' (35). The play thus characterizes writing about the past paradoxically as a state of silence, an almost death.

Ostensibly, the autobiographical mission of the Writing Room is to fill time, giving these remaining citizens something to do. It is 'a hobby for old folks ... a pastime for amateurs' (25), but the result is that these writers reach the point where they have substituted life in the present for the historical narrative of the past. Their habit of recording the past with words comes to invade the present. In the immediate aftermath of the flood, William and Dorothy have crafted written responses to the event: William's is titled 'God's Incontinence,' Dorothy's, 'A Dress for Eternity.' Martha arrives with her piece 'Return of the Young People.' Claire's con-tribution, which she presents to the audience in private monologue, is titled 'Martha's Cat is Dead.' Documenting not just the recent past, these writers become self-scripting in the immediate present, translating expe-rience into autobiography as it is happening (shades of Twitter and Face-book). For example, Danny, the only young person left in the village, narrates himself into the Writing Room, speaking as he enters: 'Danny the lonely child entered the big writing room. For ages he'd been won-dering how he'd make his entrance into that place forbidden to those who'd never taken pen in hand there. It is a solemn occasion. His heart is beating fast. Danny the lonely child, who talks alone; who walks alone, enters the writing roon where time stands still ...' (53). When Dorothy argues with her brother Samuel and moves to depart the Writing Room, she turns to her husband, William, saying, 'Let's go, William.' Samuel vents his anger on William, 'Follow her, William. "Shadow of His Old Lady!" How's that for a title?' (47), neatly reducing William himself to a story and relegating him to a fictional frame.

For Claire, this present-tense narrativization manifests as self-framing in the way she is hemmed in by figures of speech. Claire has a senti-ment for every situation, dispensing quotable gems which she attributes variously to *Let's Laugh, House and Garden, The Farmer's Almanac,* and a Chinese fortune cookie. Claire also is confounded by figures of speech, which she persists in understanding literally. When she finds Martha's cat dead, Claire stores it in her handbag. She feels compelled to tell Martha that she has found her cat. But at the same time she fears Martha will revile her as the bearer of this bad news. Specifically, she fears that Martha will not distinguish between the story of the event and the event itself, equating the teller of the story of the dead cat with the one actually responsible for the cat's demise. So, the cat remains in her bag while she thinks about what to do. As one might expect with this set up, there comes a moment when Samuel turns on Claire, pressuring her to reveal publicly her desire to leave town and start a new life with Samuel's sister Martha, and he says, 'Come on! Let the cat out of the bag!' Claire reacts almost hysterically, 'How did you know? How did you know he was in there?' Shouting 'You can't know what's in my bag!' she runs out of the Writing Room (46).

These characters have become trapped inside their own autobiographical frames. As part of the typical structure of autobiographical performance, the past is reified in the present, blending these two time frames. As I have demonstrated, in the context of the plays discussed in previous chapters, the ontological interchange between the past as history and the past reconstructed as a fictional present encourages cross-world transference. It is this transference that enables the autobiographical subject to imagine new identities and new avenues of experience. Yet, in counterpoint to the push of this hopeful future-oriented potential, there exists an inertial pull in the opposite direction that keeps the subject in the thrall of the past, artificially alive in the present. In *Written on Water*, that is what happens to these elderly autobiographers; they succumb to the comfort of living inside the fictional world of world[b] rather than in the fully 'real' but unpredictable world of world[a]. Then, the flood uproots everything, breaks the frame, and casts them out. Michel Marc Bouchard in his author note 'Memories and Floods' identifies the flood as marking a border 'that represents the end of one world and the beginning of another' (11). For these autobiographers, the flood metaphorically duplicates the ontological border between fictional worlds, curtailing their sustained autobiographical project (world[b]) and ejecting them back into life outside the Writing Room (world[a]).

Outside the Writing Room, young people return to the village in large numbers – youthful volunteers arriving to aid the town: 'They say there are two hundred young volunteers. For seventy-two inhabitants. That makes three each' (37). These young workers are associated with the town's 'lost' children. Samuel is the most suspicious of these interlopers: 'Extraordinary! Harmless young people who'll do everything they can to make us feel attached to them, and then they'll take off and abandon us. Don't you remember what we went through?' (38). Whereas the elderly people are constituted of words; the young volunteers are all bodies. They are described exclusively by their physical beauty, noting their piercings, their tattoos. Martha describes them in her writing, 'Bare chested, dressed in yellow slicker pants. The sweat of exertion gleaming on their faces, their thick locks swaying in the wind like a field of wheat. Their firm muscles, tensed and indecent' (36).

Confronted with life lived large, Dorothy, William, Claire, and Martha choose not to rewrite and so they gain their freedom from autobiography. It is Danny, the lonely child, with his omniscience and uncannily perfect memory, who becomes their recording angel.[11] Danny takes up the mantle of autobiography, scripting futures for these four. Set free from various historical obligations and inhibitions, Claire and Martha realize their love for each other. Danny narrates them: 'After trying all the figures of speech, Claire finally told Martha outright: "I want to live with you and your cat is dead. Do you want me to say it in different order: Your cat is dead and I want to live with you." "Sam is dead and I can live with you. I can live with you and Sam is dead." That's Mrs. Martha' (94). For Dorothy, her entrapment by the past is embodied not only in her autobiographical writing but also in her youthfully dark hair. In one of the early scenes of the play, Dorothy asks Samuel, as the co-owner of her duplex, to sign some financial papers which will enable her to move out of the village to a new seniors' condo in the city. He lashes out at her betrayal, teasing Dorothy about her black hair. 'You want to know where your beautiful natural hair comes from? It was stolen from a little Latin American girl while she was sound asleep ... resold it at an outrageous price so some old bag can go on believing she's eternal' (42). In the end, along with the abandonment of the nostalgic vignettes, Dorothy also abandons her pursuit of artificial youth, of a past that is inappropriately colonizing the present, and accepts her white hair. The fourth autobiographer William, with his wife Dorothy, moves to the city to be closer to his children. William (scripted by Danny) frees himself from the old restrictive story. Creating a new living story, he says, 'Our immortality is our children ... and our children's children ... and our children's children's children ... That is the true rewrite ... Tomorrow, when my grandchildren put their arms around my neck, I'll be immortal' (95). His autobiography is written in the lives of his offspring.

Samuel, by contrast, clings obstinately to the autobiographical calling of the Writing Room. The structure provided by these stories has sustained his sense of self and his place in the community. But in the upheaval of the flood, he is displaced as he discovers that the patterns he depended on are not as stable as he thought. Rather than filing the autobiographical vignettes alphabetically, Samuel had developed his own system which reflected his view of his social world. 'Alphabetical order!?!

The Gagnons next to the Goulets – impossible! One day the Goulet boy stole old man Gagnon's car. And the Gagnons next to the Gauthiers won't work either. The Gagnons' son divorced the Gauthiers' daughter. The Goulets always felt close to the Savards. The Savards had no time for the Simards who always had a lot of respect for the Blackburns. In order, that makes Goulet, Savard, Blackburn, Simard –' (21–2). But when the eavesdropping Danny is permitted entry into the Writing Room, he has a new perspective. He tells Samuel that there are serious errors in the filing system:

DANNY: It is not right for Anita Plourde to be so far from Charles Lapointe.
SAMUEL: They weren't close.
DANNY: They had a bastard child together ... One day under the East Bridge, I heard them talking. And then there's Jean-Marc Johnson who should be next to Louis-Paul Picard.
SAMUEL: They couldn't stand each other. Everybody knows that.
DANNY: Except when they were alone in the woods together.
MARTHA: Are there lots of errors like that? (80–1)

As Samuel's self-narrative crumbles around him, he does not choose life. He elects, with the help of Danny, to become fully fictionalized, 'to enter into his own writing.' Standing in the flooded cemetery, Danny improvises a story which leads Samuel to his suicide by drowning. 'I followed old Samuel from above. The moonlight glowed on his white body. He walked along the river ... When he reached the rapid, he walked into the river slowly. And under the water, he found the grave of his beloved ... The ripples of sand were erased and the laughter of children filled the air. The manuscripts washed out to sea and were read, celebrated and such by all humanity' (93–4). Samuel chooses the 'silence' of autobiography as a substitute for life, and so his death by drowning in narrative is the logical consequence.

The second play, *Scorched*, also features a character, like Samuel, who becomes trapped by narrative. Written by Wajdi Mouawad, *Scorched* is the third part of his *Le Sang des Promesses* (The Blood of Promises) trilogy. Set in Montreal, in the offices of the notary Alphonse Lebel, the first scene introduces us to twins Simon and Janine Marwan, who are here to listen to the last will and testament of their mother Nawal Marwan. Nawal, who has not spoken a word in five years, since the twins' seventeenth birthday, has outlined several upsetting strictures in this last statement. She is to be buried face down, naked, without a coffin. She adjures her children to each pour a pail of cold water on her body, before sealing the grave. She writes, 'Let no stone be placed on my grave / nor my name engraved anywhere. / No epitaph for those who don't keep their promises / And one promise was not kept. / No epitaph for those who keep the silence. / And silence was kept' (6). Finally, she has provided two sealed letters and charges the twins to deliver them. For Janine, a letter to be delivered to a father she thought was dead. And for Simon, a letter to be delivered to a brother he didn't know existed. Having set this autobiographical quest in motion, the play interleaves the twins' search for their missing family with Nawal's performed autobiography as a young woman before her emigration to Canada.

Nawal's country is hot and dusty, riven by civil war. It is ostensibly a fictional place, but it might also be understood as a lightly disguised version of Mouawad's own Lebanon. As a teenager, Nawal falls in love with Wahab. The details of the conflict are not elaborated, but it is clear that this is a star-crossed love and will not be tolerated by their communities. When Nawal becomes pregnant, Wahab is banished from the village; and when the child, a son, is born, it too is sent away. Vowing to seek the child, Nawal attempts to trace him through her war-torn country. As her unsuccessful search continues, Nawal learns to read and write. She becomes a journalist, reporting on the atrocities of the war. Eventually, she herself takes up arms in the conflict, assassinating a high-level paramilitary leader. For this crime, she is sent to the prison of Kfar Rayat. In prison, Nawal is repeatedly raped by the torturer Abou Tarek. She gives birth to twins. Upon her release from the prison, she and the babies emigrate to Canada. Years later, Nawal testifies at the trial of Abou Tarek, admitting that he is the father of her twins and boldly accusing him of unspeakable cruelties. Horrifically and unexpectedly, Nawal's search for her first-born son ends in this courtroom. When Abou Tarek, an amoral sociopath, takes the stand, he declares in his rambling testimony that the only symbol he has of his origins is a clown nose given to him by the birth mother who abandoned him. A witness in the court, Nawal recognizes this talisman as the clown nose given by her to her lost son to represent her youthful love for Wahab. Now the same nose is perceived by that child, now a grown man, as a mockery of dignity. He has misread this autobiographically weighted object as a marker of his worthlessness, replacing a mother's love with only derisive laughter. And so Nawal learns what became of her beloved son Nihad – he is the reviled Abou Tarek. Ultimately, it is not just the realization of incest that traumatizes Nawal, but the consciousness that she has broken her precious promise to her son. At his birth, she promised: 'No matter what happens, I will always love you' (21). When Abou Tarek and Nihad turn out to be the same person, Nawal is frozen by her betrayal.

Nawal's story and the plot of *Scorched* are rich with coincidence.[12] But it is these persistent coincidences that act as strong fences, forcing the story into a single 'perfect' path. Nawal's story is locked in, its outcome inescapable. Nawal is frozen by trauma, but also by the genre conventions of tragedy. The echoes of *Oedipus Rex* are loud. One of the most 'perfectly' symmetrical plots ever constructed, *Oedipus Rex* casts a long shadow over Nawal's autobiography. Nawal, here, is cast as Jocasta – the mother of a lost son who unknowingly encounters that son again as a grown man. Oedipus and Jocasta's children are the product of a loving marriage; by contrast, Nawal's son is her prison guard and rapist. Like Sophocles's plot of *Oedipus Rex*, Nawal's quest unfolds step by step following two paths simultaneously – one that seeks the father and one that seeks the son – ultimately converging on the tragic truth. But whereas Oedipus himself is the searcher, Nawal already knows the answer at the beginning of *Scorched* when she sets Simon and Janine on the two paths that are destined to intersect. Beset by hypernarrativia, Nawal is trapped by the tightly restricted path of a life already written.

Silence in *Scorched* operates in the same way as it does in *Written on Water*. Silence is a marker, not of amnesia nor of autobiographical incapacity, but paradoxically, it is the effect of too much autobiography. The excessive control of narrative over life creates a kind of short circuit. For Nawal and Samuel, the structure of their narratives lead them to a dead end as possible choices in the plot are progressively closed off. In the end, Samuel sees no way out; he chooses to submerge himself in autobiography and accepts his death in narrative. In Nawal's case, it is not clear to what extent she chooses this excess of autobiography and to what extent she is simply swept away by it. Nawal's eventual death is also causally tied to her narrative entrapment – although somewhat more loosely than Samuel's. At the moment of her revelation, Nawal is rendered mute. She writes her will and the letters to be delivered, and although it takes her five years to die, for all intents and purposes, from that moment of writing these autobiographical documents and lapsing into silence, she ceases to participate in life. The most significant difference between these two silenced autobiographers is that whereas Samuel chooses 'no story,' that is, death, even after her own 'death,' opting out of life, Nawal chooses to construct a new story. Reaching beyond her own constrictingly crafted autobiography, Nawal is the author of the auto/

biographical quest of Simon and Janine. Through the will and the letters, she lays out the plot of their search, knowing where it will take them and what they will find.

By doing so, Nawal successfully shifts the narrative. This story is no longer the tragedy of of Nawal and Nihad/Abou Tarek. The new story escapes the gravitational pull of Oedipus, presenting a different journey with subjects of a new generation. As in *Written on Water*, the way forward out of autobiography and back to life is through the children. For the twins, the discovery of their mother's tragedy (and their own) inevitably assumes for them a different pattern. Simon uses the impossible equation $1 + 1 = 1$ to express his horror at the revelation that their lost brother is also their incestuous father. But whereas for Nawal $1 + 1 = 1$ collapses into a shattering singularity, for Janine and Simon the equation also carries with it a statement of love. Restructuring the mathematical plot, Nawal divides the equation into two parts, sending Simon one direction in search of his father and Janine in ostensibly another direction in search of her brother. When these two paths meet, it is not only Nihad and Abou Tarek that are unified in the mathematical solution '1,' but Janine and Simon are also brought togther. Simon plus Janine is also 'one.' When they are first born, the janitor of Kfar Rayat who saves them mistakenly believes that there is only one child, thus reinforcing the metaphorical idea of Janine and Simon as 'one.' As Wahab says to Nawal, and as Nawal repeats, 'There is the happiness of being together.' 'Nothing is more beautiful than being together' (17, 81). In the addition of one together with another one lies strength and beauty. In this way, by passing the story to a new generation, by shifting the subjects of this auto/biographical tale, the conclusion of $1 + 1 = 1$ retains its searing pain, but is also transmuted.

From the experience of the autobiographical author-subjects of *Scorched* and *Written on Water*, it is clear that autobiography – too much autobiography – is not always a panacea, and might sometimes turn out to be a prison. Submerged in an excess of autobiography, Samuel and Nawal drown in world[b] stories and are overtaken by silence. The pull of autobiography is too strong for them and they are unable to conclude the autobiographical project and return to the business of living life, rather than writing or performing it. The immensely positive potential of fictional world constructions that escape the borders of their banks and overflow into superior worlds, influencing actual-world people and situations, need not be dismissed entirely. However, the unbridled possibility of performative creation must be stemmed by the dikes and fences of reality. This restorative balance is key. In the end, borders that have been temporarily breached by these carnivalesque cross-world intrusions of freewheeling fictional creation must again be restored.

Without naturally occuring crises in a life, some people will artificially generate scenarios with the express purpose of making a life more interesting, more worthy of autobiography. A mild form of hypernarrativia, this approach does not reshape experience as a story after the fact, nor even as it unfolds in the present, but sets out a future program of experience according to a narrative structure. Indeed, it has become a minor cottage industry for wannabe autobiographers to set themselves a particular task (the more unusual the better) for a specific length of time (usually one year) and to commit themselves to documenting the results. *Eat, Pray, Love* by Elizabeth Gilbert, *Julie & Julia*, inspired by the blog of Julie Powell who set herself the task of making all 524 recipes in Julia Child's *Mastering the Art of French Cooking* in 365 days, and *Super Size Me*, which follows film-maker Morgan Spurlock's pledge to only eat food from fast-food chain McDonalds for a month, epitomize the genre. Comparable Canadian projects include Darren Barefoot's 2011 blog (intended to to be a book someday), *One Year, One Canadian*, in which he promises to only buy Canadian products, eat Canadian food, and consume Canadian media for twelve months.[13] In 2005, Alisa Smith and J.B. Mackinnon popularized the idea of the 100-mile diet, committing themselves to only eating food sourced within a 100-mile radius of Vancouver.[14] On Canada Day, 2008, three Vancouver roommates (listed on their blog only by first names – Jen, Grant, and Rhyannon) took on the challenge to buy nothing and produce zero landfill waste for one year. Their blog, *The Clean Bin Project*, is now an award-winning film.[15] Complementing the generic literary conventions which shape autobiography, the rules for these various challenges reiteratively apply the same organizing strictures to life, making life read like a story. For each of these self-propelling autobiographical subjects, their projects not only set personal challenges to be overcome, but are expressions of their political values. This is autobiography as activism. Autobiographical performance loops with the simultaneous living of that same life, as one crafts a life that is reflective of a self-narrative while also living as a character inside that narrative construction.

Hurtling relentlessly forward in time, we seem to be compelled to find ways to pause, and in that moment of pause, to look backward and reflect on the meaning of that journey. Autobiography responds to this patent need to transpose lived experience into a story of that experience, to create art out of life. The looping autobiographical act of self-storying brings the past into focus, allowing the author-subject to live history again in the present. As shown by all the plays discussed here, this core feature of autobiographical performance that blurs the boundaries between worlds – between past and present, and between an actual-world self and a fictional version of that same self – opens up potential cross-world exchange. Out of this overlapping duality arises the possibilty for political transformation. On one hand, there is always the risk that the retrospective presentation of autobiography can fail to achieve change, simply reifying existing beliefs and fears, reinforcing the status quo through repetition. Autobiography is a fragile genre, with both the archive of memory and the voice of the story residing in one body. Threats to the story and its transmission abound. On the other hand, the reiterative and flexible nature of the fluid interplay between actual and fictional worlds encourages the author-subject as artist to reshape, reorganize, and reimagine the story of a life, forging new connections and arriving at new insights. In this way, an autobiographical story can transform a single self, allowing the performing subject to speak herself into existence, to make that unique self visible to an audience. Finally, in the fictionalizing process, the subject may author a new version of self, projecting a better self into the future. Rather than looking backward, weighted with nostalgia, autobiography instead directs our attention towards the unwritten future, demanding an answer to the question, 'What next?'

Notes

Introduction

1 Saul Steinberg, *Untitled*, 1948, ink on paper, Beinecke Rare Book and Manuscript Library, Yale University, http://www.saulsteinbergfoundation.org/gallery_untitled1948.html.

2 Philippe Lejeune, 'The Autobiographical Pact (bis),' in Paul John Eakin, *On Autobiography*, trans. Katherine Leavy (Minneapolis: University of Minnesota Press, 1989), 131–2; cf. Sprinker.

3 Susanna Egan and Gabriele Helms, 'Auto/biography? Yes, But Canadian?,' *Canadian Literature* 172 (Spring 2002): 5–16; Leigh Gilmore, *The Limits of Autobiography: Trauma and Testimony* (Ithaca: Cornell University Press, 2001); Sara Alpern, Joyce Antler, Elisabeth Israels Perry, and Ingrid Winther Scobie, *The Challenge of Feminist Biography: Writing the Lives of Modern American Women* (Urbana and Chicago: University of Illinois Press, 1992).

4 Deirdre Heddon calls this 'the quotidian turn' in the field of autobiography. Heddon, *Autobiography and Performance* (New York: Palgrave Macmillan, 2008), 161.

5 Sherrill Grace, 'Theatre and the AutoBiographical Pact: An Introduction,' in Sherrill Grace and Jerry Wasserman, eds., *Theatre and AutoBiography: Writing and Performing Lives in Theory and Practice* (Vancouver: Talonbooks, 2006), 14.

6 Gabriele Helms, 'Reality TV Has Spoken: Auto/Biography Matters,' in Marlene Kadar, ed., *Tracing the Autobiographical* (Waterloo: Wilfrid Laurier University Press, 2005), 43–63; Linda Warley, 'Reading the Autobiographical in Personal Home Pages,' in Kadar, *Tracing*, 25–42.

7 Sidonie Smith and Julia Watson, eds., *Getting a Life: Everyday Uses of Autobiography* (Minneapolis: University of Minnesota Press, 1996), 2.

8 First coming into usage in 2004, the term 'Web 2.0' denotes a set of principles and practices that position the Web as a platform. Web 2.0 shares the privileges of authorship, allowing users to manipulate, configure, and share content. No one has yet put forward a concise definition of Web 2.0, but some concepts and principles that cohere around the notion of Web 2.0 include: 'user-centred,' 'the right to remix,' 'hackability,' 'an architecture of participation,' 'software that gets better the more people use it,' 'rich user experience,' 'radically decentralized,' 'harnessing collective intelligence.' Applications that model the philosophy of Web 2.0 include Flickr, del.icio. us, Wikipedia, BitTorrent, Amazon.com reviews, and Google page rankings. Tim O'Reilly, 'What is Web 2.0: Design Models and Business Patterns for the Next Generation of Software,' 30 Sept. 2005, http://oreilly.com/web2/ archive/what-is-web-20.html.

9 A mash-up is a derivative work created through the recombination of pre-existing works. A wiki is 'a type of web page designed so that its content can be edited by anyone who accesses it, using a simplified markup language.' http://www.oed.com/. Folksonomy is portmanteau of 'folk' and 'taxonomy' to describe a grassroots mode of categorization also known as social tagging. Tags are associated with text or images in an idiosyncratic and personal way. Through accretion, these tags generate their own organizing system. Daniel H. Pink, 'Folksonomy,' *New York Times*, 11 Dec. 2005. A tag cloud 'is a visual depiction of user-generated tags, or simply the word content of a site, used typically to describe the content of web sites. Tags are usually single words and are typically listed alphabetically, and the importance of a tag is shown with font size or color definitions.' *Wikipedia*, s.v. 'Tag cloud,' http:// en.wikipedia.org/wiki/Tag_cloud.

10 See Elizabeth Podnieks, '"Hit Sluts" and "Page Pimps": Online Diaries and Their Quest for Cyber-Union,' *Life Writing* 1.2 (2004): 123–50.

11 Mor Naaman, Jeffrey Boase, and Chih-Hui Lai, 'Is It Really about Me? Message Content in Social Awareness Streams' (Conference paper presented at CSCW, Savannah, GA, 6–10 Feb. 2010), reported in Michael Kesterton, Social Studies, *Globe and Mail*, 25 Nov. 2009, L6.

12 Amy Spaulding, *The Wisdom of Storytelling in an Information Age: A Collection of Talks* (Lanham: Scarecrow Press, 2004), 2.

13 Grace, 'Introduction,' 14.

14 Robert Fulford, *The Triumph of Narrative: Storytelling in the Age of Mass Culture* (Toronto, Anansi: 1999), 14.

15 Spaulding, *Wisdom of Storytelling*, 141.

16 Fulford, *Triumph*.

17 'Citizen' journalism (also known as 'public,' 'participatory,' 'democratic,'

'guerrilla,' or 'street' journalism) is the concept of members of the public 'playing an active role in the process of collecting, reporting, analyzing and disseminating news and information.' *Wikipedia*, s.v. 'Citizen Journalism,' http://en.wikipedia.org/wiki/Citizen_journalism. A prime example is OhmyNews.com out of South Korea. 'OhmyNews.com is the most influential online news site in that country, attracting an estimated 2 million readers a day. What's unusual about OhmyNews.com is that readers not only can pick and choose the news they want to read – they also write it. With the help of more than 26,000 registered citizen journalists, this collaborative online newspaper has emerged as a direct challenge to established media outlets in just four years.' Leander Kahney, 'Citizen Reporters Make the News,' *Wired News*, 17 May 2003, http://www.wired.com/culture/lifestyle/news/2003/05/58856.

18 *Globe and Mail*, 'The Best Non-Fiction of 2008,' http://www.theglobeandmail.com/books/the-best-non-fiction-of-2008/article726321/. The books referred to are: *In the Land of Long Fingernails: A Gravedigger's Memoir* by Charles Wilkins (Viking Canada, 2008), *The Alchemy of Loss: A Young Widow's Transformation* by Abigail Carter (McClelland & Stewart, 2008), *Otherwise* by Farley Mowat (McClelland & Stewart, 2008), *A Place Within: Rediscovering India* by M.G. Vassanji (Doubleday Canada, 2008), *The Occupied Garden: Recovering the Story of a Family in the War-Torn Netherlands* by Kristen den Hartog and Tracy Kasaboski (McClelland & Stewart, 2008).

19 Charlotte Linde, *Life Stories: The Creation of Coherence* (New York: Oxford University Press, 1993), 3.

20 Throughout the book I am committed to using the word 'autobiography' to describe theatrical acts of self-storytelling and self-creation despite its etymological emphasis on 'graphy' – on writing. A possible alternative would be to use 'autoperformance'; however, I am loath to lose the 'bio' aspect of autobiography, with the three roots of the word ('auto,' 'bio,' and 'graphy') underscoring the intersections of self, life, and the creation of that self and life. Autobiography here is broadly taken to encompass non-textual creations of self including self-portraiture and self-performance. See Rosamund Dalziell, 'Speaking Volumes about Auto/Biography Studies in Canada,' *English Studies in Canada* 34.2–3 (June–Sept. 2008): 211–27.

21 Heddon, *Autobiography*, 23.

22 Although I make the observation that autobiographical drama developed more slowly in Canada than in the United States and the UK, I am hesitant here to speculate as to why this is so. In general, the same philosophical and political underpinnings were in place, but there may be material conditions

– geographic, institutional, or economic – that contributed to this delay. This is certainly a question worth pursuing.

23 The term 'autofiction' is more commonly used in French-language studies of autobiographical works. It was coined by Serge Doubrovsky in 1977.

24 Serge Doubrovsky, *Autobiographiques: De Corneille à Sartre* (Paris: Presses universitaires de France, 1988), 70; Louis Patrick Leroux, 'Tremblay's Impromptus as Process Driven A/B,' in Grace and Wasserman, *Theatre and AutoBiography*, 109.

25 Sherrill Grace, *Making Theatre: A Life of Sharon Pollock* (Vancouver, Talonbooks, 2008), 43.

26 Ibid., 234. In an early typescript draft of *Doc*, the character Catherine is named 'Sharon' and the younger Katie is called 'Sharnee,' Sharon's nickname as a child (Ibid., 236–7).

27 Sidonie Smith, 'Construing Truth in Lying Mouths: Truthtelling in Women's Autobiography,' in *Women and Autobiography*, ed. M.W. Brownley and A.B. Kimmich (Washington, DC: Scholarly Resources, 1999), 48.

28 In the Theatre Calgary premiere production of *Doc* in April 1984, the role of Katie was played by Sharon's youngest daughter, Amanda. Although she did not act on the stage, Pollock did participate in the production of the play, directing it three times between 1984 and 1991 (Grace, *Making Theatre*, 244). Pollock did finally play Catherine in a March 1991 CBC radio broadcast of the play.

29 As biography, the play is in good company with many other biographies of famous Canadians produced around the same time, including *Billy Bishop Goes to War* (1978), *Maggie and Pierre* (1980), *Gone the Burning Sun* (1984) (about Norman Bethune), *Colours in the Storm* (1990) (about Tom Thomson), *Memories of You* by Wendy Lill (1988) (about Elizabeth Smart). In addition to biographical drama in general, there are two notable plays about Emily Carr: Herman Voaden's *Emily Carr: A Stage Biography with Pictures* (1960) and Jovette Marchessault's *Le voyage magnifique d'Emily Carr* (1990; translated by Linda Gaboriau as *The Magnificent Voyage of Emily Carr* [1992]).

30 Joy Coghill, 'Notes from an Actor-Playwright: *Song of this Place … A Play Based on the Life of Emily Carr*,' *Theatre Research in Canada* 25.1–2 (2004): 202.

31 Coghill played Emily Carr in *The Heart of the Thing* (1962; CBC Television). She played Carr again recently in *An Interview between Douglas Coupland and Emily Carr*, prepared for the Vancouver Art Gallery (2010). http://www.joycoghill.com. Coghill directed the 2004 production of *Song of This Place*, and the role of Frieda was played by Donna White. http://www.theatre.ubc.ca/song/credits.htm. In this context, the role has become unmoored from its

source subject; it remains an autobiographical text from the playwright, but loses its autobiographical resonance as embodied performance. Another actress might perform Frieda as a purely fictional character without any allusion to the character's roots as a Coghill persona.

32 Roger J. Porter coined the phrase 'double-voicing' to describe autobiographical narrators that are fragmented or doubled, a position that he suggests is particularly resonant with postmodern autobiography theory which argues against a single unified self. 'These texts undermine claims of singularity, and the narratives are structured to reflect the conflict within, or the complementarity among narrating selves' (*Self-Same Songs*, 216).

33 Suzette A. Henke, *Shattered Subjects: Trauma and Testimony in Women's Life Writing*, 2nd ed. (New York: St. Martin's Press, 2000), xv–xvi.

34 Lejeune, 'Autobiographical Pact,' 5.

35 This notation system of world^a, world^b, and world^c will be used throughout this book to distinguish the various ontological levels of nested worlds within worlds. World^a is always the so-called real world. This is the world occupied by the actual author-playwright, the audience, you and me. World^b is the first fictional world, sometimes this is the principal play world, and sometimes it is a frame occupied by a narrator. Subsequent fictional worlds are named world^c, world^d, and so on. Some plays feature one or more equivalent fictional worlds. These are denoted by adding numerals to the letters, so for example world^{c1}, world^{c2}, et cetera. Overall, this system of notation, although quite mathematical in appearance, presents a smoother logical progression from one level to the next than the system suggested by Debra Malina: diegetic world (D), extradiegetic (ED), hypodiegetic (HD), hypo-hypodiegetic (H^2D), hypo-hypo-hypodiegetic (H^3D), and hypodiegetic to infinity H^nD). Malina, *Breaking the Frame: Metalepsis and the Construction of the Subject* (Columbus: Ohio State University Press, 2002), xi.

36 George Gusdorf, 'Conditions and Limits of Autobiography,' in James Olney, *Autobiography: Essays Theoretical and Critical* (Princeton: Princeton University Press, 1980), 41.

37 Patrice Pavis, 'Autobiographical Theatre,' in *Dictionary of Theatre: Terms, Concepts and Analysis*, trans. Christine Shantz (Toronto: University of Toronto Press, 1998), 31–2.

38 J.L. Austin, *How to do Things with Words*, 2nd ed., ed. J.O. Urmson and Marina Sbisà (Cambridge: Harvard University Press, 1975), 22.

39 Mikel Dufrenne, *The Phenomenology of the Aesthetic Experience*, trans. Edward S. Casey, Albert A. Anderson, Willis Domingo, and Leon Jacobson (Evanston: Northwestern University Press, 1973).

40 William F. Brewer, 'What Is Autobiographical Memory?,' in *Autobiographi-*

cal Memory, ed. David C. Rubin (Cambridge: Cambridge University Press, 1986), 25–49; Jerome Bruner, 'Life as Narrative,' *Social Research* 54.1 (1987): 11–32; Ulric Neisser, 'Five Kinds of Self-Knowledge.' *Philosophical Psychology* 1.1 (1988): 35–59.

41 Stephen Crites, 'The Narrative Quality of Experience,' *Journal of the American Academy of Religion* 39.3 (1971): 300, 297.

42 Elinor Ochs and Lisa Capps, 'Narrating the Self,' *Annual Review of Anthropology* 25 (1996): 22–3.

43 Paul John Eakin, *How Our Lives Become Stories: Making Selves* (Ithaca: Cornell University Press, 1999), 101.

44 Susanna Egan, *Mirror Talk: Genres of Crisis in Contemporary Autobiography* (Chapel Hill: University of North Carolina Press, 1999); Jean Starobinski, 'The Style of Autobiography,' in Olney, *Autobiography*, 73–83; Anthony Paul Kerby, *Narrative and the Self* (Bloomington: Indiana University Press, 1991).

45 Starobinski, 'Style of Autobiography,' 78.

46 Kerby, *Narrative*, 63.

47 Susanna Egan, 'Changing Faces of Heroism: Some Questions Raised by Contemporary Autobiography,' *biography* 10.1 (2005): 25.

48 Egan, *Mirror Talk*, 5.

49 Heddon, *Autobiography*, 2.

50 Malina, *Breaking the Frame*, 10.

51 Ibid., 10.

52 Judith Butler, *Bodies That Matter: On the Discursive Limits of Sex* (New York: Routledge, 1993); Teresa de Lauretis, 'Desire in Narrative,' in *Alice Doesn't: Feminism, Semiotics, Cinema* (Bloomington: Indiana University Press, 1984), 103–57.

53 Malina, *Breaking the Frame*, 10.

54 Gérard Genette defines metalepsis as 'any intrusion by the extradiegetic narrator or narratee into the diegetic universe (or by diegetic characters into a metadiegetic universe, etc.), or the inverse (as in Cortázar), produces an effect of strangeness that is either comical ... or fantastic.' Genette, *Narrative Discourse: An Essay in Method*, 2nd ed., trans. Jane E. Lewin (Ithaca: Cornell University Press, 1980), 234–5. Genette refers to the Julio Cortázar story 'Continuadad de los parques' (Continuity of Parks), in which a man is assassinated by a character in the book he is reading.

55 Josette Féral, 'Theatricality: The Specificity of Theatrical Language,' *SubStance* 31.2–3 (2002): 94–108.

56 Judith Milhous and Robert D. Hume, *Producible Interpretation: Eight English Plays 1675–1707* (Carbondale: Southern Illinois University Press, 1985), 3.

57 Ibid., 10.

58 Andrew Sofer, *The Stage Life of Props* (Ann Arbor: University of Michigan Press, 2003), 5.
59 The question of the authenticity of her father's grapefruit knife was featured in an untitled autobiographical solo performance presented at an undergraduate student conference (Inquiry@Queen's) by Ashley Williamson in March 2009.
60 Ric Knowles, 'Documemory, Autobiology, and the Utopian Performative in Canadian Autobiographical Solo Performance,' in Grace and Wasserman, *Theatre and AutoBiography*, 50.
61 Bert O. States, *Great Reckonings in Little Rooms: On the Phenomenology of Theater* (Berkeley: University of California Press, 1987), 34.
62 Eakin, *How Our Lives Become Stories*, x.

1. Narrative Failure and the Loss of an Autobiographical Self: *Perfect Pie* and *The Drawer Boy*

1 Neisser, 'Five Kinds of Self-Knowledge'; Brewer, 'What Is Autobiographical Memory?'; Ochs and Capps, 'Narrating the Self.'
2 Nelson Goodman, *Ways of Worldmaking* (Indianapolis: Hackett, 1978).
3 Bruner, 'Life as Narrative,' 12.
4 Ibid., 12.
5 Ibid., 13.
6 Neisser, 47.
7 *The Drawer Boy* premiered in February 1999 at Theatre Passe Muraille (Toronto). The production was directed by Miles Potter and featured in the cast Jerry Franken as Morgan, David Fox as Angus, and Tom Barnett as Miles. It was subsequently produced by Ed Mirvish Productions, which staged the play in the Winter Garden Theatre (Toronto) and the Manitoba Theatre Centre (Winnipeg) in 2001. *The Drawer Boy* won a Chalmers Award and the Governor General's Literary Award for English-language drama.
8 The premiere of Judith Thompson's *Perfect Pie* was directed by Thompson herself and featured Nancy Palk as Patsy, Sonja Smits as Francesca, Liisa Repo-Martell as Marie, and Tara Rosling as Young Patsy. The play was published by Playwrights Canada Press in 1999 in advance of its opening at Tarragon Theatre (Toronto) in January 2000.
9 Lejeune, 'Autobiographical Pact,' 5.
10 Egan, *Mirror Talk*, 7.
11 Ibid., 7.
12 Kay Young and Jeffrey L. Saver, 'The Neurology of Narrative,' *SubStance* 94–5 (2001): 75–6. Young and Saver note that 'amnestic patients have intact lan-

guage, visuospatial, and executive function, and an intact immediate attention span. They can register and hold new ideas for 30–90 seconds, but no longer. Their accessible corpus of autobiographic experience is restricted.'

13 Miles plays Morgan, and another unnamed member of the visiting acting company plays Angus. 'Miles comes out and starts with that story about the two tall English girls, and the war and all, in that funny voice, and all of sudden I realized – it's you! He's pretending to be you ... That other fella! The simple-looking fella he was telling the story to! That was me! ... That was us' (33).

14 Marlene Moser follows a similar line of thinking. She argues that Angus's cure is 'brought about through a process of education in which Angus learns to read realist narrative and theatrical conventions.' Moser, 'Ideology as Behaviour: Identity and Realism in *The Drawer Boy*,' *Modern Drama* 45.2 (Summer 2002): 231. Whereas Moser's argument concerns the processes of Method acting and realist ideology matching performance to life, I am more interested in Angus's interactions with the inevitable and ineffaceable gaps between theatre and life.

15 See Moser, 'Ideology as Behaviour'; Robert C. Nunn, 'The Meeting of Actuality and Theatricality in The Farm Show,' *Canadian Drama* 8.1 (1982): 42–54; Alan Filewod, 'Theatrical Nationhood in Radical Mobility: The Farm Show Futures and the Banner/Ground Zero Collaborations,' *Canadian Theatre Review* 125 (Winter 2006): 9–15.

16 To complicate matters, Alison Lobb is an actual world[a] person. The setting and motivating circumstances of *The Drawer Boy* piggyback on the earlier seminal Canadian theatre production *The Farm Show*. In the summer of 1972, a group of Toronto actors lived in Clinton, Ontario, with the goal of collecting stories about the life of that community and generating a play. Healey's *The Drawer Boy* fictionalizes that scenario, basing the character of Miles on an original member of the *Farm Show* collective, Miles Potter. Alison Lobb was a contemporary resident of the area around Clinton; her name appears in the acknowledgments to *The Farm Show* script. Michael Healey also thanks her in the 'Playwright's Notes' to his own play. Further, the portrayal of Alison Lobb reported by Angus cites *The Farm Show*, which also features a fictional Alison Lobb (Alison[b2]).

17 Cathy Caruth, *Unclaimed Experience: Trauma, Narrative and History* (Baltimore: Johns Hopkins University Press, 1996), 6.

18 Young and Saver, 76–7.

19 This is the interpretation promoted by the film *Perfect Pie* (2002, Dir. Barbara Willis Sweete, Perf. Wendy Crewson, Barbara Williams, Allison Pill, Rachel McAdams). Although the younger girls' world seems to overlap that

of the older women creating a somewhat magical sense of remembering, Marie/Francesca is definitely 'real' and alive. We see her onstage in the city. We see her drive to Patsy's farmhouse.

20 A monologue by Judith Thompson also titled 'Perfect Pie' (1994) closely parallels many aspects of the later play. In the first-person narrative, Patsy addresses her friend Marie. Here Patsy seems quite clear that Marie died in the train crash. 'Marie, listen to me for God's sake, even if you had lived you wouldn't have made it out of Marmora' (169). 'I feel cold to think that all that's left of you is some bones and a skull' (170). Nevertheless, in contrast with these seemingly definitive statements, Patsy tape records a letter to Marie, sends her a frozen pie, and invites her to stop by for a visit. 'I hope that we'll start up being in touch, you know, maybe just Christmas cards, or whatever, and please do enjoy the pie. Oh … Your best friend Patsy' (171).

21 Robert Nunn, 'Crackwalking: Judith Thompson's Marginal Characters,' *Siting the Other: Re-visions of Marginality in Australian and English-Canadian Drama*, ed. Marc Maufort and Franca Bellarsi (Peter Lang, 2001), 320–1; Marlene Moser, 'Identities of Ambivalence: Judith Thompson's *Perfect Pie*,' *Theatre Research in Canada* 27.1 (2006): 81–99. Bookending the play, Patsy declares: 'I will not forget you, you are carved in the palm of my hand' (3, 91). Taken from the book of Isaiah, this quotation refers to God pledging to remember his children of Zion (Isaiah 49:16). In the central image of the complete verse, Zion is a baby. Just as a mother cannot forget the child of her womb, so too God will remember and care for the people of Zion. So, more than simple remembering, this allusion also establishes the relation of mother to child, of creator to creation. And so, by extension, Patsy is again located as the godlike creator/author of Marie/Francesca.

22 William Barr, 'Types of Memory Problems,' *Epilepsy.com*, 21 Oct. 2007.

23 Herbert F. Crovitz, 'Loss and Recovery of Autobiographical Memory after Head Injury,' in Rubin, *Autobiographical Memory*, 273–90.

24 The poem 'Annabel Lee' by Edgar Allan Poe recounts the romance of the narrator and the eponymous maiden. However, this pure unrivalled love calls down the envy of the angels such 'that the wind came out of the cloud by night / Chilling and killing my Annabel Lee' (Poe, 25–6). The allusion then to beautiful frozen deaths in *Perfect Pie* is clear.

25 Patsy never recites any part of the rhyme, but I imagine that this is the one she is referring to:

> Three children sliding on the ice
> Upon a summer's day,
> As it fell out, they all fell in,

The rest they ran away.
Now had these children been at home,
Or sliding on dry ground,
Ten thousand pounds to one penny
They had not all been drowned.
You parents all that children have,
And you that have got none,
If you would have them safe abroad,
Pray keep them safe at home.
(http://www.amherst.edu/~rjyanco94/literature/mothergoose/rhymes)

26 An uncomfortable implication of the metaphorical association of Marie with a dog and with Belle in particular is that it was necessary in the tradition of the scapegoat for Marie to die to preserve the health and cohesion of the community.
27 Judith Thompson, 'Epilepsy & the Snake: Fear in the Creative Process,' *Canadian Theatre Review* 89 (1996): 6.
28 Ibid., 6.
29 Young and Saver, 78.

2. Performative Witnessing to Autobiographies of Trauma: *Goodness*

1 *Goodness* premiered in Toronto at Tarragon Theatre in October 2005, directed by Ross Manson, as a Volcano/Tarragon co-production. The cast featured Victor Ertmanis as Mathias Todd, Lili Francks as Althea, Tara Hughes as Young Althea, J.D. Nicholsen as Stephen, Jordan Pettle as Michael Redhill, and Bernadetta Wrobel as Julia. This same production with a couple of cast changes (Gordon Rand as Michael Redhill and Amy Rutherford as Julia) toured to Edinburgh (August 2006), New York (March 2007), Vancouver (June 2008), Ottawa (June 2009). In the fall of 2009, the production underwent more cast changes for a brief run in Toronto followed by a tour to Huye, Rwanda. See www.volcano.ca for the most recent information on current production plans.
2 Kelly Oliver, *Witnessing: Beyond Recognition* (Minneapolis: University of Minnesota Press, 2001), 20.
3 English lacks an appropriate word to describe the particular cognitive experience of attending a play. (French uses the verb *s'assister*, which points to active generative work being done by the audience to make the play.) Spectators merely see. Playgoers go to a play but this term doesn't indicate what they do once there. Audiences do more than the etymological root of

simply hearing (*audire*) indicates. And so audiencing is a word of my own coinage to fill this terminological gap.

4 Julie Salverson, 'Change on Whose Terms? Testimony and an Erotics of Injury,' *Theater* 31.3 (2001): 122.

5 Ibid., 119.

6 Theodor Adorno, 'Engagement,' *Noten zur Literatur*, vol.3 (Berlin: Suhrkamp, 1958), 125–7.

7 *Oxford English Dictionary Online*, s.v. 'Barbarous,' accessed 30 May 2007, http://dictionary.oed.com.

8 My thanks to my colleague Jill Scott for reminding me of the etymology of this word and connecting it to Adorno.

9 Carolyn Forché, 'Introduction,' *Against Forgetting: Twentieth Century Poetry of Witness* (New York & London: W.W. Norton & Company, 1993), 29–47; Julie Salverson, 'Anxiety and Contact in Attending to a Play about Land Mines,' in *Between Hope and Despair: Pedagogy and the Remembrance of Historical Trauma*, ed. Roger I. Simon, Sharon Rosenberg, and Claudia Eppert (Lanham: Rowman & Littlefield, 2001), 59–74; Joan Holden, 'In Praise of Melodrama,' in *Reimaging America: The Arts of Social Change*, ed. Mark O'Brien and Craig Little (Philadelphia: New Society Publishers, 1990), 278–84.

10 Silvio Gaggi, *Modern/Postmodern: A Study in Twentieth-Century Art and Ideas* (Philadelphia: University of Pennsylvania Press, 1989), 15.

11 Genette, *Narrative Discourse*, 234–5 (see introduction, note 54).

12 *The Columbia World of Quotations* (New York: Columbia University Press, 1996), 27 March 2007, www.bartleby.com/. The specific association of this quotation with genocide and with the Holocaust in particular comes from its use by William L. Shirer as the epigraph to *The Rise and Fall of the Third Reich* (1959).

13 Roman Ingarden distinguishes between a real object, which is always 'unequivocally, universally determined' and fictional objects, which may be by contrast indeterminate. For example, 'if a given real object, in a given time, is "colored," then the color quality is also unequivocally determined and is no longer differentiable. Thus, by its very nature it is impossible for a real object to be "colored" without being either "red" of a very specific shade or "yellow" (likewise in a very specific shade), etc.' Ingarden, *The Literary Work of Art: An Investigation on the Borderlines of Ontology, Logic, and Theory of Literature*, trans. George G. Grabowicz, ed. James M. Edie (Evanston: Northwestern University Press, 1973), 247. Fictional objects, however, are necessarily subject to what Ingarden calls 'spots of indeterminacy.' It is not possible to fully determine every quality of a represented object. In a literary work, an infinite list of descriptors would be required to fully render a represented

object. Although staged objects may be less indeterminate since they exist materially, nevertheless there are still myriad spots of indeterminacy in the time and space of fictional worlds of drama, encompassing unseen events and locations.

14 Dori Laub, 'Bearing Witness or the Vicissitudes of Listening,' *Testimony: Crises of Witnessing in Literature, Psychoanalysis and History*, ed. Shoshana Felman and Dori Laub (New York: Routledge, 1992), 59.

15 Ibid., 60.

16 Ibid., 62.

17 Caruth, *Unclaimed Experience*; Kali Tal, *Worlds of Hurt: Reading the Literature of Trauma* (New York: Cambridge University Press, 1996).

18 Ernest Van Alphen, 'History's Other: Oppositional Thought and Its Discontents,' in his *Caught by History* (Stanford: Stanford University Press, 1997), 36.

19 A note about the names: *Althea* in Greek means wholesome or healing; *Alethea* (a close cognate) means truth. Both are weighty associations to make with this character, associations which are invited particularly by the uncommonness of the name. Likewise, from the name Mathias Todd, we might read Todd as *tod*, in German – death. In performance, it was pronounced 'Todd' with a short o sound.

20 Richard A. Cohen, *Elevations: The Height of the Good in Rosenzweig and Levinas* (Chicago: University of Chicago Press, 1994), 147. Qtd. in Simon, 'Paradoxical Practice,' 19.

21 In subsequent productions, this role of Michael was played by Gordon Rand. The text was changed accordingly to substitute one name for the other. However, rather than substituting *Godot* for a recent credit by Rand, that is, instead of telling a real-world truth, Redhill fabricates: 'He's an excellent actor, a trained actor, who's been in many Canadian plays of repute ... but the most successful was an all-Jewish *Waiting for Godot*' ('Goodness,' New York, 3). Recognition of this fabrication undermines the strong reality effect at work when we identify Jordan Pettle and confirm his real-world status.

22 Laub, 71.

23 Ibid., 72.

24 Andrew Sofer devotes a whole chapter to the gun. He notes particularly the relationship of the gun to time. The firing of a gun may kill a character but also may kill dramatic time, bringing the play to a close. Also 'the gun could threaten, distort or even rupture time in other ways.' *Stage Life*, 170. Here the gun travels from the past into the present when Althea retrieves the mimed gun, which materializes as a real gun, and hands it to Michael.

25 As noted above, *Goodness* has had only one production to date, so in light of

this single interpretation, there has not yet been a comparative opportunity to evaluate this suggested alternate staging in performance.

26 In performance, Michael points the gun at Julia/Joanna, at the older Althea, and at his own temple. A directorial choice offered in performance, which adds significantly to the tension of this action and which is not suggested in the text, is that Michael chambers the bullet. Since we have just witnessed a gunshot at the moment of Julia's murder, the presence of another loaded and cocked gun raises the level of tension in this scene. From a static object as a repository of the memory of a past murder, the gun is made active and we are reminded that the gun retains the potential for future murder. What is lost in performance is that unlike a printed text, actual-world performance is resolutely singular and will not accommodate the proliferation of multiple possible worlds generated by the word 'or.'

27 In the world hierarchy of world^a, world^b, et cetera, employed here, world^0 denotes a supernatural world that is ontologically superior to the usually uppermost actual world of world^a. World^0 might be occupied by God or other deities that act as playwrights, directors, or audience to the theatre of human existence.

3. Setting Free Silenced Autobiographical Voices: *Eternal Hydra* and *Shadows*

1 *Eternal Hydra* had its origins as a one-act play commissioned by the Stratford Festival. The one-act version premiered in the inaugural season of the Festival's new Studio Theatre in 2002. This version was directed by Andrey Tarasiuk with Stephen Ouimette (Gordias Carbuncle), Chick Reid (Vivian Ezra/Gwendolyn Jackson), Karen Robinson (Pauline Newberry/Selma Thomas), and Paul Soles (Randall Wellington Sr/Randall Wellington Jr). The play subsequently went through a development process as it expanded to a full-length play. After a workshop production in November 2007, the Crow's Theatre production premiered at Buddies in Bad Times Theatre in May 2009 under the direction of Chris Abraham. Karen Robinson continued as Newberry/Thomas and Narrator. The other cast members were Liisa Repo-Martell (Ezra/Jackson/Sarah Briggs), Sam Malkin (Wellington Sr/Wellington Jr/Léon Labas), and David Ferry (Carbuncle/Henry Warmoth).

2 *Shadows* was commissioned by the Stratford Festival in 2001. Findley began writing the play at the Leighton Colony, Banff Centre for the Arts. The play premiered in the Studio Theatre in August 2002. Findley did not live to see the premiere; he died on 21 June. The Stratford premiere was directed by Dennis Garnhum with the following cast: Brent Carver (Ben Singer), Brenda Robins (Shelagh McIntyre), Stephen Ouimette (Daniel Storey),

Gordon Rand (Owen Barclay), Chick Reid (Kate Terry), Karen Robinson (Lily Delacourt), Kimwun Perehinec (Meredith Gryphon). Although both plays premiered in the same season, they did not appear as paired one-act plays. *Eternal Hydra* played with Paul Dunn's *High-Gravel Blind* and *Shadows* followed *Walk Right Up* by Celia McBride.

3 Egan, *Mirror Talk*, 7.

4 Philippe Lejeune, 'The Autobiography of Those Who Do Not Write,' in Eakin, *On Autobiography*, 190.

5 Eakin, *How Our Lives Become Stories*, 159.

6 G. Thomas Couser, *Vulnerable Subjects: Ethics and Life Writing* (Ithaca: Cornell University Press, 2004), x–xi.

7 Egan examines cases where questions of ethics arise in situations of unequal power relations between the ostensible biographer and her subject, drawing examples from documentary film – Michael Apted's *7 Up* series, the Canadian interview films *Talk 16* and *Talk 19* directed by Janis Lundman and Adrienne Mitchell – and from drama, notably the play *Jessica* and the subsequent *Book of Jessica* by Linda Griffiths with Maria Campbell.

8 Some of the characters have unusual names which mark them as writers. Carbuncle (and Piatigorsky) explicitly connect Vivian Ezra to the biblical scribe Ezra. In a rather hyperbolic panegyric, Carbuncle lists highlights in the history of written communication: the deciphering of the Rosetta Stone by Jean-Francois Champollion, the publication of the First Folio of Shakespeare's works, and the redaction of the bible by Ezra. He then adds Vivian Ezra's efforts to get *Eternal Hydra* published as a fourth highlight (*Eternal Hydra*, 49–50). Ben Singer's name associates him the creative process – a bardic teller of tales. We can compare this with Dan's last name, 'Storey' – the object of those tales. However, although Dan's surname and those of all the other characters in *Shadows* are printed in the dramatis personae (and presumably the program), only Ben's surname is mentioned in the play text.

9 Ingarden, *Literary Work of Art*, 246–54.

10 Wolfgang Iser, *The Act of Reading: A Theory of Aesthetic Response* (Baltimore: Johns Hopkins University Press, 1980).

11 Just as people are doubled, splitting between actual and fictional worlds, so are the play texts themselves. With an eponymous novel at its core, *Eternal Hydra* has a doubled structure at the very highest levels. The fictive Gordias Carbuncle is the author of the promised but lost *Hydra*. Anton Piatigorsky is the actual-world author of *Hydra*, which is not lost as we hold the work before us in text or performance. Despite sharing a title, however, these two *Hydra*s are decidedly different in content. *Shadows* tries to pull a related

trick and replicate itself whole. Saying goodbye to his guests, Ben muses that he ought to write a play about six playwrights in search of a commission – a joke of course on Pirandello's metatheatrical play *Six Characters in Search of an Author* (*Shadows*, 70). The play that he proposes to write would presumably be the play that we just saw. Ben tries to ascend beyond his current world frame and aligns himself with the actual playwright, offering himself as a viable substitute for Findley. Plays of this kind that reiterate the performed story as simultaneous with the writing of that story, what I am calling 'recursive narratives,' are the topic of the last chapter.

12 Adam Zachary Newton, *Narrative Ethics* (Cambridge: Harvard University Press, 1995), 19.

13 Couser, *Vulnerable Subjects*, 33.

14 See chapter 2 for a fuller discussion of the ethical implications of metatheatrically drawing the audience's attention to this relationship.

15 Heddon, *Autobiography*, 3.

16 Butler, *Bodies That Matter*, 11.

17 The published script indicates that he dims the lights via a wall rheostat as well, but there was no action to do this in performance.

18 Féral, 'Theatricality.'

19 It is interesting to note that in this foray into the nested fiction, Newberry, even as she assumes the persona of Thomas, remains 'Newberry' in the speech headers. Every other time that characters cross over into fictional worlds, the speech headers change to the name of the fictional character: Ezra becomes 'Jackson,' and in a later scene Newberry does become 'Thomas.' The list of dramatis personae simply indicates a normal doubling.

20 Another piece of evidence in favour of viewing Ezra as the primary narrator is the ghostlike status of Carbuncle. In the primary fictional world, Carbuncle is visible and audible only to Ezra and to the audience. Newberry and Wellington occasionally comment on Ezra 'talking to herself.' The suggestion is made that Ezra has conjured him, but whether he is purely an imaginative invention of hers or whether he has some independent existence is not clear. In an earlier draft of *Eternal Hydra*, Piatigorsky gives this relationship more attention, writing a farewell scene in which Ezra breaks free of the apparition.

21 Discussing the scenographic choices in the production of *Eternal Hydra*, I am referring to the Crow's Theatre 2009 production of the play as a full-length work and not to the one-act version staged at Stratford in 2002.

22 In performance, in the transition to New Orleans, just before the enactment of Chapter 72, each book on the table was picked out in a small but bright white spotlight.

23 Lubomir Doležel, *Heterocosmica: Fiction and Possible Worlds* (Baltimore: Johns Hopkins University Press, 1998).

24 Ibid., 145.

25 This story of the doomed marriage of the openly homosexual Dan to an actress closely parallels Findley's actual marriage in 1958 to actress Janet Reid. Regarding his homosexuality and their desire for children, Findley said in a CBC interview: 'She didn't want to discuss it. She didn't want to discuss my homosexuality … I loved Janet. I really loved her and I wanted to be with her and I wanted children; so did she.' Interview date: 7 December 1999, archived at: http://www.cbc.ca/lifeandtimes/findley.html. The real-world foundation of Dan's story is also alluded to by William Whitehead in his introduction to the play text.

26 Henry Warmoth (1842–1931) is the only real person to appear in either of these two plays. Born in Illinois, he was a considered a carpetbagger, arriving in Louisiana after the war. He was governor of Louisiana from 1868 until his impeachment in 1872. He married heiress Sally Durand of Newark, NJ, in May 1877, not Sarah Briggs as he does in the play (*Wikipedia*, s.v. 'Henry C. Warmoth,' http://en.wikipedia.org/wiki/Henry_C._Warmoth). Just as an aside, if we assume that these dates apply to the events of the play, then the Narrator's child conceived in early 1866 and likely born in 1867 would be between one and five years old when the Narrator takes her to see Warmoth's speech. This is only interesting as it creates a possible parallel between this child and Pauline Newberry's son, Nathaniel, who she tells us is two years old.

27 This strategy by world[a] authors to insert actual-world objects and experience into fictional worlds takes a variety of forms. As discussed earlier, in *Perfect Pie* Judith Thompson shares her experiences with epilepsy with both Marie and Patsy. Like his creator Ronnie Burkett, Billy Twinkle (*Billy Twinkle*) is also a puppeteer and shares with his creator a number of key autobiographical events. Most radically perhaps, Michael Redhill writes his own fictional twin into *Goodness*. When he displays an old photograph of his extensive family in Poland before the Holocaust, the audience must wonder if this is in fact an authentic actual-world artefact. Taking a less direct route, Michael Healey establishes cross-world connections in *The Drawer Boy*, naming his actor-character Miles – without doubt transplanting the actual *Farm Show* actor Miles Potter into this parallel fictional world. By a neat coincidence, Miles Potter several decades later directed the premiere production of *The Drawer Boy*, which also featured David Fox (another *Farm Show* alumnus) as Angus.

28 See Jenn Stephenson, 'Metatheatre and Authentication Through Metonymic Compression in John Mighton's *Possible Worlds*,' *Theatre Journal* 58.1

(March 2006) for a fuller treatment of this idea that the dissolving of a fictional-world border simultaneously brings both freedom and death.

29 Gaggi, *Modern/Postmodern*, 14.

30 Malina, *Breaking the Frame*, 10.

31 In *Narrative Discourse*, Genette recounts the story of a man who is assassinated by a character in a book that he is reading – a story by Cortazar, 'Continuidad de los Parques,' in *Final del Juego* (*End of the Game*) – 'this is an inverse (and extreme) form of the narrative figure the classics called *author's metalepsis*, which consists of pretending that the poet himself "brings about the effects he celebrates," as when we say that Virgil "has Dido die" in Book IV of the *Aeneid*' (234).

32 Gaggi, *Modern/Postmodern*, 15.

33 'Push' and 'pop' are terms from Douglas R. Hofstadter's *Gödel Escher Bach: An Eternal Golden Braid* (Basic Books: New York, 1979). 'To *push* means to suspend operations on the task you're currently working on, without forgetting where you are – and to take up a new task. The new task is usually said to be 'on a lower level' than the earlier task. To *pop* is the reverse – it means to close operations on one level, and to resume operations exactly where you left off, one level higher' (128). Hofstadter calls this process of pushing and popping 'recursion.'

34 When the play moves up to world[b], the characters reveal their 'truths' – 'Shelagh' has two sons. 'Dan' has three young kids. 'Lily's' abortion of Ben's child is true. 'Dan's' story is also true, but he claims it as someone else's (69).

35 Butler, *Bodies That Matter*, 3.

36 This doubled casting is specified in the published version of the play text.

37 The prompt script for *Shadows* confirms that this is in fact real wine and that Shelagh fills her glass just before Ben's explosive revelation. Likewise, there is no suggestion in either the script or in my own experience of this moment in performance that the audience member who samples the wine is a 'plant.'

38 For a discussion of the metatheatricality of theatrically problematic or taboo objects like alcohol, money, babies, and corpses, see Jenn Stephenson, 'Singular Impressions: Metatheatre on Renaissance Celebrities and Corpses,' *Studies in Theatre and Performance* 27.2 (Summer 2007) 137–53.

4. The Autobiographical Body as a Site of Utopian Performativity: *Billy Twinkle*

1 Until very recently, puppeteers in the European tradition made every effort to stay hidden and not to reveal the mechanisms of the puppets' animation.

Puppet éminence grise Bil Baird records that during the late 1930s, 'Frank Paris [1914–1984] was the first to operate his show in full view, wearing dark clothes and working his short-strung marionettes in a spotlight.' Bil Baird, *The Art of the Puppet* (New York: Bonanza Books, 1973), 229. Paris's 'Stars on Strings' cabaret performance featured marionette portraits of well-known personalities such as Josephine Baker and Olympic figure skater Sonja Henie (John Bell, *Strings, Hands, Shadows: A Modern Puppet History* [Detroit: Detroit Institute of Arts, 2000], 89). George Latshaw describes the advent of cabaret performance: 'Whether it was the example of the ventriloquist working out in the open, or simply an urgent need to be seen on stage, variety and nightclub performers created a sensation in the 1930s by presenting marionettes without masking. The puppeteer, working in full view of the audience, was an integral and visual part of the act. The audience loved the style and it solved a number of problems for the performer ... A variety act running 12–20 minutes, would feature trick figures, dancers and maybe a "celebrity" or two on strings. The striptease, come-apart skeleton, skater, ballerina and juggler were standard bits. Usually talk pieces were not included, although the puppeteer might MC to bridge the routines.' Latshaw, *Puppetry: The Ultimate Disguise* (New York: Richards Rosen Press, 1978), 26–8. A video of a short black-and-white film of Frank Paris and some of his marionettes in performance can be found online at http://www.youtube. com/watch?v=rJ0u6sfuO-Y. This is what Burkett says about his pioneering choice to be visible: 'Of the marionette practitioners I sought out as a child, and eventually lived and studied with, all of them told me I must never, ever stand on stage, without masking, working the puppets. The marionette operator is always hidden, thereby creating a better illusion. So they said. I introduced the notion that perhaps if the puppeteer wasn't hidden, the audience would get beyond trying to figure out the technique of the show and ease more readily and quickly into the story. I tried arguing this point with them, but they would have none of it. By the mid 1980s they had all died, and I was just about to begin Theatre of Marionettes. Since none of them were around to debate this issue with any more, I decided to just go ahead and be on stage with my marionettes.' 'The Mentored Path,' *Canadian Theatre Review* 84 (1995): 20.

2 Janne Cleveland, in her PhD dissertation on the plays of Ronnie Burkett, notes that the implications of Burkett as Stanley Rural extend well beyond a simple representation of his power: Since there is no puppet of Stanley, he cannot be wholly constituted as a subject. He only appears in memory scenes, and when he does, he is performed by Burkett. 'Thus while other characters remain characters after a performance – albeit returned to object

status – Stanley disappears altogether, leaving behind in his place only Burkett as the actor who performs him. Unlike his co-stars Stanley does not continue to exist as an object outside the space of representation' (90).

3 *Billy Twinkle: Requiem for a Golden Boy* premiered at the Citadel Theatre, Edmonton, AB, on 23 October 2008. The play was written and performed by Burkett, who also designed the marionettes, their costumes, and the set. The play has since toured extensively across Canada, Australia, and the UK. *Billy Twinkle* also received a Citation of Excellence from the Union Internationale de la Marionette USA (UNIMA).

4 Lejeune, 'Autobiographical Pact,' 5.

5 Susan Bennett, '3-D A/B,' in Grace and Wasserman, *Theatre and AutoBiography*, 41.

6 Ibid., 35.

7 Ibid., 35.

8 Knowles, 'Documemory,' 51.

9 Ibid., 49.

10 Ibid., 50.

11 Jill Dolan, *Utopia in Performance: Finding Hope at the Theatre* (Ann Arbor: University of Michigan Press, 2005), 5.

12 Liz Nicholls, 'Puppetmaster Takes a Turn in Twinkle,' *The Edmonton Journal*, 19 Oct. 2008, B1.

13 It must be acknowledged that puppets do experience superficial changes in appearance due to wear and tear – paint becomes chipped, fabric rips, joints rust – changes which seem to parallel human injury or slow decay. And yet, puppets do not grow and develop as children do, nor do they age and become grey and wrinkled as older people do. The inner experience (biological, but also emotional and psychological) of living is not reflected on the body of the puppet, as it is on humans.

14 Petr Bogatyrev, 'The Interconnection of Two Similar Semiotic Systems: The Puppet Theater and the Theater of Living Actors,' trans. Milanne S. Hahn, *Semiotica* 47.1–4 (1983): 59.

15 Baird, *Art of the Puppet*, 17.

16 Henryk Jurkowski, 'Literary Views on Puppet Theatre' (1979), in Penny Francis, *Aspects of Puppet Theatre* (London: Puppet Centre Trust, 1988), 29.

17 Roger Bensky, *Recherches sur les structures et la symbolique de la marionnette* (Paris: A.G. Nizet, 1971), 114.

18 Elizabeth A. Grosz, *Volatile Bodies: Toward a Corporeal Feminism* (Bloomington: Indiana University Press, 1994), 80, 83.

19 Egan, *Mirror Talk*, 5.

20 Starobinski, 'Style of Autobiography,' 78.

21 Kerby, *Narrative*, 63.

22 *Puppenhaft* denotes 'what is puppet-like' contrasted with *nichtpuppenhaft*
    which denotes 'that which is not puppet-like.' These terms were in common
    usage among puppet theorists beginning in the 1930s through the 1950s.
    These theorists 'looked for the essence of the puppet and for its *raison
    d'être.*' Jurkowski, 'Literary Views,' 24. See L. Buschmeyer, *Die Kunst des Pup-
    penspiels* (Erfurt, 1931); H. Sandig, *Die Ausdruckmöglichkeiten der Marionette
    und ihre dramaturgischen Konsequenzen* (Munich, 1958); Fritz Eichler, *The
    Essence of Glove and String Puppetry* (*Das Wesen des Handpuppet und Marionetten-
    spiels* [1937]); Sergei Obraztsov, 'The Importance of Puppet Theatre and Its
    Place among the Other Genres of Theatre Art,' *Teatr Lalek* 6 (Warsaw, 1958).

23 Burkett's similarities to Billy follow a path established by other playwrights
    who often flesh out their characters with shared autobiographical mate-
    rial. Just from the plays in this study, one can trace the shared biography
    of Judith Thompson and her characters' epilepsy; Dan Storey in *Shadows*
    repeats a fragment of Timothy Findley's experience of an unfortunate mar-
    riage as his own. Born in 1957, and so fifty-one years old when *Billy Twinkle*
    premiered in 2008, Ronnie and Billy share a similar chronology. Like Billy,
    Burkett became obsessed with puppets at a young age. Both grew up in
    supportive families in rural western Canada – Moose Jaw, SK, for Billy and
    Medicine Hat, AB, for Ronnie. Both travelled at a young age to puppet festi-
    vals in the United States where they were not shy about meeting established
    puppeteers and seeking mentorship. Insisting in an interview that the play
    is not autobiographical, Burkett denies that he went to a puppet festival in
    Detroit when he was twelve as Billy does in the play: 'I actually went when
    I was fourteen and it was in Lansing.' *The Walrus* interview, April 2010.
    Among Burkett's mentors whom he refers to affectionately as his 'old boys,'
    his principal mentor was Martin Stevens, known as 'Steve.' It is to him that
    Billy Twinkle is dedicated. Burkett pays tribute to the influence of Stevens
    in virtually every interview that I have read. And although Burkett insists
    that the character of Sid Diamond is an amalgamation of various mentors,
    I found a 1950 photograph of Stevens (Latshaw, *Puppetry*, 147), and the
    resemblance to the puppet Sid is unmistakable. There is also a painted
    portrait on the Internet at http://www.stevenspuppets.com/.

24 Clearly this is a very difficult routine. The night that I saw the performance,
    it was not entirely flawless and Burkett had to reach down and help pull off
    two articles of clothing that did not completely release on their own.

25 The echoes of the Frank Capra film *It's a Wonderful Life* (1947) are loud.
    Like Billy, George Bailey is poised to jump from the bridge when he is
    stopped by a supernatural guide. Like Sid, Clarence the angel will take

George on an autobiographical tour. Also like Sid, Clarence is in need of salvation. At the end, as a result of his services to George, Clarence gets his wings.

26 Sofer cites the *OED* entry for 'props': 'any portable article, as an article of costume or furniture, used in acting a play: a stage requisite, appurtenance, or accessory.' Qtd. in Sofer, *Stage Life*, 1. Sofer then opens this basic definition to consider the way that props as portable objects enact that journey. 'Props trace spatial trajectories and create temporal narratives as they track through a given performance' (2). Puppets transcend this 'portability' of props, becoming, to my mind, not props but characters, when they are animated and present the illusion of autonomous living motion.

27 It is interesting to note that structurally *Billy Twinkle* has a reverse frame. Typically, higher-order worlds frame inset lower-order worlds – the ubiquitous play-within-a-play structure. These steps are ordered sequentially as the play begins with the highest world and moves progressively downward, returning to the highest level at the end. *Billy Twinkle*, by contrast, begins in an intermediate world and moves upward into a 'supernatural' realm and returns to its initial lower-order world at the end.

28 Later, when Billy learns of Sid's death, he also learns that on that last morning Sid 'got out of bed, piled all the puppets in the backyard and set them on fire' (75). Only the total destruction of the puppets halts their capacity for oscillation, that is, to continually exist, and stop existing only to come to life again. In this way, the puppets are granted a 'human' death, where non-being is a final ending.

29 Nicholls, 'Puppetmaster.'

30 Martin Stevens, who I argue is the prototype for Sid Diamond, presented a well-known puppet production of *The Taming of the Shrew* (1947). See also a production photograph in Latshaw, *Puppetry*, 116.

31 The opening of Billy's 'Stars in Miniature' nightclub act features a full-body spotlight on Billy himself as he poses with his back to the audience. He raises his arms and wiggles his fingers. He turns to wink at us before turning around fully to present the first puppet.

32 George Speaight documents references in English miracle plays to 'gods on strings' dating from 1200. *The History of the English Puppet Theatre*, 2nd ed. (Carbondale: Southern Illinois University Press, 1990), 54.

33 Henryk Jurkowski, 'Toward a Theatre of Objects' (1984), in Francis, *Aspects of Puppet Theatre*, 40.

34 Ibid., 42.

35 Ibid., 42.

36 Ibid., 41.

37 Ronnie Burkett, 'Text and Performance' (Puppet Centre Trust: London, UK, 22 April 2007): http://www.youtube.com/watch?v=g1okMUpMSrw.
38 Ibid.
39 Ibid.
40 Jurkowski, 'Theatre of Objects,' 37.
41 Ibid., 37.
42 John Cohen, *Human Robots in Myth and Science* (London: George Allen and Unwin, 1966), 43. Qtd. in Victoria Nelson, *The Secret Life of Puppets* (Cambridge: Harvard University Press, 2001), 65.
43 Even more to this point about highlighting the objectival nature of the puppets, sometimes the trick mechanisms of the puppets themselves make this perception unavoidable. At a performance I attended, Biddy's mouth repeatedly became stuck in the open position. And repeatedly, with ad-lib comments, Burkett reached down and tapped her on the chin to close her mouth.
44 It is interesting to note in this context that Burkett reports that the title of his current show in development is *Geppetto Jones*. This is what Burkett told interviewer Liz Nicholls about the show: 'Geppetto as an old, contemporary man, long after Pinocchio has become "real" and abandoned him ... Walking home one night I passed a disheveled but somewhat elegant old street guy hauling two suitcases, and it moved me beyond sense. I thought, "That's Geppetto and those suitcases are full of puppets" Odd, huh?' Liz Nicholls, 'The Remarkable Ronnie Burkett,' *Legacy* (Spring 2009): 19. Since this interview, Burkett seems to have taken this inspiration in a new direction, or set it aside altogether. The program for *Billy Twinkle* at Place des Arts in Montreal announces that Burkett's next production is titled *Penny Plain* and that he has plans to revive his improvised *Daisy Theatre* performances.
45 Kenneth Gross, 'Love among the Puppets,' *Raritan* 17.1 (1997): 81.
46 The visitations of these three evoke a potential parallel between *Billy Twinkle* and Charles Dickens's *A Christmas Carol*. In both works, the main character undergoes a spiritual enlightenment after being confronted with his own life – past, present, and future. In this scenario, Sid Diamond is Jacob Marley; Juliet, Doreen, and Rocket represent respectively the ghosts of Christmas Past, Christmas Present, and Christmas Future. Billy reacts to Rocket as Scrooge does to the deathly spectre of the ghost of Christmas Future, fearing that he is to be dragged off to hell.
47 Stephenson, 'Singular Impressions.'
48 V. Nelson, *Secret Life of Puppets*, 20.
49 Ibid., 22–3.
50 The naming of Doreen Gray as a tongue-in-cheek homage to Dorian Gray

is a hallmark of Burkett's plays. Other such clever reworkings of famous names include Uta Häagen-Daz (*Street of Blood*), Cleo Payne (*Happy*), and a sheep named Blanche DuBaaa (*Ten Days on Earth*).

51 The choice of both boys to make the trip at Easter is curious. Billy says that he has three weeks off school at Easter break. Rocket says that he gets two weeks off school. Billy notes that Christmas is not good because he already has some puppet performances booked. Easter, of course, may be read as significant in terms of the persistent oscillating death/rebirth theme of the play.

5. Self-Authoring Characters in Recursive Autothanatography: *In On It*

1 Katherine Nelson, 'The Ontogeny of Memory for Real Events,' in *Remembering Reconsidered: Ecological and Traditional Approaches to the Study of Memory*, ed. Ulric Neisser and Eugene Winograd (Cambridge: Cambridge University Press, 1988), 265.

2 Robert Folkenflik, *The Culture of Autobiography: Constructions of Self-Representation* (Stanford: Stanford University Press, 1993), 15–16.

3 Philippe Lejeune, 'How Do Diaries End?,' trans. Victoria Lodewick, *Biography* 24.1 (Winter 2001): 111.

4 Simon Critchley, *Very Little ... Almost Nothing: Death, Philosophy, Literature* (London: Routledge, 1997), 26.

5 Jeremy Tambling, *Becoming Posthumous: Life and Death in Literary and Cultural Studies* (Edinburgh: Edinburgh University Press, 2001), ix.

6 Nancy K. Miller, 'Representing Others: Gender and the Subjects of Autobiography,' *Differences: A Journal of Feminist Cultural Studies* 6.1 (1994): 12.

7 Susanna Egan, 'The Life and Times of Autobiography' (Pain and Suffering Interdisciplinary Research Network, Department of English, University of British Columbia, 2001), http://www.english.ubc.ca/PROJECTS/PAIN/degan.htm.

8 Ivan Callus, '(Auto)Thanatography or (Auto)Thanatology? Mark C. Taylor, Simon Critchley and the Writing of the Dead,' *Forum for Modern Language Studies* 41.4 (2005): 427.

9 Alice Bennett, 'Unquiet Spirits: Death Writing in Contemporary Fiction,' *Textual Practice* 23.3 (2009): 465.

10 *In On It*, produced by da da kamera, premiered at the Vancouver East Cultural Centre in January 2001. *In On It* was directed by Daniel MacIvor, who also played the role of This One (Brad). That One (Brian) was played by Darren O'Donnell. In subsequent tours, the role of That One was played by Jim Allodi.

11 In the dramatis personae they are named as This One and That One with all their other roles, including Brad and Brian, listed in parentheses. The effect of this is to reduce the ontological level of Brad and Brian to characters performed by This One and That One. The published script, however, uses Brad and Brian for the speech headers. It is interesting to note in the names Brad and Brian the alliterative echoes of the originating creators, Daniel (MacIvor) and Darren (O'Donnell).

12 In the published version of the text, MacIvor very clearly delineates these three 'realities' and the performance and scenographic 'style' associated with each. 'In the PLAY we would both perform out – to the audience – but react as if we were actually facing one another … In the SHOW we would maintain an awareness of the audience, stage directions indicate when we addressed the audience. In the PAST we would suddenly be inside a fourth-wall reality with no awareness of the audience whatsoever' (151).

13 The pronoun 'you' used here by Brian is ambiguous. It could refer to a 'you' that is to another person – Brad – or it could also refer to Brian him-self or to just a person in general, used as a replacement for 'one.' My sense of it at this point is that Brian is imagining a car crash involving himself. Reviewer Peter Birnie suggests that This One and That One may be aspects of a single person. He draws evidence for this from the fact that Brad and Brian alternate playing roles in the play-within; for example, they each play Ray at different points. Birnie also makes the connection to other MacIvor plays that divide a single protagonist into two selves (i.e., James and Jim in *2-2 Tango* and Victor and his performance of 'Victor' in *House*).

14 Qtd. in G. Thomas Couser, 'The Shape of Death in American Autobiogra-phy,' *Hudson Review* 31.1 (1978), 57.

15 Lejeune, 'Diaries,' 100–1.

16 Ibid., 102.

17 Ibid., 103.

18 Ibid., 104.

19 Qtd. in Lejeune, 'Diaries'; Michel Leiris, *Journal 1922–1989*, ed. Jean Jamin (Paris: Gallimard, 1992), 614.

20 Qtd. in Lejeune, 'Diaries'; Leiris, *Journal*, 614–15.

21 Lejeune, 'Diaries,' 104.

22 Ibid., 104.

23 Qtd. in Sven Birkerts, *The Art of Time in Memoir: Then, Again* (Saint Paul: Graywolf, 2008), 47; Vladimir Nabokov, *Speak Memory: An Autobiography Revisited* (New York: Putnam, 1966), 47.

24 Egan,. 'Life and Times.'

25 Ibid.

26 Egan's suggestion of quilting as a spatial form of autothanatography invokes the NAMES Project AIDS Memorial Quilt. Begun in 1987, the quilt is now composed of 44,000 panels, each 3' by 6'. Most of the panels remember the life of a single individual who has died of AIDS. http://www.aidsquilt.org/history.htm.

27 Hofstadter, *Gödel, Escher, Bach*, 148–9.

28 'The Penrose stairs is an impossible object created by Lionel Penrose and his son Roger Penrose. It can be seen as a variation on the Penrose triangle. It is a two-dimensional depiction of a staircase in which the stairs make four 90-degree turns as they ascend or descend yet form a continuous loop, so that a person could climb them forever and never get any higher. This is clearly impossible in three dimensions; the two-dimensional figure achieves this paradox by distorting perspective.' *Wikipedia*, s.v. 'Penrose Stairs,' http://en.wikipedia.org/wiki/Penrose_stairs.

29 Visit http://www.youtube.com/watch?v=A41CITk85jk to listen to the Canon performed, accompanied by a visual scrolling score.

30 'A Shepard tone, named after Roger Shepard, is a sound consisting of a superposition of sine waves separated by octaves. When played with the base pitch of the tone moving upwards or downwards, it is referred to as the *Shepard scale*. This creates the auditory illusion of a tone that continually ascends or descends in pitch, yet which ultimately seems to get no higher or lower.' *Wikipedia*, s.v. 'Shepard Tone,' http://en.wikipedia.org/wiki/Shepard_tone.

31 Hofstadter, *Gödel, Escher, Bach*, 10.

32 Ibid., 709.

33 Alice Rayner, *Ghosts: Death's Double and the Phenomena of Theatre* (Minneapolis: University of Minnesota Press, 2006), x.

34 Ibid., xxi.

35 Ibid., 60.

36 Ibid., xv.

37 Ibid., 48.

38 Ibid., 48.

39 Ibid., 68.

40 Ibid., 70–1.

41 Although *In On It* premiered in Canada in January, 2001, well in advance of the events of 9/11, the play toured to P.S.122 in New York City in October, 2001. In this context, this theme of mourning emerged strongly. In her review for *Village Voice*, Alisa Solomon notes the resonance of the play and its dealing with unexpected loss in the emotional atmosphere of New York in the weeks after 11 September 2001. She asks in the first sentence of the

review: 'What kind of theater do we need now?' She concludes that the metatheatrical layering of the play is more than mere game playing. 'It also makes palpable the play's very theme: the human need to put a shape around unexpected tragedy and inconsolable loss. Somehow it's comforting that MacIvor so feelingly shows us that effort. For we are all certainly in on it now.' In the segue to a scene in world^c between Lloyd and Terry, the soundscape specifies '*distant Maria Callas which transforms into a field: birds, a plane at one point flies distantly overhead*' (169). Again, post 9/11 this seemingly bucolic sound effect of the field and the plane overhead reads entirely differently.

42 This scene is part of a sequence of remembrances from their life as a couple. Each one of these scenes is instigated by Brad, in contradistinction to Ray's scenes which all seem to be written/orchestrated by Brian. These scenes seem to be spontaneous, arising out of a trigger in the previous dialogue. All feature some musical underscoring and the majority feature music by Leslie Gore. Given the musical underscoring and the theatrical framing at work, I suggest that these scenes are not to be understood as unadulterated, unmediated views into the past, but rather as performances by Brian and Brad.

43 http://www.ehow.com/how_5590066_make-concrete-boat-float.html.

44 Sunshine, lollipops and rainbows,
Everything that's wonderful is what I feel when we're together,
Brighter than a lucky penny,
When you're near the rain cloud disappears, dear,
And I feel so fine just to know that you are mine.
My life is sunshine, lollipops and rainbows,
That's how this refrain goes, so come on, join in everybody!
Sunshine, lollipops and rainbows,
Everything that's wonderful is sure to come your way
When you're in love to stay.

45 Peter Birnie, 'Well Worth Getting In On It: The Premiere Run of Daniel MacIvor's New Work at the Cultch Is a Don't-Miss-It-No-Matter-What Proposition,' *The Vancouver Sun,* 27 Jan. 2001, H15.

46 The stage directions note that '*This moment works best if the image shown is the actual image used in publicity materials for the production*' (187). I have not tracked down the original image used in the Vancouver or New York productions in 2001. The cover of the script for *In On It* published by Scirocco Press in 2001 shows That One (Brian) facing the viewer, looking partly quizzical and partly concerned as if he is thinking, 'What is going on?' Stand-

ing very close to Brian, we see This One (Brad) in profile; he is making a grotesque face, sticking his tongue out and staring into Brian's ear. It is an arresting image.

47 Rayner, *Ghosts*, 32.
48 Tambling, *Becoming Posthumous*, 140.
49 Rayner, *Ghosts*, xxi.

Coda

1   Heddon, *Autobiography*, 172.
2   Ibid., 157.
3   Ibid., 158.
4   Paulette Regan, *Unsettling the Settler Within: Indian Residential Schools, Truth Telling and Reconciliation in Canada* (Vancouver: UBC Press, 2010), 9.
5   Ibid., 10.
6   Eakin, *How Our Lives Become Stories*, 130.
7   Ibid., 130.
8   Ibid, 135.
9   *Scorched*, the English-language version of *Incendies*, received public readings in London, UK, at the Old Vic Theatre as part of the '4play Canada' National Arts Centre English Theatre/ Canada High Commission showcase in 2005. The production premiered on 6 April 2007 in Ottawa in an NAC/ Tarragon co-production. This production was directed by Richard Rose and designed by Graeme S. Thomson and Theresa Przybylski. Sound design was by Todd Charlton. The cast included Valerie Buhagiar, Sergio Di Zio, Paul Fauteux, David Fox, Kelli Fox, Sophie Goulet, Janick Hébert, Nicola Lipman, and Alon Nashman.
10 *Written on Water* was commissioned and developed by CanStage (Toronto, Canada) and the Melbourne Festival (Melbourne, Australia). The play, directed by Micheline Chévrier, opened on 22 January 2004. In the cast were Doris Chilcott, David Fox, Jerry Franken, Barbara Gordon, Carolyn Hetherington, and Brian Marler.
11 Out of the flood debris, Danny has salvaged a pair of angel wings from the Christmas pageant, which he wears throughout. Also in Danny's autobiographical account of himself, Danny relates how he once ate a whole box of consecrated host wafers. The angel wings and the strong association of Danny with the ineffable potential of the future align him with *Billy Twinkle*'s Rocket.
12 Nelson Pressley, '"Scorched": A Searing Tale of Love and War; Twins Jour-

ney into Their Mother's Past in This Epic Tragedy,' *The Washington Post,* 7 Oct. 2010; Lyn Gardner, 'Review: Theatre: Scorched Old Vic Tunnels, London 3/5' *The Guardian,* 10 Sept. 2010.

13 http://www.oneyearonecanadian.ca/. Barefoot, on his website, characterizes this kind of project as 'stunt journalism,' a title which I think omits the key autobiographical aspect of seeing larger issues through the eyes of the writer/participant.

14 J.B. MacKinnon and Alisa Smith, *The 100-Mile Diet: A Year of Local Eating* (Toronto: Random House, 2007).

15 The people behind the The Clean Bin Project are Grant Baldwin and Jen Rustemeyer. http://cleanbinproject.com/theproject/; http://www.cleanbin-movie.com/.

Bibliography

Adorno, Theodor. 'Engagement.' In his *Noten zur Literatur*, vol. 3, 125–7. Berlin: Suhrkamp, 1958.

Alpern, Sara, Joyce Antler, Elisabeth Israels Perry, and Ingrid Winther Scobie. *The Challenge of Feminist Biography: Writing the Lives of Modern American Women.* Urbana and Chicago: University of Illinois Press, 1992.

Austin, J.L. *How to Do Things with Words.* 2nd ed. Edited by J.O. Urmson and Marina Sbisà. Cambridge: Harvard University Press, 1975.

Bainbrigge, Susan. 'Introduction.' *Forum of Modern Language Studies* 41.4 (2005): 359–64.

Baird, Bil. *The Art of the Puppet.* New York: Bonanza Books, 1973.

Barr, William. 'Types of Memory Problems.' *Epilepsy.com.* Last modified 21 Oct. 2007. Accessed 18 Feb. 2008.

Bell, John. *Strings, Hands, Shadows: A Modern Puppet History.* Detroit: Detroit Institute of Arts, 2000.

Bennett, Alice. 'Unquiet Spirits: Death Writing in Contemporary Fiction.' *Textual Practice* 23.3 (2009): 463–79.

Bennett, Susan. '3-D A/B.' In Grace and Wasserman, *Theatre and AutoBiography*, 33–48.

Bensky, Roger-Daniel. *Recherches sur les Structures et la Symbolique de la Marionnette.* Paris: A.G. Nizet, 1971.

Birkerts, Sven. *The Art of Time in Memoir: Then, Again.* Saint Paul: Graywolf, 2008.

Birnie, Peter. 'Daniel MacIvor Serves Up Subversion: The Creator of *In On It* Is a Master of Playing with Audience Expectations.' *The Vancouver Sun,* 24 Jan. 2001, B9.

– 'Well Worth Getting In On It: The Premiere Run of Daniel MacIvor's New Work at the Cultch Is a Don't-Miss-It-No-Matter-What Proposition.' *The Vancouver Sun,* 27 Jan. 2001, H15.

Bogatyrev, Petr. 'The Interconnection of Two Similar Semiotic Systems: The Puppet Theater and the Theater of Living Actors.' Translated by Milanne S. Hahn. *Semiotica* 47.1–4 (1983): 47–68.

Bouchard, Michel Marc. *Written on Water (Les Manuscrits du déluge)*. Vancouver: Talon, 2004.

Brewer, William F. 'What Is Autobiographical Memory?' In Rubin, *Autobiographical Memory*, 25–49.

Bruner, Jerome. 'Life as Narrative.' *Social Research* 54.1 (1987): 11–32.

– 'The Narrative Construction of Reality.' *Critical Inquiry* 18.1 (1991): 1–21.

Bruss, Elizabeth. *Autobiographical Acts: The Changing Situation of a Literary Genre*. Baltimore: Johns Hopkins University Press, 1976.

Burkett, Ronnie. *Billy Twinkle: Requiem for a Golden Boy*. Toronto: Playwrights Canada Press, 2008.

– 'The Mentored Path.' *Canadian Theatre Review* 84 (1995): 16–21.

– *Street of Blood*. 1998. In *String Quartet: Four Plays by Ronnie Burkett*, 75–146. Toronto: Playwrights Canada Press, 2010.

– 'Text and Performance.' Puppet Centre Trust. London, UK. Last modified 23 Apr. 2007. http://www.youtube.com/watch?v=g1okMUpMSrw.

– *Tinka's New Dress*. 1994. In *String Quartet: Four Plays by Ronnie Burkett*, 1–74. Toronto: Playwrights Canada Press, 2010.

Butler, Judith. *Bodies That Matter: On the Discursive Limits of 'Sex'*. New York: Routledge, 1993.

Callus, Ivan. '(Auto)Thanatography or (Auto)Thanatology? Mark C. Taylor, Simon Critchley and the Writing of the Dead.' *Forum of Modern Language Studies* 41.4 (2005): 427–38.

Carlson, Marvin. *The Haunted Stage: The Theatre as Memory Machine*. Ann Arbor: University of Michigan Press, 2003.

Carr, David. *Time, Narrative, and History*. Bloomington: Indiana University Press, 1986.

Carter, Kathryn. 'Death and the Diary, or Tragedies in the Archive.' *Journal of Canadian Studies* 40.2 (Spring 2006): 42–59.

Caruth, Cathy. *Unclaimed Experience: Trauma, Narrative and History*. Baltimore: Johns Hopkins University Press, 1996.

Cleveland, Janne. 'Getting in the Car to Weirdsville: Taking a Trip with Ronnie Burkett Theatre of Marionettes.' PhD diss., Carleton University, 2008.

Coghill, Joy. 'Notes from an Actor-Playwright: *Song of this Place* ... A Play Based on the Life of Emily Carr.' *Theatre Research in Canada* 25.1–2 (2004): 202–13.

– *Song of This Place*. Toronto: Playwrights Canada Press, 2003.

Cohen, John. *Human Robots in Myth and Science*. London: George Allen and Unwin, 1966.

Cohen, Richard A. *Elevations: The Height of the Good in Rosenzweig and Levinas.* Chicago: University of Chicago Press, 1994.

Couser, G. Thomas. 'The Shape of Death in American Autobiography.' *Hudson Review* 31.1 (1978): 53–66.

– *Vulnerable Subjects: Ethics and Life Writing.* Ithaca: Cornell University Press, 2004.

Critchley, Simon. *Very Little … Almost Nothing: Death, Philosophy, Literature.* London: Routledge, 1997.

Crites, Stephen. 'The Narrative Quality of Experience.' *Journal of the American Academy of Religion* 39.3 (1971): 291–311.

Crovitz, Herbert F. 'Loss and Recovery of Autobiographical Memory after Head Injury.' In Rubin, *Autobiographical Memory,* 273–90.

Dalziell, Rosamund. 'Speaking Volumes about Auto/Biography Studies in Canada.' *English Studies in Canada* 34.2–3 (June–Sept. 2008): 211–27.

De Lauretis, Teresa. 'Desire in Narrative.' In *Alice Doesn't: Feminism, Semiotics, Cinema,* 103–57. Bloomington: Indiana University Press, 1984.

Dolan, Jill. *Utopia in Performance: Finding Hope at the Theatre.* Ann Arbor: University of Michigan Press, 2005.

Doležel, Lubomir. *Heterocosmica: Fiction and Possible Worlds.* Baltimore: Johns Hopkins University Press, 1998.

Doubrovsky, Serge. *Autobiographiques: De Corneille à Sartre.* Paris: Presses universitaires de France, 1988.

Dufrenne, Mikel. *The Phenomenology of the Aesthetic Experience.* Translated by Edward S. Casey, Albert A. Anderson, Willis Domingo, and Leon Jacobson. Evanston: Northwestern University Press, 1973.

Eakin, Paul John. *Fictions in Autobiography: Studies in the Art of Self-Invention.* Princeton University Press, 1985.

– *How Our Lives Become Stories: Making Selves.* Ithaca: Cornell University Press, 1999.

Eakin, Paul John, ed. *On Autobiography.* Translated by Katherine Leavy. Minneapolis: University of Minnesota Press, 1989.

Egan, Susanna. 'Changing Faces of Heroism: Some Questions Raised by Contemporary Autobiography.' *Biography* 10.1 (2005): 20–38.

– 'The Life and Times of Autobiography.' Pain and Suffering Interdisciplinary Research Network, Dept. of English, University of British Columbia, 2001. http://www.english.ubc.ca/PROJECTS/PAIN/degan.htm.

– *Mirror Talk: Genres of Crisis in Contemporary Autobiography.* Chapel Hill: University of North Carolina Press, 1999.

Egan, Susanna, and Gabriele Helms. 'Auto/biography? Yes – But Canadian?' *Canadian Literature* 172 (2002): 5–16.

Féral, Josette. 'Theatricality: The Specificity of Theatrical Language.' *SubStance* 31.2–3 (2002): 94–108.

Filewod, Alan. 'Theatrical Nationhood in Radical Mobility: The Farm Show Futures and the Banner/Ground Zero Collaborations.' *Canadian Theatre Review* 125 (Winter 2006): 9–15.

Findley, Timothy. 'Shadows.' *Canadian Theatre Review* 114 (2003): 54–71.

Folkenflik, Robert, ed. *The Culture of Autobiography: Constructions of Self-Representation.* Stanford: Stanford University Press, 1993.

Forché, Carolyn. Introduction to *Against Forgetting: Twentieth Century Poetry of Witness*, 29-47. New York & London: W.W. Norton & Company, 1993.

Francis, Penny, ed. *Aspects of Puppet Theatre: A Collection of Essays.* London: Puppet Centre Trust, 1988.

Friedlander, Saul. *Memory, History, and the Extermination of the Jews of Europe.* Bloomington: Indiana University Press, 1993.

Fulford, Robert. *The Triumph of Narrative: Storytelling in the Age of Mass Culture.* Toronto: Anansi, 1999.

Gaggi, Silvio. *Modern/Postmodern: A Study in Twentieth-Century Arts and Ideas.* Philadelphia: University of Pennsylvania Press, 1989.

Genette, Gérard. *Narrative Discourse: An Essay in Method.* 2nd ed. Translated by Jane E. Lewin. Ithaca: Cornell University Press, 1980.

Gilmore, Leigh. *The Limits of Autobiography: Trauma and Testimony.* Ithaca: Cornell University Press, 2001.

Goodman, Nelson. *Ways of Worldmaking.* Indianapolis: Hackett, 1978.

Grace, Sherrill. *Making Theatre: A Life of Sharon Pollock.* Vancouver: Talonbooks, 2008.

– 'Performing the Auto/biographical Pact: Towards a Theory of Identity in Performance.' In Kadar, *Tracing the Autobiographical*, 65–79.

– 'Theatre and the AutoBiographical Pact: An Introduction.' In Grace and Wasserman, *Theatre and AutoBiography*, 13–29.

Grace, Sherrill, and Jerry Wasserman. eds. *Theatre and AutoBiography: Writing and Performing Lives in Theory and Practice.* Vancouver: Talonbooks, 2006.

Griffiths, Linda. *Alien Creature: A Visitation from Gwendolyn MacEwen.* Toronto: Playwrights Canada Press, 2000.

Gross, Kenneth. 'Love among the Puppets.' *Raritan* 17.1 (1997): 67–82.

Grosz, Elizabeth. *Volatile Bodies: Toward a Corporeal Feminism.* Bloomington: Indiana University Press, 1994.

Gusdorf, Georges. 'Conditions and Limits of Autobiography.' In Olney, *Autobiography*, 28–48.

Healey, Michael. *The Drawer Boy.* Toronto: Playwrights Canada Press, 1999.

Heddon, Deirdre. *Autobiography and Performance.* New York: Palgrave Macmillan, 2008.

Helms, Gabriele. 'Reality TV Has Spoken: Auto/biography Matters.' In Kadar, *Tracing the Autobiographical,* 43–63.

Henke, Suzette A. *Shattered Subjects: Trauma and Testimony in Women's Life-Writing.* New York: St. Martin's Press, 2000.

Hinz, Evelyn J. 'Mimesis: The Dramatic Language of Auto/Biography.' In *Essays on Life Writing: From Genre to Critical Practice,* edited by Marlene Kadar, 195–212. Toronto: University of Toronto Press, 1992.

Hofstadter, Douglas. *Gödel, Escher, Bach: An Eternal Golden Braid.* Rev. ed. New York: Basic Books, 1999.

Holden, Joan. 'In Praise of Melodrama.' In *Reimaging America: The Arts of Social Change,* edited by Mark O'Brien and Craig Little, 278–84. Philadelphia: New Society Publishers, 1990.

Ingarden, Roman. *The Literary Work of Art: An Investigation on the Borderlines of Ontology, Logic, and Theory of Literature.* Translated by George G. Grabowicz. Studies in Phenomenology and Existential Philosophy, edited by James M. Edie. Evanston: Northwestern University Press, 1973.

Iser, Wolfgang. *The Act of Reading: A Theory of Aesthetic Response.* Baltimore: Johns Hopkins University Press, 1980.

Jenner, C. Lee. 'Working with Puppets: Interviews with Bruce D. Schwartz, Theodora Skipitares, Julie Taymor.' *Performing Arts Journal* 7.1 (1983): 103–16.

Jurkowski, Henryk. 'Literary Views on Puppet Theatre.' 1979. In Francis, *Aspects of Puppet Theatre,* 1–36.

– 'Towards a Theatre of Objects.' 1984. In Francis, *Aspects of Puppet Theatre,* 37–43.

Kadar, Marlene, ed. *Tracing the Autobiographical.* Waterloo: Wilfrid Laurier University Press, 2005.

Kerby, Anthony Paul. *Narrative and the Self.* Bloomington: Indiana University Press, 1991.

Knowles, Ric. 'Documemory, Autobiology, and the Utopian Performative in Canadian Autobiographical Solo Performance.' In Grace and Wasserman, *Theatre and AutoBiography,* 49–71.

Latshaw, George. *Puppetry: The Ultimate Disguise.* New York: Richards Rosen Press, 1978.

Laub, Dori. 'Bearing Witness or the Vicissitudes of Listening.' In *Testimony: Crises of Witnessing in Literature, Psychoanalysis and History,* edited by Shoshana Felman and Dori Laub, 57–74. New York: Routledge, 1992.

Leiris, Michel. *Journal, 1922–1989.* Edited by Jean Jamin. Paris: Gallimard, 1992.

Lejeune, Philippe. 'The Autobiographical Pact.' In Eakin, *On Autobiography*, 3–30.
– 'The Autobiographical Pact (bis).' In Eakin, *On Autobiography*, 119–37.
– 'The Autobiography of Those Who Do Not Write.' In Eakin, *On Autobiography*, 185–215.
– 'How Do Diaries End?' Translated by Victoria A. Lodewick. *Biography* 24.1 (Winter 2001): 99–112.
Leroux, Louis Patrick. 'Tremblay's Impromptus as Process-driven A/B.' In Grace and Wasserman, *Theatre and AutoBiography*, 107–23.
Linde, Charlotte. *Life Stories: The Creation of Coherence.* New York: Oxford University Press, 1993.
MacIvor, Daniel. 'In On It.' 2001. In *I Still Love You: Five Plays by Daniel MacIvor*, 149–99. Toronto: Playwrights Canada Press, 2006.
Malina, Debra. *Breaking the Frame: Metalepsis and the Construction of the Subject.* Columbus: Ohio State University Press, 2002.
Milhous, Judith, and Robert D. Hume. *Producible Interpretation: Eight English Plays 1675–1707.* Carbondale: Southern Illinois University Press, 1985.
Miller, Nancy K. 'Representing Others: Gender and the Subjects of Autobiography.' *Differences: A Journal of Feminist Cultural Studies* 6.1 (1994): 1–27.
Moser, Marlene. 'Identities of Ambivalence: Judith Thompson's *Perfect Pie.*' *Theatre Research in Canada* 27.1 (2006): 81–99.
– 'Ideology as Behaviour: Identity and Realism in the *Drawer Boy.*' *Modern Drama* 45.2 (Summer 2002): 231–45.
Mouawad, Wajdi. *Scorched (Incendies).* Translated by Linda Gaboriau. Toronto: Playwrights Canada Press, 2005.
Nabokov, Vladimir. *Speak, Memory: An Autobiography Revisited.* New York: Putnam, 1966.
Neisser, Ulric. 'Five Kinds of Self-Knowledge.' *Philosophical Psychology* 1.1 (1988): 35–59.
Nelson, Katherine. 'The Ontogeny of Memory for Real Events.' In *Remembering Reconsidered: Ecological and Traditional Approaches to the Study of Memory*, edited by Ulric Neisser and E. Winograd, 244–76. Cambridge: Cambridge University Press, 1988.
Nelson, Victoria. *The Secret Life of Puppets.* Cambridge: Harvard University Press, 2001.
Neuman, Shirley. 'The Observer Observed: Distancing Self in Autobiography.' *Prose Studies* 4.3 (1981): 317–36.
Newton, Adam Zachary. *Narrative Ethics.* Cambridge: Harvard University Press, 1995.

Nicholls, Liz. 'Puppetmaster Takes Star Turn in Twinkle.' *Edmonton Journal*, 19 Oct. 2008, B1–.
– 'The Remarkable Ronnie Burkett.' *Legacy* (Spring 2009): 16–19.
Nunn, Robert. 'Crackwalking: Judith Thompson's Marginal Characters.' In *Siting the Other: Re-visions of Marginality in Australian and English-Canadian Drama*, edited by Marc Maufort and Franca Bellarsi, 311–23. Brussels: Peter Lang, 2001.
– 'The Meeting of Actuality and Theatricality in The Farm Show.' *Canadian Drama* 8.1 (1982): 42–54
Ochs, Elinor, and Lisa Capps. 'Narrating the Self.' *Annual Review of Anthropology* 25 (1996): 19–43.
Oliver, Kelly. *Witnessing: Beyond Recognition*. Minneapolis: University of Minnesota Press, 2001.
Olney, James, ed. *Autobiography: Essays Theoretical and Critical*. Princeton: Princeton University Press, 1980.
Pavis, Patrice. 'Autobiographical Theatre.' In *Dictionary of the Theatre: Terms, Concepts, and Analysis*, translated by Christine Shantz, 31–2. Toronto: University of Toronto Press, 1998.
Piatigorsky, Anton. 'Eternal Hydra.' One-act version, 2002. *Canadian Theatre Review* 115 (2003): 66–87.
– *Eternal Hydra*. Toronto: Coach House, 2009.
Podnieks, Elizabeth. '"Hit Sluts" and "Page Pimps": Online Diarists and Their Quest for Cyber-Union.' *Life Writing* 1.2 (2004): 123–50.
Poe, Edgar Allan. 'Annabel Lee.' Poemhunter.com. Accessed 31 May 2012. http://www.poemhunter.com/poem/annabel-lee/.
Pollock, Sharon. *Doc*. Rev. ed. Toronto: Broadview, 2003.
Porter, Roger J. *Self-Same Songs: Autobiographical Performances and Reflections*. Lincoln: University of Nebraska Press, 2002.
Rak, Julie. 'Introduction: Widening the Field: Auto/biography Theory and Criticism in Canada.' In *Auto/biography in Canada: Critical Directions*, 1–29. Waterloo: Wilfrid Laurier University Press, 2005.
Rayner, Alice. *Ghosts: Death's Double and the Phenomena of Theatre*. Minneapolis: University of Minnesota Press, 2006.
Regan, Paulette. *Unsettling the Settler Within: Indian Residential Schools, Truth Telling and Reconciliation in Canada*. Vancouver: UBC Press, 2010.
Redhill, Michael. *Goodness*. Toronto: Coach House, 2005.
– 'Goodness.' New York draft. Unpublished manuscript, 11 Jan. 2007.
Rubin, David C., ed. *Autobiographical Memory*. Cambridge: Cambridge University Press, 1986.

Salverson, Julie. 'Anxiety and Contact in Attending to a Play about Land
   Mines.' In Simon, Rosenberg, and Eppert, *Between Hope and Despair*, 59–74.
– 'Change on Whose Terms? Testimony and an Erotics of Injury.' *Theater* 31.3
   (2001): 119–25.
Sears, Djanet. *Afrika Solo*. Toronto: Sister Vision, 1990.
Seremba, George. *Come Good Rain*. Winnipeg: Blizzard, 1993.
Simon, Roger I. 'The Paradoxical Practice of Zakhor: Memories of "What
   Has Never Been My Fault or My Deed."' In Simon, Rosenberg, and Eppert,
   Between Hope and Despair, 9–25.
Simon, Roger I., Sharon Rosenberg, and Claudia Eppert, eds. *Between Hope and
   Despair: Pedagogy and the Remembrance of Historical Trauma*. Lanham: Rowman
   & Littlefield, 2000.
Smith, Sidonie. 'Construing Truth in Lying Mouths: Truthtelling in Women's
   Autobiography.' In *Women and Autobiography*, edited by M.W. Brownley and
   A.B. Kimmich, 33–52. Washington, DC: Scholarly Resources, 1999.
Smith, Sidonie, and Julia Watson, eds. *Getting a Life: Everyday Uses of Autobiogra-
   phy*. Wilmington: University of Minnesota Press, 1996.
Sofer, Andrew. *The Stage Life of Props*. Ann Arbor: University of Michigan Press,
   2003.
Solomon, Alisa. 'The Age of Anxiety.' *Village Voice*, 2 Oct. 2001.
Spaulding, Amy E. *The Wisdom of Storytelling in an Information Age: A Collection of
   Talks*. Lanham: Scarecrow Press, 2004.
Speaight, George. *The History of the English Puppet Theatre*. 2nd ed. Carbondale:
   Southern Illinois University Press, 1990.
Sprinker, Michael. 'Fictions of the Self: The End of Autobiography.' In Olney,
   Autobiography, 321–42.
Starobinski, Jean. 'The Style of Autobiography.' In Olney, *Autobiography*, 73–83.
States, Bert O. *Great Reckonings in Little Rooms: On the Phenomenology of Theater*.
   Berkeley: University of California Press, 1987.
Stephenson, Jenn. 'Metatheatre and Authentication through Metonymic Com-
   pression in John Mighton's *Possible Worlds*.' *Theatre Journal* 58.1 (2006): 73–93.
– 'Singular Impressions: Metatheatre on Renaissance Celebrities and Corpses.'
   Studies in Theatre and Performance 27.2 (2007): 137–53.
Tal, Kali. *Worlds of Hurt: Reading the Literature of Trauma*. New York: Cambridge
   University Press, 1996.
Tambling, Jeremy. *Becoming Posthumous: Life and Death in Literary and Cultural
   Studies*. Edinburgh: Edinburgh University Press, 2001.
Theatre Passe Muraille. *The Farm Show: A Collective Creation*. Toronto: Coach
   House, 1976.

Thompson, Judith. 'Epilepsy & the Snake: Fear in the Creative Process.' *Canadian Theatre Review* 89 (1996): 4–7.

– 'Perfect Pie.' In *Solo*, edited by Jason Sherman, 163–71. Toronto: Coach House, 1994.

– *Perfect Pie*. Toronto, Playwrights Canada Press Press, 1999.

Van Alphen, Ernest. *Caught by History: Holocaust Effects in Contemporary Art, Literature, and Theory*. Stanford: Stanford University Press, 1997.

Warley, Linda. 'Reading the Autobiographical in Personal Home Pages.' In Kadar, *Tracing the Autobiographical*, 25–42.

White, Hayden. 'The Value of Narrativity in the Representation of Reality.' *Critical Inquiry* 7 (1980): 5–27.

Young, James E. *At Memory's Edge: After-Images of the Holocaust in Contemporary Art and Architecture*. New Haven: Yale University Press, 2000.

Young, Kay, and Jeffrey L. Saver. 'The Neurology of Narrative.' *SubStance* 94–5 (2001): 72–84.

Index

actuality, 18, 79, 178, 205
amnesia, 19, 24, 26–9, 35–7, 39, 41–2,
  44, 71, 104, 155, 160, 166
arrested narration, 19, 27–8, 36
Austin, J.L., 12–13
authentication, 41, 88
authenticity, 21, 47, 57, 75, 87–8,
  90–1, 105, 107, 109, 111, 177
author-subject, 11–12, 15, 21, 25–6,
  32, 37, 76, 104, 130, 169
auto/biography, 8, 26–7, 32, 36,
  69–70, 74–5, 80, 93, 101, 104
autobiographers: silenced, 166; vulnerable, 75, 156, 160
autobiographical body, 21, 105, 108,
  157
autobiographical frames, 122, 162
autobiographical objects, 20
autobiographical pact, 25–6, 30–3,
  104–5, 204
autobiographical performance, 3, 8,
  10, 14, 19, 21–2, 70, 76, 100, 105–6,
  108, 126, 133, 150, 154
autobiographical process, 12, 17–18,
  109, 112, 158–9, 167
autobiographical roles, 21, 26, 105
autobiographical storytelling, 6, 10,
  20, 25, 155, 157, 169

autobiographical subject, 11–12, 16,
  19, 21, 105–6, 112, 131, 133, 151,
  155, 162, 167–8
autobiographical voice, 4
autobiography: excess of, 166–7;
  shared, 155
autofiction, 8–9, 174
autothanatography, 22, 132, 134, 136,
  143–4, 158, 195

Billy Twinkle, 18, 21, 104–5, 109,
  111–12, 116, 122, 157, 191
biographer, 26, 34, 69–70, 73–4, 79, 86
biographical subject, 26, 69–70, 72,
  76, 79
biography, 9, 26, 28, 30, 65, 68–72, 76,
  85–6, 99, 101, 105, 134, 137, 155,
  174
body, 10, 13, 21, 38, 86, 99–101,
  104–8, 111–12, 157, 169, 189;
  actual, 100, 106–7, 111, 157
borders, 13, 17, 19–20, 37, 47, 50, 65,
  76–9, 81, 84, 87, 91, 100, 114–15,
  167–9
Bouchard, Michel Marc, 18, 160, 162
Brechtian mode, 92
Burkett, Ronnie, 18, 21, 103–4,
  109–10, 112–13, 117, 119, 188

Carr, Emily, 9, 174
Coghill, Joy, 9, 174
control, 20, 55–8, 64, 74–5, 77, 80–2,
    88, 90, 93, 96–7, 100, 136, 141
creation, 3, 41–2, 44, 47, 49, 63, 71,
    75, 77, 83, 85, 90–3, 99, 110–11,
    118
creator, 3, 12, 26, 42, 88, 90, 93, 97,
    109–11, 118, 136, 179, 186, 194
crisis, 6–7, 15–17, 21, 112–14, 121,
    126, 133, 160

Dawe, TJ, 105
death, 21–2, 39–40, 64, 114, 116,
    130–4, 139, 141–4, 146, 148, 151,
    153, 158, 161, 166
diaries, 4–5, 142–4
Doc, 8–9, 174
documentary realism, 45–6
The Drawer Boy, 18–19, 24, 27–8, 36,
    44, 69–71, 75, 104, 155, 159, 177–8,
    186
dysnarrativias, 19, 71

Eakin, Paul John, 22, 159
Egan, Susanna, 26, 112, 132, 143–4
epilepsy, 35, 39, 41–2, 186, 190
episodic memory, 24, 27, 29–30, 34–
    5
Escher, M.C., 144, 153, 195
Eternal Hydra, 18, 20, 68, 73–4, 81,
    83–4, 88, 93, 101, 183–5
extended self, 19, 24–5, 29, 35, 41

fictional frame, 13, 106–7, 126, 141,
    161
Findley, Timothy, 89, 183, 185–6
Fox, David, 177, 197
freedom, 17, 49, 64, 72–3, 87, 91, 97,
    99, 129–30, 163, 187

Gaggi, Silvio, 91–2
gender, 6, 76, 86
Genette, Gerard, 176
genocide, 17, 46–7, 49–50, 59–60,
    63–4, 156, 181
ghosts, 64, 132–3, 142, 145–50, 152–3,
    158–9
Goodness, 18–20, 45–55, 59–60, 65–7,
    69, 75, 108, 133, 141, 156, 180, 182,
    186
Grace, Sherrill, 4, 8

Hamlet, 13, 30, 88, 108, 145
Healey, Michael, 18–19, 24, 178, 186
history, 11, 28, 41, 46–7, 124, 155, 162;
    oral, 47, 55, 141; personal, 14, 47,
    87, 112, 134; somatic, 105; unspeak-
    able, 46; verifiable authentic, 155
Hofstadter, Douglas, 144–5
hypernarrativia, 159, 166, 168

identity, 4, 8, 12, 15–16, 19, 22, 75–6,
    87, 105–6, 139, 143, 159
In On It, 18, 22, 135, 145–6, 148,
    150–3, 157, 159, 193, 195–6, 199
intersubjectivity, 106–8, 111–12, 122,
    129

Jurkowski, Henryk, 118–19, 190

Laub, Dori, 48, 52
Lejeune, Philippe, 3, 11–12, 25, 27–8,
    104, 131, 142–3, 145
life stories, 4, 7, 15, 79, 104, 132, 137
Lobb, Alison, 29, 178

MacIvor, Daniel, 18, 22, 134, 193–4,
    196
Malina, Debra, 17, 92, 175
marionettes, 21, 103–4, 109, 112–15,

117, 119–20, 122–4, 128, 188–90, 200

memoir, 4, 6–7, 132

meta-autobiography, 11–12, 17, 22–4, 30

metalepsis, 17, 19, 47, 50, 52, 59, 65–6, 91–2, 176

metatheatre, 47, 186–7, 206

mirror, 25–8, 32, 34, 37, 41, 69, 100

mirror talk, 176–7, 184, 189, 201

Moser, Marlene, 178

Mouawad, Wajdi, 18, 160, 164–5

mourning, 147–50, 152–3, 159, 195

murder, 20, 50, 58–60, 62, 64, 155, 183

narrative, 7, 14–16, 26, 29, 33, 41, 69, 72, 81–2, 88, 91, 101, 112, 134, 144

narrative capacity, 20, 71, 159

narrative construction, 168

narrative process, 24, 34

narrative roles, 25, 31, 104

narrative self, 26, 28, 71

narrative structures, 37, 76, 168

narrative voice, 11, 81–2

narrator, 11, 15, 21, 25–6, 28, 30–2, 34, 36–7, 41, 51, 53–4, 76, 80–8, 90, 104–5; anonymous, 74, 76, 83, 94, 96, 101

objects, 19–21, 55, 64, 76, 90, 102, 111, 115, 118–20, 147, 149, 158, 182; actual, 88, 97, 181, 186; fictional, 181

ontological split, 124

ontological status, 25, 30, 114–15, 136, 141, 146

ontological structure, 12, 14, 17, 41, 78–9, 81, 110, 152, 175, 194

Ouimette, Stephen, 183

parody, 46, 117–18

Penrose Stairs, 144, 195

Perehinec, Kimwun, 100

Perfect Pie, 17, 19, 24, 35–8, 40–1, 69–71, 75, 104, 132, 135, 155, 159

performative autobiography, 19, 24, 27, 44, 99, 153

performative identities, 100–1

performative language, 13, 19, 27, 37, 43, 53, 64–5, 76, 87, 100

performative power, 4, 27, 53–4, 57, 59, 64, 72, 75, 136, 140, 153, 155, 157

performative witness, 45, 53, 59, 64–6

Pettle, Jordan, 52, 63, 75, 180, 182

phenomenological frisson, 21, 106–7, 112

phenomenology, 131

Piatigorsky, Anton, 18, 20, 68, 73, 90, 184–5

Pinocchio, 116, 121, 127–8, 130, 192

Pirandellian mode, 91, 98, 185

Pollock, Sharon, 8–9, 174

Potter, Miles, 177–8, 186

power, 6, 14, 27, 52, 55, 60, 64–5, 68, 70–1, 81, 84, 90, 100, 130, 141

procedural memory, 24, 27, 30, 34, 37, 44

Producible Interpretation, 18

props, 64, 81, 90, 109, 115, 119, 122–3, 146–7, 191

Prospero, 91, 123, 129–30, 158

puppetry, 110, 119, 188–91, 202–3

puppets, 9, 21, 103–5, 108–12, 115–30, 157, 187–92; autonomous, 123, 126, 128; hand, 21, 104, 113, 126, 130, 133; self-similar, 105, 110, 157; short-strung cabaret, 116, 121, 128

Rand, Gordon, 180, 182, 184
Rayner, Alice, 145, 147, 197
recursion, 144, 187
Redhill, Michael, 18, 45, 50–1, 53–4,
   69, 75, 155, 180, 186
Reid, Chick, 183–4
repetition, 16, 45, 49–50, 54, 66, 108,
   141, 145–6, 148, 169
responsibility, 5, 34, 59, 64, 70
Robinson, Karen, 84, 105, 183–4

Salverson, Julie 46
Scorched, 18, 160, 164, 166–7, 197
self, 3, 7–9, 14–15, 17, 20, 22–4, 26–7,
   41, 70–1, 85–6, 92–3, 125, 154–5,
   157, 173; actual-world, 11–12, 73,
   106–7, 110, 112, 117, 169; autobiographical, 107; generated, 21, 23,
   27; invention, 4, 19, 22, 27, 159,
   173; storying, 3–4, 10, 14, 18, 20, 70,
   80, 100, 136, 142, 155, 160, 169
Shadows, 18, 20, 68, 72, 74, 77–9, 81,
   89, 91–2, 97–9, 101, 114, 136, 156,
   183–4
silence, 48, 61, 66, 91, 94, 101, 138,
   146, 156, 160–1, 164–7
Smith, Sidonie, 206
Sofer, Andrew, 18, 182, 191
Stevens, Martin, 190–1
storytelling, 6, 14, 20, 24, 34, 36, 45,
   64–6, 70, 94, 156, 160; biographical,
   73; daily, 159; personal, 5; reiterative, 44
Stratford Festival, 74, 99, 156, 183
subject, 3, 10–11, 16–17, 24–6, 31–2,
   41, 69–74, 85–6, 93, 97, 104–6,
   109–11, 142–3, 157–8, 167; actual-
   world, 14, 71, 87, 112; performing,
   10, 154, 169
subject creation, 16, 77, 79

subject-self, 41, 72, 122
survival, 16, 19, 45, 49, 59, 93

testimony, 47–9, 53–4, 60, 64
theatrical duality, 29–30, 32–3, 109,
   142
theatricality, 18, 47, 78, 115
Thompson, Judith, 18–19, 24, 38, 40,
   42, 177, 179, 190
trauma, 19–20, 35, 40–2, 46, 49, 52,
   71, 152, 156–7, 166
truth, 3, 8, 11–12, 19, 46, 53, 61, 74,
   78, 97, 100, 104, 182, 187

unbounded narration, 19, 34, 36
utopian performativity, 21

ventriloquism, 75, 100–1
violence, 16–17, 35, 63, 68, 71, 76, 79,
   91–2
voice, 10, 13, 19, 25, 38, 52, 84, 87–8,
   96, 102, 110, 156, 169

witnessing, 12, 17, 19, 45–6, 48, 50,
   52–9, 61–4, 66, 98, 106, 156, 165
worldmaking, 23, 28
worlds, 6–8, 36–7, 47–8, 50, 63–6,
   71–4, 76–9, 81–8, 90–3, 96–8, 107–9,
   113–15, 136–8, 146, 151–6; actual, 9,
   11–13, 15, 23, 25, 48–9, 59, 66, 71–2,
   78, 98, 100–1, 124–5, 129–30, 157–8;
   fictional, 10–11, 13, 17, 47–9, 56,
   65–6, 71–2, 75–6, 78–9, 81–4, 86–90,
   92–3, 97, 108–9, 184–6; lower-order,
   72, 82, 86, 114, 124; nested, 25, 43,
   47, 54, 98, 109, 117, 157–8, 175;
   superior, 89–90, 122, 167
Written on Water, 18, 160, 162, 166–7,
   197